JANE AUSTEN

OTHER TITLES IN THE GREENHAVEN PRESS LITERARY COMPANION SERIES:

AMERICAN AUTHORS

Nathaniel Hawthorne
Ernest Hemingway
Herman Melville
Arthur Miller
John Steinbeck
Mark Twain

WORLD AUTHORS

Sophocles

BRITISH LITERATURE

The Canterbury Tales
Shakespeare: The Comedies
Shakespeare: The Sonnets
Shakespeare: The Tragedies

THE GREENHAVEN PRESS
Literary Companion
TO BRITISH AUTHORS

JANE AUSTEN

David Bender, *Publisher*

Bruno Leone, *Executive Editor*

Scott Barbour, *Managing Editor*

Bonnie Szumski, *Series Editor*

Clarice Swisher, *Book Editor*

Greenhaven Press, San Diego, CA

Library of Congress Cataloging-in-Publication Data

Readings on Jane Austen / Clarice Swisher, book editor.
      p.   cm. — (The Greenhaven Press literary
companion to British authors)
    Includes bibliographical references and index.
    ISBN 1-56510-578-8 (lib. bdg. : alk. paper). —
ISBN 1-56510-577-X (pbk. : alk. paper)
    1. Austen, Jane, 1775–1817—Criticism and interpreta-
tion. 2. Women and literature—England—History—19th
century. I. Swisher, Clarice, 1933– . II. Series.
PR4037.R43   1997
823'.7–dc20
                                          96-32264
                                             CIP

Cover photo: Archive Photos

Copyright ©1997 by Greenhaven Press, Inc.
PO Box 289009
San Diego, CA 92198-9009
Printed in the U.S.A.

"It is a truth universally acknowledged, that a single man in possession of a good fortune, must be in want of a wife.**"**

–Jane Austen
Pride and Prejudice

CONTENTS

Foreword   10

Introduction   12

Jane Austen: A Biography   13

Chapter 1: Jane Austen's Relationship to Her Times and Her Critics

1. **England in Austen's Time** *by Fay Weldon*   34
Life for most women in Austen's time was harsh by modern standards. Because they had few career choices, many women endured loveless marriages with few rights and many duties. Austen's novels, however, never betray this harsh reality.

2. **Austen's Women in a Conservative Society**
by David Monaghan   42
Austen disagreed with the way women were thought of in her time; that, lacking intelligence, their only purpose was to procreate and serve submissively. But although Austen promotes women's power and achievements, she does not think they should come at the expense of the established social order.

3. **Nineteenth-Century Criticism of Austen's Novels**
by John Halperin   51
Jane Austen's novels received scant attention throughout the nineteenth century because novels were generally held in disrepute by serious readers and because Austen lived and published quietly. The few serious critics who reviewed her books, however, made worthwhile observations.

Chapter 2: Themes in Jane Austen's Novels

1. **Sex and Social Life in Austen's Novels**
by Jan Fergus   60
Broadly defined as energetic attraction between men and women, sexuality pervades the action and dialogue in Austen's books. Austen takes liberties with the prevailing rules of conduct and creates heroines who merit admiration while subtly defying the rules.

2. **Humor in Austen's Novels** *by A.C. Bradley*   70
Austen evokes laughter by detailing the gap between reality and illusion in order to highlight the ridiculous. Each

novel contains scenes and characters that could be played almost unaltered on the comic stage.

3. **Austen Portrays a Small World with Humor and Detachment** *by J.B. Priestley*   78
Austen deliberately chose to write about a small world of changing social classes in early nineteenth-century England. In a good-natured way, she uses irony to criticize the snobbery and pettiness of characters scrambling for social position.

Chapter 3: Techniques and Devices in Jane Austen's Novels

1. **Stylistic Devices That Create Irony** *by Andrew H. Wright*   85
In all of her novels, Austen's style creates a tone of irony, which she uses to criticize snobbery and foolishness. She achieves her style with pompous words and convoluted sentences, understatement, antiphrasis, the illusion of logic, and clichés.

2. **Games as a Device in Austen's Novels** *by Alistair M. Duckworth*   93
Ordinary social games played in family settings reflect serious themes in Austen's novels. Austen first associates games with shallow characters; she later uses them as a device to show relationships between morality and society.

Chapter 4: Jane Austen's Early Novels

1. **Satire and Realism in *Northanger Abbey*** *by Norman Sherry*   104
Through heroine Catherine Morland, Austen both satirizes romantic novels of her day and advocates the superiority of reality in ordinary life. Innocent Catherine suffers imaginative excesses in the unfamiliar social world of Bath but is brought to earth by Henry Tilney, who marries her in the end.

2. ***Sense and Sensibility* Has Little Irony** *by John Odmark*   112
Of all Austen's novels, *Sense and Sensibility* contains the least opportunity for irony. Because Austen so clearly agrees with the superiority of Elinor's point of view, the reader rarely sees things differently or knows more than the main character.

3. **Minor Characters Reflect the Theme of *Sense and Sensibility*** *by Howard S. Babb*   117
The minor characters in *Sense and Sensibility* reinforce the theme that people need a balance of emotion and sense, but none of the minor characters grows beyond his or her own self-interest.

Chapter 5: *Pride and Prejudice*

**1. The Best Qualities of *Pride and Prejudice*
by W. Somerset Maugham**   125

Pride and Prejudice deserves to be considered one of the
ten best novels ever written because of its humor and for
presenting a limited world with uncommon wit. The engaging novel makes the reader eager to turn each page.

**2. Clashes and Compromises in *Pride and Prejudice*
by Laura G. Mooneyham**   131

Austen structures *Pride and Prejudice* around the relationship of Elizabeth and Darcy. The novel is divided almost
equally between their conflicts and their resolution, but
both parts depend on the couple's balanced attraction, intelligence, and strength of character.

**3. The Significance of Pictures in *Pride and Prejudice*
by Tony Tanner**   140

Austen uses paintings to convey meaning. For example,
when Elizabeth tours Pemberley, she is shown a large portrait of Darcy. Her discovery while studying it marks a
turning point in the novel.

**4. Good Manners Mirror Good Morals in *Pride and
Prejudice* by Jane Nardin**   147

In *Pride and Prejudice*, Austen makes the assumption that
a character's outward manners reveal his or her inner
morality. Austen establishes two principles on which to
judge proper behavior and illustrates the stupidity and immorality of those who violate these principles.

Chapter 6: Jane Austen's Late Novels

**1. Portraits of People in Austen's *Emma*
by Richard Church**   156

Emma is a logically developed story of fate and punish-
ment and, as a comedy, final happiness. In addition, the
novel is a masterpiece of clearly drawn and interesting
major and minor characters.

2. Emma: A Heroine with Faults by *Douglas Jefferson*   162

Emma is a multidimensional, imperfect character. Austen
allows the reader to get close enough to Emma's inner life
to view her buoyancy and confidence, her worries and
snobbery.

**3. *Mansfield Park*: The Portrayal of Quiet, Complex
Love** by *June Dwyer*   168

In *Mansfield Park*, Austen presents an alternative to the
energetic, attractive heroine who finds equality in marriage. In this novel, the plain, shy heroine Fanny embodies
the virtues of loyalty, duty, and affection and first finds
love in a platonic fondness before finding romantic love.

4. *Persuasion*: Austen's New Kind of Novel
  by Marvin Mudrick   178
  In her final novel, Austen presents a heroine of greater
  feeling and sarcastically criticizes characters caught up in
  materialism. As a new kind of heroine, Anne Elliot edu-
  cates herself and finds her own fulfillment before she is
  reunited with Wentworth, the man she loves.

5. *Persuasion* and the Cinderella Story
  by D.W. Harding   186
  Persuasion, the story of Anne Elliot, resembles a more
  complex version of the Cinderella tale. Anne is more responsible for her sadness and alienation, and she takes a
  more active role in finding her prince. Despite the differences, the tale helps to clarify Austen's theme.

Organizations to Contact   192

Chronology   194

For Further Research   198

Works by Jane Austen   201

Index   202

Foreword

> *"'Tis the good reader that*
> *makes the good book."*
>
> Ralph Waldo Emerson

The story's bare facts are simple: The captain, an old and scarred seafarer, walks with a peg leg made of whale ivory. He relentlessly drives his crew to hunt the world's oceans for the great white whale that crippled him. After a long search, the ship encounters the whale and a fierce battle ensues. Finally the captain drives his harpoon into the whale, but the harpoon line catches the captain about the neck and drags him to his death.

A simple story, a straightforward plot—yet, since the 1851 publication of Herman Melville's *Moby-Dick*, readers and critics have found many meanings in the struggle between Captain Ahab and the whale. To some, the novel is a cautionary tale that depicts how Ahab's obsession with revenge leads to his insanity and death. Others believe that the whale represents the unknowable secrets of the universe and that Ahab is a tragic hero who dares to challenge fate by attempting to discover this knowledge. Perhaps Melville intended Ahab as a criticism of Americans' tendency to become involved in well-intentioned but irrational causes. Or did Melville model Ahab after himself, letting his fictional character express his anger at what he perceived as a cruel and distant god?

Although literary critics disagree over the meaning of *Moby-Dick*, readers do not need to choose one particular interpretation in order to gain an understanding of Melville's novel. Instead, by examining various analyses, they can gain numerous insights into the issues that lie under the surface of the basic plot. Studying the writings of literary critics can also aid readers in making their own assessments of *Moby-Dick* and other literary works and in developing analytical thinking skills.

The Greenhaven Literary Companion Series was created with these goals in mind. Designed for young adults, this unique anthology series provides an engaging and comprehensive introduction to literary analysis and criticism. The essays included in the Literary Companion Series are chosen for their accessibility to a young adult audience and are expertly edited in consideration of both the reading and comprehension levels of this audience. In addition, each essay is introduced by a concise summation that presents the contributing writer's main themes and insights. Every anthology in the Literary Companion Series contains a varied selection of critical essays that cover a wide time span and express diverse views. Wherever possible, primary sources are represented through excerpts from authors' notebooks, letters, and journals and through contemporary criticism.

Each title in the Literary Companion Series pays careful consideration to the historical context of the particular author or literary work. In-depth biographies and detailed chronologies reveal important aspects of authors' lives and emphasize the historical events and social milieu that influenced their writings. To facilitate further research, every anthology includes primary and secondary source bibliographies of articles and/or books selected for their suitability for young adults. These engaging features make the Greenhaven Literary Companion series ideal for introducing students to literary analysis in the classroom or as a library resource for young adults researching the world's great authors and literature.

Exceptional in its focus on young adults, the Greenhaven Literary Companion Series strives to present literary criticism in a compelling and accessible format. Every title in the series is intended to spark readers' interest in leading American and world authors, to help them broaden their understanding of literature, and to encourage them to formulate their own analyses of the literary works that they read. It is the editors' hope that young adult readers will find these anthologies to be true companions in their study of literature.

INTRODUCTION

This literary companion provides teachers and students with a wide variety of analysis and opinion about Jane Austen's novels. A superficial glance through her books may lead readers to conclude mistakenly that her stories are all the same. True, they are about wealthy people—some intelligent and witty, some foolish—who entertain themselves by visiting one another and giving and attending parties and balls. But there are noticeable differences among the novels.

This volume includes a wide range of scholars and critics. One essay is written by a novelist, another by a student of Shakespearean drama. Five of the essays are authored by women scholars. Although a few essays date from the eighteenth and nineteenth centuries, the majority of essays have been written during the last two decades, representing a resurgence of interest in Austen, perhaps prompted by the bicentennial of her birth in 1975.

Readings on Jane Austen includes many special features that make research and literary criticism accessible and understandable. An annotated table of contents lets readers quickly preview the content of individual essays. A chronology features a list of significant events in Austen's life placed in a broader historical context. The bibliography provides sources that include books on Austen's time and additional critical sources suitable for further research. In addition, names and addresses of two Austen societies make additional information available.

Each essay has aids for clear understanding. The introductions serve as directed reading for the essays by explaining the main points, which are then identified by subheads within the essays. Footnotes identify uncommon references and define unfamiliar words. Inserts, many taken from Austen's novels, illustrate points made in the essays. Taken together, these aids make Greenhaven Press's *Literary Companion Series* an indispensable research tool.

JANE AUSTEN: A BIOGRAPHY

Jane Austen, considered England's first great woman novelist, was born in the village of Steventon, Hampshire, on December 16, 1775, and lived her whole life within a small area in southwestern England. Though Austen lived during the Napoleonic Wars, the American and French Revolutions, and the Industrial Revolution, she ignored the world at large and focused her writing on middle- and upper-class social life in England's small villages and rural areas. Determined to write only about what she knew, she observed behavior with a perceptive eye and portrayed human traits realistically. She is the author of six major novels, three written in her early twenties and three in her late thirties. Her letters to her sister Cassandra and to other family members have also been published, and remain a valuable resource for biographers, scholars, and critics.

Austen grew up in England during the late eighteenth century in a society with strict social classes and clearly defined roles. At the top of the social order was the aristocracy, men and women with titles and enough inherited wealth to live comfortably without working. Next was the middle class, called the gentry, composed of wealthy landowners, prosperous businessmen, military officers, and professional people. Below the gentry were paid laborers, ordinary soldiers and sailors, and subsistence farmers. At the bottom of the social order were the servants, who lived and worked on the estates of the upper classes for little pay. While the women in the lower classes worked hard at physical tasks to help feed, clothe, and shelter their families, women in the upper classes were expected to follow strict rules of decorum that governed their conversation in social situations and their relations with men. Women were trained in music, drawing, and the domestic arts of embroidery and sewing. They could not attend universities and were expected to have no opinions about intellectual matters or political issues.

Three choices were available to them: They could marry, preferably landing a prosperous husband; they could spend their lives as spinsters living in their parents' or other relatives' homes; or they could become governesses or teachers and be sustained in the homes of the wealthy.

AUSTEN'S FAMILY

Jane Austen's ancestors on her father's side were gentry from near Canterbury in Kent in southeastern England. Dating back to the Middle Ages, her ancestors raised sheep and manufactured clothing; eventually, one branch of the family carried on the business and became very wealthy, and the other branch entered professions. Jane's father, George Austen, the son of a surgeon, was orphaned before he was nine and left penniless; however, his wealthy uncle Francis Austen, a lawyer, raised him as one of his own children. He sent George to St. John's College at Oxford, where he became a distinguished scholar and fellow, or teacher. An unusually good-looking man, he was known at the university as "the handsome proctor." After teaching for a time, he took Holy Orders, making him eligible to be a rector in the Anglican Church. It was the custom for wealthy persons to act as patrons and pay the living expenses of ministers. George's distant cousin, Thomas Knight, purchased a position for George Austen at the rectory in Steventon, and his Uncle Francis purchased the rectory for him at Deane, the neighboring church.

Jane Austen's ancestors on her mother's side, dating back to the Norman Conquest of England in 1066, settled in the west near Windsor. Jane's mother, Cassandra Leigh, descended from a distinguished line including Sir Thomas Leigh, lord mayor of London, and Oxford scholars Sir Thomas White, founder of St. John's College; Theophilus Leigh, a well-known wit of the time and master of Balliol College; and Thomas Leigh, her father, fellow at All Souls College. Cassandra Leigh met the handsome George Austen at the university's social gatherings in Oxford. Cassandra's family was upper gentry and George's family lower gentry, but the couple fell in love and were married at Walcot Church in the city of Bath on August 26, 1764. They settled first at Deane and shortly after at Steventon.

Jane was the seventh of eight children born to George and Cassandra Austen between 1765 and 1779. James, the oldest, followed in his father's footsteps and became rector of Steventon when his father retired. Nothing is known about George, who had physical and mental disorders, except that he lived in the area near Steventon. Third son Edward, adopted by Thomas Knight, a wealthy, childless distant relative, grew up in Kent in the Knight household and took the Knight name in order to inherit the family estate. Jane's favorite brother Henry, especially charming and good-looking, served as a colonel in the Oxfordshire militia before becoming a London banker and eventually a clergyman. Cassandra, two years older than Jane, was Jane's confidante and closest companion throughout her life. Francis, called Frank, entered the navy at twelve, reached the rank of admiral, and was knighted for his bravery and service in battle. Like Frank, Charles, the youngest Austen child, had a distinguished navy career. The Austens were devoted parents who nurtured bright, spirited children. In *A Memory of Jane Austen*, Jane's nephew James E. Austen-Leigh describes the congeniality and closeness of the Austen family:

> This was the small circle.... There was so much that was agreeable and attractive in this family party that its members may be excused if they were inclined to live somewhat too exclusively within it. They might see in each other much to love and esteem, and something to admire. The family talk had abundance of spirit and vivacity, and was never troubled by disagreements even in little matters, for it was not their habit to dispute or argue with each other; above all, there was strong family affection and firm union, never to be broken but by death.

George Austen lived the life of a gentleman and scholar at Steventon and provided well for his family. Besides his work as the clergyman of two churches, he supplemented his income by farming the land around the rectory and by tutoring not only his own sons, but also boys from other families who paid for his services as teacher. With sufficient income to build additions to the house and improve the grounds, he made their home superior to other country parsonages, and with his status and money, he provided what his family needed to enjoy the social life on the level of an English country gentleman. The Austens had horses and carriages, which symbolized wealth. The family visited relatives and friends and hosted return visits in the style of the aristocracy and gentry, whose outlook, manners, and language were alike. In *A Portrait of Jane Austen*, biographer and critic David Cecil clarifies a few differences between the two ruling classes:

> The Steventon district had its great nobles, ... who were on sufficiently equal terms with their humbler gentry neighbours to invite them to a big ball or a garden fête once or twice in the year. But they did not expect to be invited back, and at other times they did not mix with them. . . . Well-connected, well-mannered and traditionally Tory, the Austens were qualified in every respect to be welcomed into the inner circle of this society; and all the more because Thomas Knight, chief landowner of the district, lived in Kent, leaving George Austen as his representative to be consulted and deferred to as an acting squire.

AUSTEN'S EDUCATION AND EARLY WRITING

The values and status of Jane's family definitely affected her education. Her mother oversaw her training in needlework, music, and dancing. In 1782, when Cassandra was eight, the family arranged to send her to Mrs. Cawley's school in Oxford, and because Jane so closely identified with her sister, they sent her too, even though she was only six. Mrs. Austen described Jane's attachment to her sister by saying, "If Cassandra were going to have her head cut off, Jane would insist on sharing her fate." After one year, Mrs. Cawley moved her school to Southampton, but an epidemic of a disease similar to typhus called putrid throat broke out, and the girls returned home. The family sent them to the Abbey School in Reading, a loosely run school with few lessons and much play. Jane attended the Abbey School until she was eleven, when she returned home to be taught by her father.

Jane continued her education in a variety of ways. In addition to her father's lessons, Jane learned French and some Italian and studied history. She read widely from the numerous books in her father's library. George Austen had an extensive library, which included all of Shakespeare's plays and the English novels of Henry Fielding, George Smollett, and Oliver Goldsmith. His library also included contemporary popular stories; for example, *Evelina* and *Cecilia*, written by Fanny Burney, the originator of the English novel of domestic life. Moreover, Mr. Austen read to his family regularly in the evening and the children habitually read aloud to each other. Jane was much better educated than most girls in the late eighteenth century, as critic and biographer John Halperin comments in *The Life of Jane Austen*:

> While her education was somewhat haphazard, it was a liberal one. ... She was taught to question rather than to accept

blindly; and the satirical vein very early became a favourite with her, not least because she could be certain of addressing an audience—the family—familiar with the objects of her mirth and sympathetic to her irreverent treatment of them.

Jane began writing when she was ten or eleven years old. Her copybooks containing tales she composed as a young girl have survived. Many are flimsy and nonsensical stories, but they are all written with high spirit. She also composed plays for family parties and usually preceded them with a grandiloquent dedication, such as the one for "The Mystery. An Unfinished Comedy": "*To the Rev. George Austen.* Sir,—I humbly solicit your patronage to the following Comedy, which, though an unfinished one, is, I flatter myself, as complete a *Mystery* as any of its kind. I am, Sir, Your most humble Servant, The Author." The copybooks also record a history that Jane wrote and Cassandra illustrated. In *Jane Austen,* biographer Victor Lucas calls it

> a delightful spoof on that kind of history book which is concerned less with the facts of history than with an historian's prejudice for or against historical characters. She called it *The History of England by a Partial Prejudiced and Ignorant Historian.* It begins "Henry the 4th ascended the throne of England, much to his own satisfaction, in the year 1399." Already she is doing what she will do many times in her books—giving us, in an economical phrase, and with a twinkle of humour, an insight into the character of the person she is describing.

Cassandra depicted King Henry VIII wearing a red nightcap, appropriate headgear, the girls concluded, for a king who had no fewer than six wedding nights.

Critics refer to Austen's childhood works as "the Juvenalia," ninety-thousand words written between 1787 and 1795, including short tales, sketches, fictional letters, scraps of epistolary novels, bits of plays, and the English history. At sixteen, Jane copied all of her early works into three notebooks, entitled *Volume the First, Volume the Second,* and *Volume the Third.* Halperin observes: "As an adolescent she already viewed popular and sentimental fiction with the critical eye of a satirist; her early works ridicule the sentimental excesses and sensational unrealities of current popular fiction."

AUSTEN'S SOCIAL LIFE

Jane was actively involved in the family's social life. Though the Austens' favorite society was their own immediate family, many aunts, uncles, and cousins visited from Bath or Kent and stayed for a week or more. The Austens met regularly with local families to exchange morning visits, dinners, and evenings of card playing and games. They and their neighbors particularly enjoyed putting on amateur theatricals at Christmas and during the summer when the young people were home from school. Young Jane wrote prologues for the plays and helped with production while the older siblings and neighbors took the acting parts. They rehearsed such well-known comedies as Richard Sheridan's *The Rivals* as well as less well known plays such as *High Life Above Stairs, High Life Below Stairs, The Wonder: A Woman Keeps a Secret,* and *The Chances,* performing in the Austens' barn in the summer and in the dining room in the winter. These amateur theatricals were common pastimes between 1784 and 1790; Jane would draw on these experiences when writing the theatricals in *Mansfield Park.*

Much of Steventon social life revolved around public and private balls. Jane was an excellent dancer and often attended formal balls held in the town hall in Basingstoke, a nearby village. Besides its function as an important site of amusements, the ballroom served as a meeting place for young people in search of future husbands or wives. Unmarried girls attended formal balls in the company of chaperones, often their older married sisters. A master of ceremonies made the introductions and then opened the ball by partnering one of the young ladies in the first dance. To the music of a harpsichord, gentlemen and ladies, holding hands at arm's length, danced the stately minuet and quadrille. The polite society in which Jane lived considered the waltz scandalous because, as Lucas explains, "in this daring innovation from Germany [the lady and gentleman] embraced each other, quite close, their arms around each other's waists, looking into each other's eyes, and did not let go until the music stopped." At informal dances held in homes, often at the home of Jane's neighbor and friend Mrs. Anne Lefroy, the fiddle provided music for lively country dances in which everyone participated. Young girls dancing to harpsichords or fiddles had but few years to find a husband before they were considered too old to be attractive, suitable wives.

From Cassandra's portraits and relatives' accounts, it appears that Jane Austen was considered by most an attractive young woman. In *Jane Austen and Steventon*, niece Emma Austen-Leigh reports that the earliest recorded description of Jane comes from her cousin Philadelphia Walter, who in 1788 praised Cassandra's looks but said that Jane was "not at all pretty and very prim, unlike a girl of twelve," but Mrs. Lefroy's visiting brother said that when he knew Jane at that age, "my eyes told me she was fair and handsome, slight and elegant, but with cheeks a little too full." Her nephew J.E. Austen-Leigh gives a detailed description in *A Memoir of Jane Austen*:

> In person she was very attractive; her figure was rather tall and slender, her step light and firm, and her whole appearance expressive of health and animation. In complexion she was a clear brunette with a rich colour; she had full round cheeks, with mouth and nose small and well formed, bright hazel eyes, and brown hair forming natural curls close round her face. If not so regularly handsome as her sister, yet her countenance had a peculiar charm of its own to the eyes of most beholders.

Jane grew out of her twelve-year-old primness and improved in appearance; in 1791 another cousin, Eliza, spoke of both Cassandra and Jane as "perfect beauties" who were gaining "hearts by the dozens," and called the sisters "two of the prettiest girls in England."

AUSTEN AS A YOUNG WOMAN

By the time Jane reached adolescence, her comfortable, secure world had begun to expand and change. Until she was twelve, Jane had never traveled beyond Bath, about a hundred miles away, to visit her mother's brother's family, the Leigh-Perrots. At twelve, she and Cassandra traveled by carriage with their parents to Kent, stopping in London on the way, a trip requiring several days. This was the first of many trips she made to London and Kent. During her teen years, her immediate family shrank when two of her brothers went away to college at Oxford and two joined the navy. But her extended family grew as cousins and older brothers married and had children. Births and deaths followed one another: Her cousin Eliza, educated in France, had married a French aristocrat, the Comte de Feuillide, who became embroiled in the politics of the French Revolution and was executed by guillotine early in 1774. The following year Anne, wife of her brother James, died, leaving a two-year-old daughter, Jane, to be raised at Steventon by her grandparents and aunts.

During the 1790s, new developments affected Cassandra's and Jane's personal lives. Cassandra fell in love with Thomas Fowle, a former pupil of her father who had gone on to the university and become a clergyman. The couple were engaged in 1795, but because his rectory living was insufficient to support a family, he went to the West Indies as a chaplain to earn and save money. While in Santo Domingo he contracted yellow fever and died in 1797, leaving his £1000 earnings to his betrothed. Cassandra was distraught and lived an isolated life for two years, during which time Jane, as her close companion, suffered with her. Cassandra never married; indeed there are no indications that she ever considered marriage again.

Jane also had a romantic interest, a flirtation with Tom Lefroy, an Irish nephew visiting the Lefroy rectory at Ashe only a few miles from Steventon. Jane's letters to Cassandra from 1796 leave it unclear if this was a mere flirtation or a serious relationship. In one letter, Jane says, "I am almost afraid to tell you how my Irish friend and I behaved. Imagine to yourself everything most profligate and shocking in the way of dancing and sitting down together. . . . He is a very gentlemanlike, good-looking, pleasant young man, I assure you." In another letter, she says she is giving up all of her other admirers "as I mean to confine myself in the future to Mr. Tom Lefroy, for whom I do not care sixpence." In another letter, she says, "I am to flirt my last with Tom Lefroy, and when you receive this it will be over. My tears flow as I write at the melancholy idea." Both Cassandra and Mrs. Lefroy were concerned that the relationship was serious and warned Jane that Tom was too young and too poor to marry. The Lefroys sent him home to Ireland, and within a year he was engaged to a woman with a large fortune.

AUSTEN'S FIRST NOVELS

The years 1796 through 1799 were significant in Jane Austen's career as a writer. By 1796 she had written part of an epistolary novel she called *Elinor and Marianne*. Setting it aside in October, she began a conventional novel called *First Impressions* and completed it in August 1797; the novel was later retitled *Pride and Prejudice*. By November 1797 she was busy recasting the correspondence of *Elinor and Marianne* as a narrative; she retitled it *Sense and Sensibility*. That same November saw her first attempt to find a publisher for

First Impressions. Austen's father sent the following letter to Cadell, a London publisher:

> Sir,—I have in my possession a manuscript novel, comprising 3 vols., about the length of Miss Burney's "Evelina." As I am well aware of what consequence it is that a work of this sort shd make its first appearance under a respectable name, I apply to you. I shall be much obliged, therefore, if you will inform me whether you choose to be concerned in it, what will be the expense of publishing it at the author's risk, and what you will venture to advance for the property of it, if on perusal it is approved of. Should you give any encouragement, I will send you the work.
>
> > I am, sir, your humble servant,
> > George Austen.
> > Steventon, near Overton, Hants,
> > 1st Nov., 1797.

Cadell rejected the manuscript, and it was left to George to so inform his daughter. In *The Story of Jane Austen's Life*, Oscar Fay Adams comments on the difficulty for the father: "For knowing as we do how closely the welfare of any particular Austen was interwoven with that of all, we may be very sure that here was a painful task for the affectionate father, so proud of his daughter's dawning talent."

The rejection disappointed Jane but did not dampen her desire for writing. She finished the new version of *Sense and Sensibility* in early 1798 and immediately began another novel, which she finished within a year. Her third novel, *Susan*, later retitled *Northanger Abbey*, differs from the first two. Instead of being set in a village, it is set in the city of Bath and in a remote country house. Almost entirely a satire on the romantic novels of the time, it has a heroine with whom the author has little sympathy, unlike the heroines of the first two novels, whom Austen clearly likes. In *Susan*, the hero, Henry Tilney, more closely represents Austen's ironic viewpoint and has engaging traits similar to those of heroines Elinor and Elizabeth. In the spring of 1803, Austen revised the manuscript and sold it to the publisher Crosby for £10. Though Crosby advertised the book as *"Susan:* a Novel in 2 Volumes," he never published it. In 1809, he agreed to sell the manuscript back to the author for the same amount he paid for it, but Jane could not produce the £10.

Austen's letters to her sister, Cassandra, date from 1796. Whenever one of the girls traveled, the sisters exchanged letters. Cassandra saved many but not all of Jane's letters to her, but destroyed all of the letters she wrote to Jane. The bulk of Jane's surviving letters to Cassandra contain information and impressions that typically interest single, young sisters, sharing her daily activities and those of other family members. The most complete edition of Austen's letters, including numerous letters to other relatives, was published in two volumes in 1932 by R.W. Chapman. Entitled *Jane Austen's Letters to Her Sister Cassandra and Others,* the collection has been an important source for biographers and critics searching both to define Jane Austen as a person and to interpret her novels.

AUSTEN'S PERSONALITY

Given Austen's prolific correspondence, the biographical memoir written by her nephew J.E. Austen-Leigh just over fifty years after Austen's death, and the numerous diary entries of other relatives, it seems Austen's personality and character would be obvious and indisputable, but that is not the case. Scholars and biographers have trouble reconciling relatives' portrayal of Jane as a model of sweetness with rather nasty lines from her letters and books that sarcastically skewer others. Some scholars argue that her satiric remarks reflect a detached and ironic style Austen cultivated for the sake of humor. Others argue that beneath the author's sweet, polite surface lurks a streak of bitterness and anger.

Austen is fondly remembered in J.E. Austen-Leigh's *Memoir.* Nieces and nephews recalling their aunt after her death particularly note her popularity with children. One remembers "her great sweetness of manner. She seemed to love you, and you loved her in return." Another remembers her aunt's helpfulness. "She would furnish us with what we wanted from her wardrobe; and she would be the entertaining visitor in our make-believe house." Yet another niece recalls her "being so playful, and her long circumstantial stories so delightful." A nephew remembers her as a community member. Her love for children was apparent, he says,

> but her friends of all ages felt her enlivening influence. Her unusually quick sense of the ridiculous led her to play with all the commonplaces of everyday life, whether as regarded persons or things; but she never played with its serious duties or responsibilities, nor did she ever turn individuals into ridicule. With all her neighbours in the village she was on friendly, though not on intimate, terms. She took a kindly interest in all their proceedings, and liked to hear about them.

Austen-Leigh concludes his chapter on his aunt by saying, "She was, in fact, as ready to comfort the unhappy, or to nurse the sick, as she was to laugh and jest with the light-hearted."

Meanwhile, scholars point to situations and lines in Austen's novels and comments in her letters to Cassandra that make it hard to believe that Jane was always sweet, charming, and good-natured. In *Pride and Prejudice*, Elizabeth says to her sister, "There are few people whom I really love, and still fewer of whom I think well. The more I see of the world, the more am I dissatisfied with it." In one of her letters to Cassandra, she writes: "Mrs. Hall, of Sherborne, was brought to bed yesterday of a dead child, some weeks before she expected, owing to a fright. I suppose she happened unawares to look at her husband." From another letter: "Mrs. Portman is not much admired in Dorchester; the good-natured world, as usual, extolled her beauty so highly, that all the neighbourhood have had the pleasure of being disappointed." Another letter says, of a maid apprenticed to a dressmaker, "we may hope to see her able to spoil gowns in a few years." She tells her sister that a neighbor's wife is "discovered to be everything that the Neighbourhood could wish her, silly & cross as well as extravagant." She writes that an upcoming ball will probably be "very stupid, there will be nobody worth dancing with, and nobody worth talking to."

Examples like these appear throughout Austen's writing, even in the Juvenalia, and their frequency raises questions about the extent to which sarcastic and cynical comments reveal Austen's personality. Critic Marvin Mudrick says of Jane's youthful writing that she has "close observation without sympathy, common sense without tenderness, densely imagined representation without passion." British novelist Virginia Woolf thinks that Jane Austen "had few illusions about other people and none about herself." Of *Sense and Sensibility*, Halperin comments, "The world of this tale is a dark, dark place, populated by the most astonishing cast of villainous characters assembled by the novelist in any of her books." Of the same book, Virginia Woolf remarks, "It seems as if her creatures were born merely to give Jane Austen the supreme delight of slicing their heads off."

Explanations for the sarcasm and cynicism vary widely. Perhaps Austen used sarcasm as a defense and poked fun so that she did not despair over the evil and foolishness she saw in society. Perhaps Austen, like other satirists, found laughter a better technique for effecting reform than complaint. If her style does indeed reflect real anger and bitterness, Austen's situation perhaps justifies it. She was a bright, educated woman with ambition to become a serious novelist, but she lived in a society that imposed strict expectations and limitations on women. Knowing that she had no income and would have no inheritance, she was faced with finding a husband or having to depend on others for her keep. In Austen's time, the oldest child inherited the estate of the parents.

David Cecil takes all of the speculation about personality less seriously, however:

> Jane Austen was always to delight in her fools: without compunction she mocks their follies so as to get all the amusement out of them she can. But, just because she enjoyed them so much, they do not put her out of temper; rather she recognizes them as an addition to the pleasures of life. This was true of her at seventeen as at thirty.... The outstanding characteristic of these early works is their rollicking high spirits. From these alone we could deduce that the young Jane Austen enjoyed her existence.

Nevertheless, her enjoyable existence in Steventon came to an abrupt end in 1801 when George Austen retired and moved his wife and daughters to Bath. In November 1800, Jane returned home with her friend Martha Lloyd to find Mrs. Austen at the door announcing, "Well, girls! it is all settled. We have decided to leave Steventon and go to Bath." Though Jane was not ordinarily overwhelmed, at this news she fainted in the doorway. She was deeply attached to Steventon; Austen-Leigh points out that

> this was the residence of Jane Austen for twenty-five years. This was the cradle of her genius. These were the first objects which inspired her young heart with a sense of the beauties of nature. In strolls along those wood-walks, thick-coming fancies rose in her mind, and gradually assumed the forms in which they came forth to the world. In that simple church she brought them all into subjection to the piety which ruled her in life.

Jane had never liked Bath, but by the time of the move in 1801, she was resigned and at least outwardly cheerful. She was unhappy, however, when the family sold five hundred books and Jane's pianoforte because their new quarters were smaller. The heroine of *Persuasion*, a novel Austen wrote in 1816, has a similar experience in which she is forced to leave a home she loves and move to Bath.

Before settling in their new home in the city, George

Austen took his wife and daughters on a six-week vacation by the sea, visiting several resorts along the coast. At one stop, Jane had a brief romance. After years of waiting, she found a man she could love and respect, and her family approved of the match. It appears the man had to leave the party for a while but planned to rejoin them later in the vacation. Then Jane received news from his brother that her suitor had died suddenly. Nothing is known about the man besides family gossip, not even his name. As is the case during other periods of troubled emotions, no letters remain, this time for a period of three years.

ROOTLESS YEARS IN BATH AND SOUTHAMPTON

The Austens returned to Bath in the fall, and Jane spent five troubled years in the city. In 1802, while Jane and Cassandra were visiting the Bigg-Withers at their home, Manydown, near Steventon, Harris, the youngest son and heir to the estate, proposed marriage to Jane and was accepted. He was twenty-one and she twenty-six, considered at that time the beginning of middle age. During the night, she realized she could not marry a man she did not love just to have a suitable husband, and in the morning, she broke the engagement. Distressed and embarrassed, she and Cassandra went to her brother at Steventon and insisted on his taking them to Bath immediately. A second disappointment came in 1803, when she sold *Susan* to the publisher who advertised but never published the book. And in 1804 Jane suffered the loss of her good friend and adviser, Mrs. Anne Lefroy, who was killed in a fall from a horse.

The most serious loss was her father's death. In January 1805, after a two-day illness, George Austen died and was buried in a crypt in Walcot, the Bath church where he was married. His death was particularly upsetting to Jane, who loved her father and got on well with him; in contrast, her relationship with her mother was uneasy and often filled with stress. Now the three Austen women were alone and without money. Each of the Austen brothers responded with a £50 annual stipend, and Cassandra could count on interest income from the money her fiancé had left her, but Jane had nothing. In the summer of 1805, Jane's unmarried friend Martha Lloyd, left homeless at the death of her mother, came to live with them. These four women lived together for the rest of Jane's life.

In 1804 and 1805 while living in Bath, Jane tried to write but with little success. She recast *Lady Susan*, a very early epistolary novel written in 1793 or 1794, into story form. The book is a dark tale of the proud, greedy, dishonest Lady Susan, who hates her own daughter. Austen's characters were modeled on people she had only heard about, in a social setting she was acquainted with but had not inhabited. She never tried to publish this novel and never again tried to write about what she did not know firsthand. Then she began *The Watsons*, a realistic and ironic study of women's place in society that discusses four sisters in search of husbands. The story has a dark tone and portrays the women's lives as unfulfilling, devoid of security or happiness; she portrays men as inconstant, vain, and materialistic. After sixty-thousand words, she abandoned the novel. Both of these unfinished pieces were published posthumously in 1870 with Austen-Leigh's *Memoir*.

Early in 1806 the decision was made that Jane, Cassandra, their mother, and Martha would leave Bath—a decision that particularly pleased Jane—and accept Frank Austen's invitation to live with him and his new wife, Mary, in Southampton. Late in the summer, the newlyweds and the four women moved into a large house at 2 Castle Square in Southampton, where they stayed until 1809. Little of significance happened in Jane's life during these years in Southampton. She received invitations for morning visits, dinners, card playing, and even an occasional ball, but her letters describe day-to-day events with little enthusiasm and only a sprinkling of the wit found in her earlier letters. In one letter to Cassandra, she writes, "I see nothing to be glad of." Now that Martha Lloyd lived with them, there was another person to care for Mrs. Austen, whose health had declined, giving Jane and Cassandra more opportunity to travel.

On a trip in the summer of 1808 to visit her brother Edward at Godmersham Park in Kent, Austen twice stopped in London to attend plays and visit art galleries, both favorite activities. While in Kent she received another proposal, this one from Edward's brother-in-law Edward Bridges, a clergyman four years younger than Jane, who was thirty-two. Again she turned down the opportunity for marriage because she did not love the man, but apparently she handled this refusal more gracefully than that to Harris Bigg-Withers. Later that same summer, Cassandra went to Godmersham

Park for several weeks to help Edward's wife, Elizabeth, before the birth of her eleventh child. Tragically, ten days after the child's birth, Elizabeth died. (All of Jane's brothers lost their first wives, and only Edward never remarried.) Though Cassandra stayed on to help with the children after Elizabeth's death, Jane, reputed to be concerned, caring, and helpful, volunteered only to care for two of the boys during their brief visit to Southampton.

A HOME IN CHAWTON

By 1809 Edward had inherited the Knight estate, Godmersham Park, and the Knight Hampshire houses in Chawton that George Austen had overseen. Edward offered the cottage to his mother, sisters, and Martha Lloyd and kept the great house for himself and his children for their visits there. Chawton is a small village, a mile from the larger village of Alton, and fifteen miles from Winchester and from Jane's former home in Steventon. The four women moved into the Chawton cottage on July 7, 1809. Within three weeks, Jane sent a lighthearted poem to her brother Frank about the "many comforts" of their Chawton home, rejoicing that with the completion of the remodeling "It will all other Houses beat." Clearly, Jane was happy to have a secure home and to return to a small village.

The cottage, a two-story brick house with a tiled roof, is hardly spectacular; now, restored, it serves as a museum for manuscripts, documents, and objects from the lives of Jane and her relatives. Perhaps formerly an inn, it stands adjacent to the road between London and Winchester. The sitting rooms, kitchen, and offices are on the first floor of the L-shaped house, and the second floor comprises six bedrooms, enough for the Austen women, Martha Lloyd, servants, and visitors (Jane and Cassandra shared one of the bedrooms). A bake house and a shed for their donkey and cart stand out back, and flower and vegetable gardens, orchards, and hedged walks surround the buildings.

Most of the housekeeping at Chawton fell to Jane and Cassandra since Mrs Austen, now seventy, devoted her time to gardening and embroidery. Jane was responsible for the wine making and helped with the gardening and cooking. The women often spent evenings making quilts together. On a typical day, Jane arose early and practiced on her new pianoforte before she made breakfast. Afternoons she spent walking in the gardens or along the hedges, doing errands in Alton, or visiting neighbors. For her private amusement, she made music books of pieces to practice; she wrote them out by drawing the lines by hand and neatly making every note with pen and ink. And secretly she wrote, at a small table with a piece of blotting paper in front of her; if someone came, she quickly hid the manuscript under it. Likewise, she refused to oil a squeaky door as it served as a warning of someone's approach, giving her time to hide her work. Her brother James likened her to some little bird who "builds of the materials nearest at hand, of the twigs and mosses supplied by the tree in which it is placed: curiously constructed out of the simplest matters." She was now seen always wearing her white muslin cap, the sign of a woman in middle age. David Cecil explains: "Indeed her establishment at Chawton marks the turning point in her story. Nothing more was to happen to Jane Austen the woman; from now on her history is that of Jane Austen the artist."

PUBLICATION OF AUSTEN'S EARLY NOVELS

Beginning in 1810, Jane stayed home and secretly worked on her writing. She revised *Sense and Sensibility* and *Pride and Prejudice*, but she could do nothing with *Susan* while the publisher Crosby held the manuscript. Fearing another rejection of *Pride and Prejudice*, she chose to submit the manuscript for *Sense and Sensibility* to a publisher first. Her brother Henry, the banker who lived in London, served as her literary agent, and Thomas Egerton of the Military Library, Whitehall, agreed to publish *Sense and Sensibility* at the author's risk; that is, Jane had to sign an agreement to reimburse the publisher for all losses. While waiting between acceptance and publication, she wrote, "I am never too busy to think of *S&S*. I can no more forget it, than a mother can forget her sucking child." She started immediately to save money, but the thousand copies of the first edition, which came out in November 1811, sold out in twenty months. The book's sale not only covered the costs of publication, but also earned £140 for Jane, considerably increased by sales of the second edition.

Only the most intimate family members knew that Jane was a published author; the title page of *Sense and Sensibility* read only "By a Lady." One day when Jane was in the Alton library with her niece Anna, Jane casually pointed out

Sense and Sensibility as one of the books newly arrived from London. Anna picked it up, looked at the cover, and said, "With a title like that it must be rubbish," and put it down. Encouraged by the success of her first publication, Jane risked submitting *Pride and Prejudice* again. She wanted £150 for it, but Egerton offered to pay £110, and she took his offer. *Pride and Prejudice* appeared in January 1813, "By the Author of *Sense and Sensibility*." When the newly published copies arrived, Jane wrote, "I have got my own darling child from London.... I must confess that I think [the heroine, Elizabeth] as delightful a creature as ever appeared in print, and how I shall be able to tolerate those who do not like *her* ... I do not know." *Pride and Prejudice* was an immediate success, soon a popular topic of dinner-table conversation and the object of critics' praise. Jane's nephew James-Edward read and enjoyed both of the published novels without knowing that his aunt was their author.

THREE NEW NOVELS

Jane began to write *Mansfield Park* in 1812 and completed the rough draft by July 1813, revising until late into December. A mature woman now, Austen addressed the deeper subjects of social changes emerging in England and the moral and immoral perceptions about events and behavior. Its main character is the unassuming but courageous Fanny Price, many readers' favorite Austen heroine. Egerton published the book in May 1814, "By the Author of *Sense and Sensibility* and *Pride and Prejudice*," and the fifteen hundred initial copies sold within six months. For financial advantages, Henry arranged for a second publisher to issue the second edition of *Mansfield Park*, but the book did not continue to sell well. About this time, Henry leaked the secret of her identity. Though sworn not to divulge any information about his sister's authorship, he could not resist dropping hints when London readers speculated about who the author might be. When, finally, the news was out, Jane said of her newfound fame, "What a trifle it all is to the really important points of one's existence."

Austen's next novel, *Emma*, took her fourteen months to write, from the beginning of January 1814 to the end of March 1815; it was published on her fortieth birthday, December 16, 1815. After a series of coincidences, Jane dedicated this novel to England's prince regent, the future

George IV. Jane was in London nursing her brother Henry through a serious illness, about which his physician, Charles Thomas Haden, consulted a colleague who happened to be one of the prince's personal physicians. By this time Jane was well known, and the physician mentioned that the prince liked Jane's books and kept a set in each of his residences. Through the grapevine, the prince learned that his physician saw Jane Austen regularly at her brother's bedside. The prince directed his librarian and chaplain, James Stanier Clarke, to call on her and invite her to tour Carlton House, one of the prince's residences. During her visit on November 13, 1815, Clarke informed her that she was free to dedicate her next book to the prince. Jane, however, strongly disapproved of the future king and planned to ignore the invitation. Through correspondence, Jane learned, however, that being "free to" really meant that she was "expected to." So she dedicated *Emma* to the future George IV "By His Royal Highness's Permission, Most Respectfully," by "His Royal Highness's Dutiful and Obedient Humble Servant, the Author." Austen and the publisher honored the prince with special copies bound in red.

Three months after she had completed *Emma*, Jane began writing *Persuasion*, which she worked on through the winter months. The financial success of *Emma* allowed her to buy back the manuscript of *Susan* from Crosby, but she had to be discreet to keep him from finding out that he owned a manuscript by the author of four successful novels. Jane enlisted Henry as her agent, and he secured the manuscript before he told the astonished publisher that Jane Austen was its author. In the spring of 1816, Jane was occupied with three projects: finishing *Persuasion*, revising *Susan*, and writing "Plan of a Novel," a burlesque on romantic fiction. She completed the burlesque in the spring, finished the final revisions of *Persuasion* on August 6, changed the title of *Susan* to *Northanger Abbey* and the name of the heroine to Catherine and then put it on the shelf. *Persuasion* and *Northanger Abbey* were published together the year after Jane's death.

FAILING HEALTH

By the time she finished *Persuasion*, Jane was desperately ill with a form of tuberculosis that attacked the adrenal glands. At that time, the disease had no name; it was named Addison's disease in 1849, and today it is treated with cortisone. Its symptoms are blotchy skin, erratic body temperature, low blood pressure, nausea, and vomiting. Jane became weaker by stages: When she could no longer walk to Alton, she rode the donkey; when riding the donkey was too taxing, she rode in the cart. Finally, she spent most of her days lying on a couch made by arranging two or three chairs. Yet she kept writing, and her letters to relatives repeatedly note that she thought she was getting better. On January 29, 1817, she began another book entitled *Sandition.* It is an attack on improvers and developers who flaunt tradition and destroy the countryside. By March 18, she had written twenty-five thousand words, but could write no more. Except for a half-dozen letters, her work on *Sandition,* not published until 1925, was her last writing.

On April 27, 1817, Austen made a will, leaving all of her money to Cassandra, except for £50 bequeathed to Henry's housekeeper, who had lost money when Henry's bank failed. She left a necklace to Louisa Knight and a lock of her hair to her favorite niece, Fanny. Because her doctor lived in Winchester, the family moved her there to be closer to his care. On May 24, the carriage came from Steventon and took Jane and Cassandra in a downpour to lodgings in Winchester. Her brother Henry and Edward Knight's nineteen-year-old son, William, rode on horseback, one on each side. Cassandra nursed Jane as her health deteriorated rapidly. Early in the morning of Friday, July 18, the end near, Cassandra asked Jane if she wanted anything, and Jane replied: "Nothing but death, God grant me patience, Pray for me oh pray for me." Medicated, she was soon unconscious. She lay with her head on a pillow in Cassandra's lap and died at 4:30 in the morning.

Early in the morning on July 24, Austen was buried in Winchester Cathedral, attended only by three brothers and a nephew. Cassandra watched from the lodging window as bearers carried her body to the church. The family arranged to have her grave marked with a black marble slab and wrote the following inscription for it. It is noteworthy that the inscription makes no mention of her as a novelist.

In Memory of
JANE AUSTEN
youngest daughter of the late
Rev GEORGE AUSTEN

formerly Rector of Steventon in this county
she departed this life on the 18th of July, 1817,
aged 41, after a long illness supported with
the patience and the hopes of a Christian.

The benevolence of her heart,
the sweetness of her temper, and
the extraordinary endowments of her mind
obtained the regard of all who knew her, and
the warmest love of her intimate connections.

Their grief is in proportion to their affection
They know their loss to be irreparable
but in their deepest affliction they are consoled
by a firm though humble hope that her charity,
devotion, faith and purity have rendered
her soul acceptable in the sight of her
REDEEMER

In the middle of the nineteenth century, one of the vergers in Winchester Cathedral wondered why so many people asked for directions to Jane Austen's grave. "Was there," he asked, "anything particular about that lady?" In 1872 a brass tablet was added on the north wall of the cathedral near her grave. It says

JANE AUSTEN
known to many by her writings,
endeared to her family
by the varied charms of her Character
and ennobled by Christian faith and piety,
was born at Steventon in the County of Hants.

Dec. xvi mdcclxxv,
and buried in this Cathedral
July xxiv mdcccxvii

"She opened her mouth with wisdom
and in her tongue is the law of
kindness."

Prov. xxxi. v. xxvi

CHAPTER 1

Jane Austen's Relationship to Her Times and Her Critics

READINGS ON
JANE AUSTEN

England in Austen's Time

Fay Weldon

In the form of a letter to her niece Alice, novelist Fay Weldon explains the discrepancy between the harsh society in which Jane Austen lived and the gentler society she portrays in her novels. According to Weldon, women in the late eighteenth century lacked basic rights and endured all kinds of dangers and duties. Conceding that the real life of women in Austen's time must seem unbelievable to a modern English girl like Alice, Weldon suggests that Austen may simply have created an idyllic fictional world as an alternative to the unpleasantness she nevertheless took for granted in the real world. Novels, Weldon reminds her niece, are inventions of the imagination, not records of history. After studying economics and psychology, Fay Weldon turned to writing. She has published numerous stories and novels, among them *Down Among Women, The Life and Loves of a She-Devil, Polaris and Other Stories,* and *Puffball;* several plays, among them *Mixed Doubles* and *Jane Eyre: An Adaptation;* and a biography, *Rebecca West.*

My dear Alice,

... I do believe it is the battle the writer wages with the real world which provides the energy for invention. I think Jane Austen waged a particularly fearful battle, and that the world won in the end and killed her: and we are left with the seven great novels. I know you've been told six. But she did write another, *Lady Susan,* a diverting, energetic and excellent novel, when she was very young, at about the same time as she wrote the comparatively tedious and conventional *Sense and Sensibility* (please don't read it first). She put *Lady Susan* in a drawer. She did not attempt to have it published; nor, later, did her family. My own feeling is that they simply did not like it.

They thought it unedifying and foolish, and that wicked adventuresses should not be heroines, and women writers should not invent, but only describe what they know. They had, in fact, a quite ordinary and perfectly understandable desire to keep Jane Austen respectable, ladylike and unalarming, and *Lady Susan* was none of these things.....

You must understand, I think, the world into which Jane Austen was born. I do not think the life or personality of writers to be particularly pertinent to their work.... But I do think *the times* in which writers live are important. The writer must write out of a tradition—if only to break away from it.... He, or she, writes out of a society: links the past of that society with its future....

Jane Austen concerned herself with what to us are observable truths, because we agree with them. They were not so observable at the time. [In reading *Pride and Prejudice*] we believe with her that Elizabeth should marry for love, and that Charlotte was extremely lucky to find happiness with Mr Collins, whom she married so as not, in a phrase dating from that time, to be left on 'the shelve'. She believed it was better not to marry at all, than to marry without love. Such notions were quite new at the time. It surprises us that in her writing she appears to fail to take the pleasures of sex into account, but that was the convention at the time: we disapprove, where her society most approves. She is not a gentle writer. Do not be misled: she is not ignorant, merely discreet: not innocent, merely graceful. She lived in a society which assumed—as ours does—that its values were right. It had God on its side, and God had ordained the ranks of His people; moreover, He had made men men and women women, and how could a thing like that be changed? It is idle to complain that Jane Austen lacked a crusading zeal. With hindsight, it is easy to look at the world she lived in, and say she should have. What she did seems to me more valuable. She struggled to perceive and describe the flow of beliefs that typified her time, and more, to suggest for the first time that the personal, the emotional, is in fact the *moral*—nowadays, of course, for good or bad, we argue that it is political. She left a legacy for the future to build upon.

English Life in Austen's Time

I want you to conceive of England, your country, two hundred years ago. A place without detergents or tissues or tarmaced roads or railway trains, or piped water, let alone electricity or gas or oil; where energy (what a modern term) was provided by coal, and wood, and the muscle of human beings, and that was all. Where the fastest anyone could cover the ground was the speed of the fastest horse, and where, even so, letters could be posted in London one evening and be delivered in Hereford the next morning. Because people were so poor—most people—they would run, and toil, and sweat all day and all night to save themselves and their children from starvation. Rather like India is today. If you were a child and your parents died, you lived on the streets: if you were a young woman and gave birth out of wedlock you would, like as not, spend the rest of your life in a lunatic asylum, classified as a moral imbecile. If you tried to commit suicide to save yourself from such a life, you would be saved, and then hanged. (These last two 'ifs', incidentally, applied as recently as fifty years ago.) If you stole anything worth more than £5 you could be hanged, or transported to a penal colony for life. If it was under £5 there were long, harsh prison sentences in unspeakable prisons, and the age of criminal liability was seven. No casual vandals or graffiti writers then.

Child, you don't know how lucky you are. If you cheat on the Underground[1] they give you a psychiatrist. If you break a leg, there's someone to mend it. If you have a cold in the nose, you use a tissue and flush it down the W.C. [toilet]: Jane Austen used a pocket handkerchief, and had a maid to boil it clean. Fair enough, if you're Jane Austen, but supposing you were the maid? You would be working eighteen hours a day or so, six-and-a-half days a week, with one day off a month, and thinking yourself lucky.

EMPLOYMENT CHOICES FOR WOMEN

If you weren't the maid, you might well be working on the land. Well into the nineteenth century, agriculture was the largest single source of employment for women. And do not think for one moment women of the working classes did *not* work, or had husbands able and willing to support them. A young country girl (and only fifty per cent of the population lived in towns) would be on the farm, cooking, cleaning, washing clothes—and carrying the water, and chopping the

1. the underground train system

wood and lighting the boiler to heat it—feeding animals, milking cows, planting, gleaning, gathering hay. If you worked in the dairy you would at least have the pleasure of developing skills, and would be better paid, but your day would start at 3 A.M. and end in the late evening. Your reward would be in heaven. The Bible rather rashly claimed that that was where the poor went, thus giving the rich every justification for preserving their poverty. No one's health was good—T.B. [tuberculosis] afflicted a sizeable proportion of the population. If you, as a young woman, fled to the city to improve your life, you could, with difficulty, become an apprentice and learn the traditional women's trades of millinery, embroidery, or seaming; or you could be a chimney sweep (from the age of six) or you could become a butcher (a nasty trade, despised by men) or a prostitute—70,000, they reckoned, in London at the turn of the century, out of a population of some 900,000.

MARRIAGE AS AN OPTION

Or you could marry.

The trouble was that you had to be able to *afford* to marry. You were expected to have a dowry, provided by your parents or saved by yourself, to give to your husband to offset your keep. For this great reason, and a variety of others, only thirty per cent of women married. Seventy per cent remained unmarried. It was no use waiting for your parents to die so that you could inherit their mansion, or cottage, or hovel, and so buy yourself a husband—your parents' property went to your brothers. Women inherited only through their husbands, and only thus could gain access to property. Women were born poor, and stayed poor, and lived well only by their husbands' favour. The sense of sexual sin ran high: the fear of pregnancy was great—you might well estimate that half the nation's women remained virgins all their lives....

So to marry was a great prize. It was a woman's aim. No wonder Jane Austen's heroines were so absorbed by the matter. It is the stuff of our women's magazines but it was the stuff of their life, their very existence. No wonder Mrs Bennet, driven half-mad by anxiety for her five unmarried daughters, knowing they would be unprovided for when her husband died, as indeed would she, made a fool of herself in public, husband-hunting on her girls' behalf. Politeness warred, as always, with desperation. Enough to give anyone the vapours!

Women survived, in Jane Austen's day, by pleasing and charming if they were in the middle classes, and by having a good, strong working back if they were of the peasantry. Writing was, incidentally, one of the very few occupations by which impoverished and helpless female members of the gentry could respectably—well, more or less—earn money. To be a governess was another, much fabled, occupation. Beautiful and talented governess, handsome scion of ancient housing, marrying where he loved and not where he ought. . . . It was a lovely, if desperate, fantasy. (See Elizabeth and Darcy in *Pride and Prejudice.*)

The average age of puberty, incidentally, was later in their day than it is now. In 1750 we know it to have been between eighteen and twenty. General malnutrition and low female body weights were no doubt the cause. Marriage was later, too: on average between twenty-five and twenty-eight, though Jane Austen's heroines seem to have started panicking in their early twenties. Lydia, in *Pride and Prejudice*, managed it at the age of sixteen, and shocked everyone by revealing everyone's true feelings—trailing her hand with its new wedding-ring out of the carriage window as she rode triumphantly into town, so that everyone would know. Married! Jane Austen herself put on her cap when she was thirty. That is, she announced herself by her dress as out of the marriage market, now resigned to growing old with as much grace and dignity as she could muster. Thirty!

WOMEN LACKED RIGHTS

Once you were married, of course, life was not rosy. Any property you did acquire belonged to your husband. The children were his, not yours. If the choice at childbirth was between the mother or child, the mother was the one to go. You could not sue, in your own name. (By the same token at least you could not be sued.) He could beat you, if he saw fit, and punish your children likewise. You could be divorced for adultery, but not divorce him for the same offence. Mind you, divorce was not a way out of marital problems. Marriage was for ever. Between 1650 and 1850 there were only 250 divorces in England.

You put up with the sex life you had, and were not, on the whole, and in the ordinary ranks of society, expected to enjoy it. It tended to result, for one thing, in childbirth. Contraception was both wicked and illegal, against God's law and the land's. Abstinence was the decent person's protection against pregnancy. There were, of course, then as now, libidinous sections of society, the wild young of the upper classes, and free thinkers, who saw sexual freedom as the path to political liberty: and, of course, there were married couples who did find a real and sensual satisfaction in each other—but this was a bonus, not something to be taken for granted: certainly nothing you could go to a Marriage Counsellor about.

The fact that there were 70,000 prostitutes in London in 1801, out of a female population of some 475,000, indicates that your husband at least would not be virginal on marriage. He would quite possibly be diseased. Venereal disease was common, and often nastily fatal.

Alice, by your standards, it was a horrible time to be alive. Yet you could read and read Jane Austen and never know it. And why should you? Novelists provide an escape from reality: they take you to the City of Invention. When you return you know more about yourself. You do not read novels for information, but for enlightenment. I don't suppose Jane Austen thought particularly much about the ills of her society. All this, for her, was simply what the world was like. . . .

WOMEN'S DUTY TO BEAR CHILDREN

Now, Alice, there you are, a typical young woman of the 1799s. We're supposing you're working on the land, and of peasant stock. You've scraped your dowry together and you've found your young (or old, often quite old!) man, and got yourself married. Your prime duty is to have children. The clergyman has told you so at the wedding ceremony. 'Marriage is designed by God for the procreation of children. . . .' Everyone believes it. (If you turned out to be barren, that was a terrible disaster, not just personally but socially. It made you a non-woman. . . . But such disasters apart, you're likely to be pregnant within a year of marriage and carry one child successfully to term every two years until the menopause. This seems to be the rate which nature, uninterfered with, decrees for human reproduction. Fifty per cent of all the babies would die before they were two: from disease due to malnutrition, ignorance, or infection. Every death would be the same misery it is today. Your many pregnancies would be plentifully interrupted by miscarriages, and one baby in every four would be still-born.

Midwives, mercifully, did not customarily allow imperfect babies to live, nor were they expected to. Child delivery was primitive and there were no analgesics. Child care was not considered a full-time job. Babies were swaddled and hung on pegs out of the way while mothers went on keeping the wolf from the door. If the mother's milk failed, the babies would be fed on gruel, soaked into sacking and sucked out by the baby.

Your own chances of dying in childbirth were not negligible and increased with every pregnancy. After fifteen pregnancies (which meant something like six babies brought to term and safely delivered) your chances of dying were (Marie Stopes later claimed) one in two. . . .

Back to you, Alice, mother of six, aged thirty, with your backache and your varicose veins and your few teeth, carrying water from the village well for all your family's needs, and water is about as heavy a soul's task as you can get, and you have to choose if they're going to be clean or you're going to be ill. . . .

So you must understand there were compensations to be found in virginity, in abstinence, in fidelity, and in spinsterhood, which are not found today, and read Jane Austen bearing this in mind.

MODEST COMPENSATIONS

There were more positive compensations for living in this terrible time. The countryside must have been very, very pretty. The hedgerows and blasted oaks had not been rooted out by agro-industrialists, and wild flowers and butterflies flourished to brighten the gentle greyish greens of the landscape. These days the greens are brighter and the fields are smoother, thanks to insecticides, nitrates and herbicides. And everything you looked at would have been lovely: furniture (if you had any) made of seasoned oak, and by craftsmen working out of a tradition unequalled anywhere in the world—usefulness working in the service of grace. New and different buildings going up everywhere, as the population grew and the middle classes with it. . . .

Perhaps landscape, buildings and objects had to be beautiful to compensate for the ugliness of the people. Malnutrition, ignorance and disease ensured a hopping, shuffling, peering, scrofulous population, running short of eyes and limbs. Crutches, peg-legs, glass-eyes and hooks were much in demand. If the children had pink cheeks it was because they had T.B. Do not be deceived by the vision of Georgian England as a rural idyll. Artists of the time liked to depict it as such, naturally enough . . . and so did writers, and while you are reading Jane Austen you are perfectly entitled to suspend your disbelief, as she was when she wrote. Fiction, thank God, is not and need not be reality. The real world presses forcibly enough into the imaginative adventure that is our life, without fiction aiding and abetting.

CHANGES FOR THE BETTER

During Jane Austen's lifetime—she was born in December 1775 and died in July 1817—attitudes, they say, changed significantly. They became, for a time, before the rigours of Victorian puritanism set in, more relaxed. The age of puberty declined; sexual activity in women was less surprising and less alarming; young women, increasingly, chose to marry for love and not at their parents' choosing. There was an increase in the marriage rates, a lowering of the age of marriage, and a dramatic rise in the illegitimacy rate. Women became more fertile, for good or bad. The rate of infant mortality decreased. . . .

Why, you ask? Better nutrition, a new understanding of hygiene, the aftermath of the French Revolution, the loosening of the stranglehold of the Church, more novels and better novels read by more people in the opinion-forming ranks of society, better poetry—not wide-sweeping social changes, waves in the body politic but the sharp focusing power of individuals. . . .

Any theory will do until the next one replaces it. Being a writer, I like the better-novels theory, which I hereby give you. If the outer world is a mere reflection of the inner one, if as you refine the person so the outer aspects of the world are refined, so will social change work from the inside out, from the individual out into the wider community. Enlighten people, and you enlighten society. How's that? That is enough for now. . . .

With love,
Aunt Fay

Austen's Women in a Conservative Society

David Monaghan

Eighteenth-century women were thought to have minds too feeble to be educated and were expected only to serve the needs of their family and husbands. Critic David Monaghan argues that Austen, while disagreeing with these attitudes, does not advocate changing the system. According to Monaghan, Austen condemns meekness in her women characters and believes that they are indeed capable of learning and should be educated. Monaghan describes Austen's nonetheless conservative view: By concerning themselves with manners and educating their children properly, women foster a moral society and preserve its stability, and they make great contributions as skillful managers of their households. Monaghan points out that in her late works, however, Austen recognizes that the old order is beginning to crumble and that new roles for women are emerging. David Monaghan is an associate professor at Mount Saint Vincent University, Halifax, Nova Scotia. He is the author of *Jane Austen: Structure and Social Vision* and several articles on Jane Austen as well as other English, American, and Canadian novelists.

Women can rarely have been held in lower esteem than they were at the end of the eighteenth century.... The notion that women not only are but should be the intellectual inferiors of men was so fundamental to Dr Gregory's thinking that, in all seriousness, he advises any woman who might have offended against nature by cultivating her mind to conceal the fact: 'But if you happen to have any learning, keep it a profound secret, especially from the men, who generally look

From "Jane Austen and the Position of Women" by David Monaghan, in *Jane Austen in a Social Context*, edited by David Monaghan. Copyright ©1981 by David Monaghan. Reprinted by permission of Macmillan Ltd.

with a jealous and malignant eye on a woman of great parts,[1] and a cultivated understanding'.[2].... Most governesses and academies for young ladies sought to avoid overtaxing the limited minds of their charges by substituting accomplishments such as piano-playing, drawing and dancing for intellectual pursuits....

As adults women found their opportunities for self-assertion severely restricted. According to Hannah More, 'to women moral excellence is the grand object of education; and of moral excellence, domestic life is to a woman the appropriate sphere'.[3] For Gisborne, too, a woman's life must be centred on the home, and according to him her main responsibilities involve 'contributing daily and hourly to the comfort of husbands, of parents, of brothers and sisters . . . in the intercourse of domestic life'.[4] Even within this narrow domestic world women were, of course, expected to be subservient to their husbands.... Outside the family the only role offered to the woman was that of arbiter of manners....

AUSTEN DISAGREES WITH PREVAILING STANDARDS FOR WOMEN

Demeaning as these views may appear to us, few women expressed any dissatisfaction with their lot in the final years of the eighteenth century, and Mary Wollstonecraft's call for the assertion of the Rights of Woman[5] went almost entirely unheeded.... Jane Austen's disagreements with the prevailing attitudes of her time are fairly apparent.... Like Mary Wollstonecraft, for instance, Jane Austen operates on the assumption that women are inherently as intelligent and rational as men....

Only slightly less radical than her faith in the power of the female mind is Jane Austen's belief that intellectual abilities are as desirable in the woman as in the man. This re-evaluation of standards of female worth informs the treatment of some of the main female characters in *Pride and Prejudice*. Jane Bennet and Miss Bingley both have qualities which were regarded as marks of feminine excellence in an age which advised women to conceal any mental accomplishments. Jane has a benevolent attitude towards the world, and hers is a soft and yielding temperament; Miss Bingley is

1. talents   2. from "Dr. Gregory's Legacy to His Daughters," published in *Angelica's Ladies Library*   3. from *Strictures on the Modern System of Female Education*   4. from *An Enquiry into the Duties of the Female Sex*   5. from *A Vindication of the Rights of Women*

accomplished, elegant and physically attractive. Yet neither is judged the equal of Elizabeth Bennet because they lack her 'quickness of observation' and 'judgment'. This standard of excellence is made explicit by Darcy, who comments that while a woman should cultivate accomplishments such as 'music, singing, drawing, dancing and the modern languages . . . , to all this she must add something more substantial, in the improvement of the mind by extensive reading'. . . .

AUSTEN VALUES EDUCATION

In a letter dated November 12, 1800, to Martha Lloyd Austen, wife of her brother Francis Austen, Jane discusses an upcoming visit with her sister-in-law and her desire for animated conversation. Jane describes her recent readings in history and her hopes of sharing her knowledge with Martha. The letter is included in Penelope Hughes-Hallett's collected correspondence of Austen, My Dear Cassandra.

To Martha Lloyd
STEVENTON WEDNESDAY EVENG. NOVR 12 [1800]
My dear Martha
. . . You distress me cruelly by your request about books; I cannot think of any to bring with me, nor have I any idea of our wanting them. I come to you to be talked to, not to read or hear reading. I can do *that* at home; and indeed I am now laying in a stock of intelligence to pour out on you as *my* share of conversation. I am reading Henry's History of England, which I will repeat to you in any manner you may prefer, either in a loose, desultory, unconnected strain, or dividing my recital as the historian divides it himself, into seven parts, The Civil and Military—Religion—Constitution—Learning and Learned Men—Arts and Sciences—Commerce Coins and Shipping—and Manners; so that for every evening of the week there will be a different subject; the Friday's lot, Commerce, Coin and Shipping, you will find the least entertaining; but the next eveng:'s portion will make amends. We all unite in best love, and I am

Yr very affecte *J.A.*

Jane Austen's view of marriage is also at odds with the mainstream of contemporary thought. For her, the proper marriage is one in which the two parties operate on a basis of mutual respect. [In *Persuasion,*] the reader is offered a symbol of this ideal in the description of the way in which Admiral and Mrs Croft handle their carriage:

> But by coolly giving the reins a better direction herself, they happily passed the danger; and by once afterwards judiciously putting out her hand, they neither fell into a rut, nor ran foul of a dung-cart; and Anne, with some amusement at their style of driving, which she imagined no bad representation of the general guidance of their affairs, found herself safely deposited by them at the cottage.

What Jane Austen suggests here is that the Crofts manage to stay upright, in their married life as much as in their carriage, because, rather than blindly obeying her husband, Mrs Croft corrects his faults and supports his endeavours. Whenever a wife is overindulgent towards her husband in Jane Austen's novels we get the kind of imbalance that characterises the Palmers' relationship in *Sense and Sensibility*. The more Mrs Palmer remains good-natured in the face of her husband's displays of childish bad temper, the more excessive and self-indulgent his conduct becomes.

Jane Austen is equally hostile to the view that meekness is the major feminine virtue. So far as she is concerned, Elizabeth Bennet behaves far more admirably when she ignores decorum and tramples across muddy fields to visit the sick Jane, than does the young Fanny Price when she creeps timidly around Mansfield Park. Indeed, in *Mansfield Park* Jane Austen goes so far as to argue that meekness is a fault rather than a virtue. For much of the novel Fanny is, by Fordyce's standards, the ideal woman in that she is religious, morally upright and, above all, subservient to others. However, for Jane Austen, Fanny's lack of self-assertion constitutes a serious deficiency because it ensures that she is unable to exercise any influence and hence to do anything to halt the gradual corruption of the Bertram family. . . .

MANNERS CONTRIBUTE TO MORAL STABILITY

Yet, for all Jane Austen's sense of female worth, nowhere in her novels, with the significant exception of *Persuasion*, to which I will return later, does she follow Mary Wollstonecraft in expressing discontent at the woman's restricted role. None of her heroines has any ambition to be admitted into the professions, to manage an estate or to join the army. Instead, they concentrate their energies into the world of manners until, at the conclusions of the novels, they add to this the concerns of marriage. Only one of Jane Austen's major characters, Jane Fairfax in *Emma*, is faced with working for a living, and the prospect is viewed with horror: "'I did not mean, I was not thinking of the slave-trade", replied Jane, "governess-trade, I assure you, was all I had in view; widely different certainly as to the guilt of those who carry it on; but as to the greater misery of the victims, I do not know where it lies"'. A paradox thus seems to emerge. However, it can be resolved once we realise that, for Jane Austen, the restrictions imposed on the woman's social role do not diminish its importance. Rather, basing her case on contemporary conservative philosophy, she argues that those who control manners and the home have a crucial role to play in preserving the *status quo*. . . .

The link between manners and social stability is made explicit by Edmund Burke:[6]

> Manners are of more importance than laws. Upon them, in a great measure, the laws depend. The law touches us but here and there, and now and then. Manners are what vex and soothe, corrupt or purify, exalt or debase, barbarise or refine us. . . . They give their whole form and colour to our lives. According to their quality, they aid morals, they supply them, or they totally destroy them.

WOMEN'S IMPORTANT DUTIES

. . . Because her novels are primarily concerned with young, single heroines rather than with married life, Jane Austen tends to place her main emphasis on the part played by women in preserving manners and morals. Nevertheless, she is also very much concerned with demonstrating the larger social consequences of their familial functions.

Of the various duties of women as wives and mothers, Jane Austen singles out the education of young children for particular attention. This is because she perceives direct links between the child's ability to effect the transition into adulthood and the kind of training she has received from her mother. . . . All of the Bennet sisters suffer from their mother's deficiencies. Lydia and Kitty simply learn her silliness and concern for the surface of life; Jane remains uncorrupted by Mrs Bennet, but, lacking any positive direction, ends up with an untrained and undiscriminating mind; and Elizabeth and Mary, in trying to compensate for this absence of maternal

6. British politician and writer, author of "First Letter on a Regicide Peace"

guidance, are forced to pursue programmes of self-education based in the first instance on Mr Bennet's cynicism and in the second on his books. The result is complete failure to achieve maturity on the part of Kitty, Lydia and Mary, and a difficult period of initiation for Jane and Elizabeth. . . .

The implications of household management, the other main aspect of the woman's domestic role, are stressed less frequently, but become very clear if we examine the symbolic use of houses in *Mansfield Park* and *Persuasion.* Mansfield Park represents English society at a time when its rural ideal of order and repose is being threatened by new values brought in from effete aristocratic circles. . . . *Persuasion* opens with an account of domestic problems at Kellynch Hall. So long as Lady Elliot lived the Kellynch estate was run with 'method, moderation, and economy'. However, since her death Sir Walter Elliot has given free rein to his natural extravagance until, burdened with debt, he is finally forced to rent out his estate and retire to Bath. . . .

In both novels . . . Jane Austen is saying, symbolically, that those who order their houses well are securing the health of the nation, while those who neglect them are damaging it. However, what we must recognise is that she is not simply employing household management as a convenient symbol, but is also expressing her quite literal belief in the domestic environment as a microcosm of the nation. It is not just the Mansfield Parks and Kellynch Halls of her novels that take on larger implications, but all households. Hence, every housewife has a crucial role to play in preserving the *status quo.*

This should help us to understand why Jane Austen reserves some of her sharpest irony in *Sense and Sensibility* for Mrs Dashwood's deficiencies as a household manager: 'In the mean time, till all these alterations could be made from the savings of an income of five hundred a-year by a woman who never saved in her life, they were wise enough to be contented with the house as it was'. Were it not that Elinor introduces some method into her dealings, Mrs Dashwood would be guilty of damaging the fabric of English society, and thus deserves to suffer the lash of Jane Austen's tongue. . . .

FAMILIES AND VILLAGES AS MICROCOSMS OF SOCIETY

It is, of course, impossible to demonstrate very explicitly this link between individual manners and the moral health of the nation, since the equation is an almost indefinable one, depending as it does on an infinite number of tiny gestures. However, in some of her novels Jane Austen is able to show very precisely what function manners play in the life of the village, which is, for her and her age, a microcosm of the larger society. . . .

The larger implications of manners can be similarly perceived if we examine some of the symbolic aspects of Elizabeth Bennet's relationship with Darcy in *Pride and Prejudice.* The differences which keep Elizabeth and Darcy apart for much of the novel have social roots. He assumes that anyone with middle-class associations must be unworthy, while she believes that the aristocracy are merely snobs. Both, of course, are guilty of misunderstanding a central tenet of conservative social philosophy, which is that all ranks have a common interest and are motivated by the same ideals of duty and respect for others. In each case, this deficient social outlook manifests itself in bad manners. Elizabeth is consistently pert and rude towards Darcy, while he acts arrogantly towards the inhabitants of Meryton. Repeated displays of bad manners by both parties serve only to widen the gap between them and, symbolically, to create a rift between the aristocracy and the gentry-middle-class which threatens the structure of English society. The union of ranks necessary for the continuing health of society is achieved only after Darcy and Elizabeth come to understand the worth of each other's groups and correct their manners. Elizabeth learns respect for the aristocracy as a result of her experiences at Pemberley and Darcy is made to realise the limitations of his outlook by the gentlemanly behaviour of the tradesman, Mr Gardiner. As a result, Darcy politely invites Elizabeth and the Gardiners to dine at Pemberley, and Elizabeth, who now recognises the great honour involved in such an invitation, accepts graciously. Such proper manners guarantee that society will flourish, and the harmonious relationship thus established between the ranks is represented symbolically by the marriage between Elizabeth and Darcy. . . .

The lives of Jane Austen's heroines, who spend much of their time at balls, dinners and on extended visits, should not, therefore, be considered trivial. Essentially they are engaged in receiving an education in manners, the subtleties of which can be fully explored only in the context of the formal social occasion, and are thus being prepared for their role as arbiters of manners and preservers of morals. By undergoing this process, and by eradicating the deficiencies in manners from which all but Elinor Dashwood and Anne Elliot suffer, the heroines eventually become as useful to society as any politician, soldier or clergyman. . . .

CHANGING SOCIETY MEANS CHANGING ROLES FOR WOMEN

Lest there be any temptation to suspect that Jane Austen's acceptance of conventional female roles was simply a rationalisation of her unwillingness to mount the challenge to the *status quo* which her perception of women's innate equality with men might seem to indicate as appropriate, we must turn finally to *Persuasion.* By the time she wrote this novel, Jane Austen . . . had begun to realise that the old order of things was breaking down. Two aspects of this breakdown were particularly significant for women. First, manners were ceasing to function as a source of moral communication. For the decadent old order, as represented by the Elliots and the Dalrymples, they were becoming little more than vehicles for empty display and the emerging naval classes were as yet too unsophisticated to understand the intricacies of polite codes. Second, the home and the family were declining in importance. . . .

The woman's *raison d'être*[7] is thus seriously undermined. By the standards established in the earlier novels Anne Elliot is perhaps the most perfect of all Jane Austen's women—she possesses an 'elegant and cultivated mind', is an excellent surrogate mother to Mary's children, is highly accomplished, and has impeccable manners. . . .

Jane Austen responds to this new set of social facts by making some tentative proposals for a redefinition of the female role. Deprived of their function the 'quiet, confined' lives to which women have traditionally been limited are transformed into sources of frustration rather than of fulfilment. In such circumstances a woman's 'feelings prey upon' her, and she becomes subject to 'all manner of imaginary complaints'. What she needs, then, is a new arena of 'exertion', and through her presentation of Mrs Croft Jane Austen suggests that it will be found in fields of endeavour previously reserved for men. When Admiral Croft goes to sea, his wife accompanies him; when it comes time to rent Kellynch

7. reason for being

Mrs Croft 'asked more questions about the house, and terms, and taxes, than the admiral himself, and seemed more conversant with business'; and when the Admiral talks to his naval friends, Mrs Croft joins in 'looking as intelligent and keen as any of the officers around her'. . . .

The affection with which Austen portrays Mrs Croft suggests that what is important to her is not some *a priori*[8] definition of the proper female, but that women should seek out a role in society that will allow them to be fulfilled as 'rational creatures'. Control of manners and the family satisfy Jane Austen only because she regards these as being functions of crucial importance to society and not because they are in any absolute sense suitable occupations for women. Thus, once the society begins to change and the importance of manners and the family is diminished, then the woman must move into other areas of activity and must adopt a personal style appropriate to her new role, however 'unfeminine' this style may be.

Jane Austen's attitude to women, then, while growing directly out of the social and philosophical environment in which she lived reveals the workings of a keen individual intelligence. She may be committed in general to the *status quo*. Nevertheless, she is not prepared to go along with prevailing views about innate female intelligence and abilities. The fact that her contemporaries' view of women was demeaning does not, however, tempt her to follow Mary Wollstonecraft in demanding a complete reorganisation of society. Instead, she takes a clearsighted look at the functions performed by women and finds that, regardless of the very low esteem in which their sex is held, they are given a role substantial enough to satisfy the needs of such intelligent and capable people as Elinor and Marianne Dashwood, Elizabeth Bennet, Fanny Price and Emma Woodhouse. Only when the society changes does Jane Austen look for a change in the woman's area of activity.

8. already established or presumed

Nineteenth-Century Criticism of Austen's Novels

John Halperin

John Halperin gives several reasons why Jane Austen received little critical acclaim during the nineteenth century. Halperin explains that fiction was considered unimportant, and most novels of the time were poorly written sentimental stories. Consequently few critics paid serious attention to another novelist writing about domestic affairs. Moreover, Austen's name did not appear on the title pages of her books while she was alive, nor was she known in London literary circles, since she lived secluded in a village in the southwest. Yet she had a few quiet admirers among writers, a few who gave mild approval, and a few who disliked her work. Poet William Wordsworth and novelists Charlotte Brontë and Mark Twain attacked Austen's work in scathing commentary. According to Halperin, the critics who admired Austen's work offered significant analysis that was taken up by critics in the twentieth century. John Halperin teaches English at Vanderbilt University. He is the author of *The Language of Meditation: Four Studies in Nineteenth-Century Fiction; The Theory of the Novel: New Essays, Egoism and Self-Discovery in the Victorian Novel*; and many journal essays on Jane Austen and other novelists.

At the time Jane Austen published her novels—that is, during the second decade of the nineteenth century—women did not attend the universities. Men did not study English literature as part of any academic curriculum. Fiction was not deemed an important branch of the literary arts, and readers and critics did not look upon novelists as a literary

From "Introduction: Jane Austen's Nineteenth-Century Critics: Walter Scott to Henry James" by John Halperin, in *Jane Austen: Bicentenary Essays*, edited by John Halperin. Copyright ©1975 Cambridge University Press. Reprinted by permission of the author and Cambridge University Press.

species likely to add to the world's storehouse of significant art. Fiction was considered a leisurely amusement ('Castle-building,' as Charles Jenner put it in 1770 in *The Placid Man*) and worse, and novelists were rarely esteemed. The novel as serious literature . . . had been replaced by the novel of their imitators, the novel of sentimentality and sensibility, the circulating library novel. (In 1775, the year of Jane Austen's birth, Sheridan in *The Rivals* has Sir Anthony Absolute tell Mrs Malaprop: 'A circulating library in a town is an ever-green tree of diabolical knowledge!') The rush to the libraries in the latter half of the eighteenth century provoked anti-fiction diatribes, based to some extent on fears of the effects of democratized reading habits on 'people who had no business reading,' from a number of different sources; and, as Richard D. Altick points out, the appearance of hundreds of 'trashy' novels in the later years of the eighteenth century encouraged this reaction against fiction.

> Among the pessimists and optimists alike sprang up a rigid . . . association of the mass reading public with low-grade fiction. This was to have far-reaching consequences during the nineteenth century, for out of it grew the whole vexatious 'fiction question'. . . . [O]pposition to fiction on religious and moral principles became a convenient stalking-horse for the other motives which it [became] less politic to avow. This tendency was already marked in the eighteenth century; people who, for social or economic reasons, opposed the expansion of the reading public found it handy to conceal their true purposes by harping on the common reader's notorious preference for the novel.

NOVELS CONSIDERED TO BE DISREPUTABLE

The campaign against fiction was one of the most strenuous activities of both the Evangelical and the Utilitarian movements in the first third of the nineteenth century. Both groups regarded all forms of imaginative literature, and especially the novel, with suspicion. Novels were held to be dangerous because they over-excited the imagination of young people; they were linked to corruption, dissipation and all sorts of immorality, including adultery and divorce. Imaginative literature was considered frivolous; Bentham,[1] of course, excluded it from his ideal republic because it had no practical utility. Random reading was regarded as a

1. Jeremy, philosopher and reformer who developed the ethical philosophy: Good is "the greatest happiness of the greatest number"

waste of time; literature, after all, did not teach skills. Various Methodist tracts even argued that it could be proven from Scripture that God specifically forbade the reading of novels; one of the Utilitarian organs announced to its readers that 'Literature is a seducer; we had almost said a harlot.' No wonder lighter literature was often kept out of the libraries; indeed, many of the early mechanics' institute libraries allowed only books on or about the various branches of science within their walls.

IN PRAISE OF *PRIDE AND PREJUDICE*

An anonymous review of Pride and Prejudice, *published in 1813 in the* British Critic, *praises the novel for its superior portrayal of domestic life and for its finely drawn characters, especially Elizabeth Bennet.*

Elizabeth's sense and conduct are of a superior order to those of the common heroines of novels. From her independence of character, which is kept within the proper line of decorum, and her well-timed sprightliness, she teaches the man of Family-Pride to know himself. . . .

An excellent lesson may be learned from the elopement of Lydia:—the work also shows the folly of letting young girls have their own way, and the danger which they incur in associating with the officers, who may be quartered in or near their residence. The character of Wickham is very well pourtrayed. . . . Many such silly women as Mrs. Bennet may be found; and numerous parsons like Mr. Collins, who are every thing to every body; and servile in the extreme to their superiors. Mr. Collins is indeed a notable object.

We cannot conclude, without repeating our approbation of this performance, which rises very superior to any novel we have lately met with in the delineation of domestic scenes. Nor is there one character which appears flat, or obtrudes itself upon the notice of the reader with troublesome impertinence. There is not one person in the drama with whom we could readily dispense;—they have all their proper places; and fill their several stations, with great credit to themselves, and much satisfaction to the reader.

By 1800 novels were so numerous and in such bad repute that respectable journals such as the *Scots* and *Gentlemen's* magazines ceased to notice them at all. The reading public had convincingly demonstrated its size and enthusiasm in the 1790s, when Burke's *Reflections on the Revolution in France* sold in the thousands, Tom Paine's rejoinder in *The Rights of Man* sold in the hundreds of thousands, and the Cheap Repository Tracts of Hannah More and others sold, unbelievably enough, in the millions. Political and religious controversy provided stimuli for reading in the nineties and on into the 'teens when thousands of workingmen subscribed to Cobbett's radical journal, the *Political Register*; and some began to fear that it had been a mistake to teach reading to working-class children in Robert Raikes's Sunday schools.

The reading of novels, however, was always considered, by the various Establishments, the most frivolous and dangerous form of reading for the half-educated. Coleridge,[2] certainly no literary Establishmentarian, nevertheless spoke for many when he asserted in 1808 that 'where the reading of novels prevails as a habit, it occasions in time the entire destruction of the powers of the mind.' As late as 1826 the publisher Constable launched a series of cheap and popular publications that did not include fiction, and two years later the competing Murray's Family Library did the same. (Things had changed by 1865, however, when the founders of the *Fortnightly Review*, described by Anthony Trollope as 'the most serious, the most earnest, the least devoted to amusement, the least flippant, the least jocose' of literary periodicals, decided that their new journal must always contain a novel.)

REASONS WHY AUSTEN IS UNKNOWN

These things help explain, I think, why there is little serious criticism of Jane Austen during the first half of the nineteenth century. Attention to her work grows somewhat in the second half, particularly during the period 1859–1870. But between Jane Austen's death in 1817 and G.H. Lewes's 'The Novels of Jane Austen' in 1859, her work attracts little criticism of enduring interest, and only two essays of any distinction whatever (those by Scott and Archbishop Whately). Even from 1870 until the first decades of the twentieth century, Jane Austen criticism—with a few notable exceptions—is scanty and undistinguished. Edmund Wilson is surely wrong when he observes that 'only two reputations have never been affected by the shifts of fashion' in literary taste during the period 1820–1945: Shakespeare's and Jane Austen's. We may

2. Samuel Taylor, Romantic poet

agree with him when he goes on to say that Jane Austen's pre-eminent place has remained unchallenged for some years now and that it is likely to remain substantially untouched by future revolutions of taste.

But Jane Austen has been a long time getting to the top of the greasy pole; as late as 1900 she was nowhere near it. It is the case, however, that when attention to her novels finally did revive in the twentieth century, its directions and interests were often those of the nineteenth century. Thus, although the nineteenth century contributed only a little to Jane Austen's subsequent literary reputation, what little it did contribute often anticipated and helped to shape the thrust of the later criticism with which most of us are more familiar.

An additional reason for this dearth of early criticism is that the anonymous mode of publication obscured the authorship of Jane Austen's novels for some years (her name never appeared on a title-page during her lifetime; indeed, even her nosy putative cousin Egerton Brydges did not know, as late as 1803, that Jane Austen was 'addicted to literary composition,' as he puts it). The novelist's nephew, J.E. Austen-Leigh,[3] tells us that few of her readers

> knew even her name, and none knew more of her than her name. I doubt whether it would be possible to mention any other author of note, whose personal obscurity was so complete. . . . Seldom has any literary reputation been of such slow growth. . . . Her works were at first received [coldly], and . . . few readers had any appreciation of their peculiar merits. . . . To the multitude her works appeared tame and commonplace, poor in colouring, and sadly deficient in incident and interest. . . . Her reward was not to be the quick return of the cornfield, but the slow growth of the tree which is to endure to another generation.

AUSTEN UNRECOGNIZED IN THE LITERARY WORLD

And clearly Jane Austen had neither the inclination nor the means to 'puff' her work herself, in the manner of Trollope's Lady Carbury. She lived 'in entire seclusion from the literary world: neither by correspondence, nor by personal intercourse was she known to any contemporary authors. It is possible that she never was in company with any person whose talents or whose celebrity equalled her own. . . . Even during the last two or three years of her life, when her works

---

3. in *A Memoir of Jane Austen*

were rising in the estimation of the public, they did not en-
large the circle of her acquaintance.' Her novels were fashionable with some highbrow readers, who admired her wit
and her incisive picture of provincial life; yet even her admirers sometimes tended to see her fiction as having only a
narrow range and a limited kind of seriousness. That many
early-nineteenth-century readers and critics found her classical sense of control and decorum unappealing is borne out
in B.C. Southam's calculation that only twelve contemporary
reviews and notices of her work are known to exist (the actual number is probably fifteen rather than twelve) and that
up to 1870 (the year of Austen-Leigh's *Memoir*, which stim-
ulated a mild rediscovery of Jane Austen) 'fewer than fifty
articles mention Jane Austen at any length and of these only
six take her as the principal subject.'

Many of the major literary figures of the nineteenth century say little about Jane Austen, and the little they do say is
often uncomplimentary. To the extent that she was popular
at all, she was more so with professional critics than with
professional writers. There is evidence that her work was
quietly admired by such different characters as Southey, Coleridge, Henry Crabb Robinson, Miss Mitford, Tennyson,
Macaulay, and Guizot[4]; but Wordsworth, according to Sara
Coleridge in 1834, 'used to say that though he admitted that
her novels were an admirable copy of life, he could not be
interested in productions of that kind; unless the truth of nature were presented to him clarified, as it were, by the per-
vading light of imagination, it had scarce any attractions in
his eyes.' (Wordsworth's dislike of Jane Austen can probably
be attributed more to his deficient sense of humor than to
any particular theory of composition.) Such luminaries as
Madame de Staël, Macready, Newman, and the American
poet Longfellow were lukewarm or less in their assessments
of Jane Austen. Carlyle pronounced her novels mere 'dish-
washings!' And later in the century, Jane Austen was
roundly attacked by such important yet diverse writers as
Charlotte Brontë and Mark Twain.

BRONTË AND TWAIN CRITICAL OF AUSTEN

Charlotte Brontë's outburst came in private letters rather
than in published essays, and Twain's in a few essentially

4. Nineteenth-century writers, critics, and intellectuals

offhand remarks and one rather obscure essay; since their opinions do not properly belong to the history of systematic critical perspectives on Jane Austen formally published in the nineteenth century, I shall mention them briefly here.

Charlotte Brontë's famous attack consists in three letters, two to Lewes and one to her publisher's reader, W.S. Williams of Smith and Elder. In her 1848 letters to Lewes, Charlotte Brontë describes Jane Austen's novels as resembling

> an accurate daguerreotyped portrait of a commonplace face; a carefully fenced, highly cultivated garden, with neat borders and delicate flowers; but [there is] no glance of a bright, vivid physiognomy, no open country, no fresh air, no blue hill, no bonny beck. I should hardly like to live with her ladies and gentlemen in their elegant but confined houses. . . . Miss Austen being . . . without 'sentiment,' without *poetry*, maybe *is* sensible, real (more *real* than *true*), but she cannot be great.

In her letter to Williams, written in 1850, Charlotte Brontë is more abusive:

> anything like warmth or enthusiasm; anything poignant, heartfelt, is utterly out of place in commending these works: all such demonstration the authoress would have met with a well-bred sneer, would have calmly scorned as outré and extravagant. She does her business of delineating the surface of the lives of genteel English people curiously well; there is a Chinese fidelity, a miniature delicacy in the painting: she ruffles her reader by nothing vehement, disturbs him by nothing profound: the Passions are perfectly unknown to her; she rejects even a speaking acquaintance with [them]; even to the Feelings she vouchsafes no more than an occasional graceful but distant recognition; too frequent converse with them would ruffle the smooth elegance of her progress. Her business is not half so much with the human heart as with the human eyes, mouth, hands, and feet; what sees keenly, speaks aptly, moves flexibly, it suits her to study, but what throbs fast and full, though hidden, what the blood rushes through, what is the unseen seat of Life and the sentient target of death—*this* Miss Austen ignores; she no more, with her mind's eye, beholds the heart of her race than each man, with bodily vision sees the heart in his heaving breast. Jane Austen was a complete and most sensible lady, but a very incomplete, and rather insensible (*not senseless*) woman.

What Charlotte Brontë objects to in Jane Austen's novels is a restricted focus which ignores the *feelings* in its pursuit of a surface realism. It is odd that a writer like Charlotte Brontë, so conscious as she is in her own novels of the psychology of her characters, should have failed to recognize the same preoccupation in the fiction of her greater predecessor—but such is the case. (Surely she cannot have read *Emma* with much care.) Interestingly enough, however, Charlotte Brontë's comparison of Jane Austen's art with the painting of miniatures corresponds almost exactly to Jane Austen's own modest assessment of her art (then unpublished) in a famous letter (1816) to her brother Edward as being confined to a 'little bit (two Inches wide) of Ivory' on which she works 'with so fine a Brush, as produces little effect after much labour.'

Twain, describing a ship's library in *Following the Equator* (1897), exulted that 'Jane Austen's books . . . are absent. . . . Just that one omission alone would make a fairly good library out of a library that hadn't a book in it.' In an essay (only recently published) entitled simply 'Jane Austen,' Twain says that reading a Jane Austen novel makes him feel 'like a barkeeper entering the Kingdom of Heaven.' He dislikes the propriety and stiff decorum of her characters, finds them unreal and unappealing, and, like Charlotte Brontë, complains of their passionlessness. He dislikes Jane Austen's preoccupation with the genteel and the artificial, and finally casts her into the abyss of the Puritan tradition, a tradition which always enraged him.

There are other, later depreciations of Jane Austen (most notably and surprisingly one by Henry James in 1905); and there are too a number—not large, but significant nonetheless—of thoughtful and more comprehensive nineteenth-century critical discussions of her which are more friendly. . . . There are several important issues with which Jane Austen criticism has been occupied from its beginnings, and it should be instructive to see how and where and when some of these issues first surfaced. What nineteenth-century criticism of Jane Austen there is is often as incisive as the criticism of our own day, and it certainly helps to illuminate the critical road.

CHAPTER 2

Themes in Jane Austen's Novels

Sex and Social Life in Austen's Novels

Jan Fergus

Jan Fergus argues that sexuality—defined as the energy attracting men and women—pervades Austen's books. Fergus explains the restrictive social rules set down for women in Austen's time and shows how Austen takes liberties with these rules. Austen's heroines express their feelings more openly than the rules of conduct allow; they are strong and establish equal partnerships with husbands. Emma and Elizabeth, Fergus points out, even test their relationships before marriage to assure that they have found love and equality. Jan Fergus is assistant professor at Lehigh University and has taught at Brooklyn College, City University of New York. She has written about Jane Austen and morality in literature.

The definitive twentieth-century opinion of sexuality in Jane Austen's novels was uttered at one of Gertrude Stein's parties in Montparnasse:[1] "'You are talking of Jane Austen and sex, gentlemen?' said a tweedy Englishman with a long ginger moustache. 'The subjects are mutually exclusive.'" The subjects exclude one another, however, only when 'sex' is narrowly defined as explicit, exhaustive detail about what people do and feel in bed. Austen's own understanding of sexuality is much less narrow. She is interested in dramatising sex in everyday social life—in the drawing room rather than the bedroom. The courtship plots she creates allow her to explore the relations between sex and moral judgement, sex and friendship, sex and knowledge—that is, between sex and character. In this sense, there is no escaping sexuality in Austen's novels. It is always present, treated with a variety

---

1. an area in Paris where Gertrude Stein and other expatriate American writers gathered

From "Sex and Social Life in Jane Austen's Novels" by Jan Fergus, in *Jane Austen in a Social Context*, edited by David Monaghan. Copyright ©1981 by Jan S. Fergus. Reprinted by permission of the author and Macmillan Ltd.

and freedom that most modern readers overlook and that the novels of most of her contemporaries were unable, for various reasons, to achieve. . . .

The very publicity[2] of sex in Austen's novels—the constant awareness, the relentless dramatisation—is what makes her examination of it in social life so extensive and powerful. . . . Private sexual behaviour, and even private sexual attitudes, are notoriously likely to diverge from publicly proclaimed norms and are, for this reason, rarely documented and very hard to establish. . . . Courtship, however, because it is the one publicly approved form of sexuality, is fully documented by both public and private sources during this period. Courtship is also the focus of didactic[3] novelists and of Austen herself.

PROPER BEHAVIOR FOR YOUNG MEN AND WOMEN

Publicity is not merely sanctioned in courtship but required. A secret engagement like that between Frank Churchill and Jane Fairfax in *Emma* is felt to be reprehensible because it defies or mocks 'the world'; properly, Highbury should be aware of their relation and Enscombe should endorse it. All available eighteenth-century records—journals, letters, sermons, conduct books, essays and novels—insist that every possible stage of courtship must be reached in full view of the public eye. These stages—initial attraction, flirtation, infatuation and love develop within a social world and are subject to intense social scrutiny. Moreover, the public eye is readily offended by any deviation from the various courtship conventions which operate, to some extent, both in life and in literature. . . .

Initial attraction between the sexes is a subject of many warnings, for example, in conduct books addressed to young women. Love at first sight is particularly reprobated. The likely consequence—a marriage based on 'mere personal liking, without the requisite foundation of esteem, without the sanction of parental approbation'—can produce only 'misery and shame'. . . .

Although the conduct books only rarely warn young women against the seducing effects of good looks in men, such works continually put them on their guard against the seducing effect of their own charms on themselves, that is,

2. in the public's view   3. teaching a moral lesson

against the 'consciousness of being distinguished by personal attractions'. This consciousness makes women particularly susceptible to the elaborate compliments of flirtation, known also as gallantry, coquetry and polite raillery. Although women are adjured in the strongest terms not to coquet, much more frequent are exhortations to close their ears to compliments.... In conduct books and novels, then, vanity is the likeliest source of a woman's misconduct or undoing....

The rule that a woman must not love until she is beloved is, of course, wholly contradicted in life, as private journals and letters witness. But even there, women are usually determined to conceal their love from 'the world' if not from themselves.... A modest woman will always feel 'shame', or even that 'violence' has been done 'both to her pride and to her modesty', if she harbours love with any doubt 'of a return'....

A woman's love, according to the conduct books and many novels, is founded on gratitude and esteem and does not vary; a man's love is acknowledged to be more capricious, but esteem should be its foundation also.... Love unfounded on esteem never prospers in didactic novels. And for women, other initial sources of love are usually ignored. Before Austen's novels, the possibility that antagonism can include a form of sexual attraction or grow into love is seldom recognised....

AUSTEN TREATS CONDUCT RULES WITH IRONY

The prescriptions for courtship in conduct books and didactic novels may differ slightly, but both sources emphatically agree that any violation of the elaborate and unreasonable conventions that they prescribe will be punished. Austen's freedom from the constraints imposed by these social and literary conventions was first noticed, with a sense of enormous relief, by Richard Whately[4] in 1821:

> Her heroines are what one knows women must be, though one never can get them to acknowledge it. As liable to 'fall in love first', as anxious to attract the attention of agreeable men, as much taken with a striking manner, or a handsome face, as unequally gifted with constancy and firmness, as liable to have their affections biassed by convenience or fashion, as we, on our part, will admit men to be.

Austen subjects all the conventions of courtship to the scrutiny of irony and commonsense as part of her attempt to

4. educator, theologian, and author who reviewed Austen's books in *Quarterly Review*

dramatise the relations between character and sexuality within everyday social life. Informing this scrutiny in all the novels is a favourite perception: that good looks and charm inevitably create favourable responses and biased judgement. Such bias is at work when Elizabeth Bennet honours Wickham for his sentiments toward Mr Darcy's father and thinks him 'handsomer than ever' as he utters them, or when she reflects that Wickham's 'very countenance may vouch for [his] being amiable'. This simplest and most instinctive sexual response is always taken for granted in Austen's novels, not criticised or investigated. Bingley is immediately attracted to Jane Bennet, 'the most beautiful creature I ever beheld!', as Jane is to Bingley, although her account is rather less candid:

> 'He is just what a young man ought to be', said she, 'sensible, good humoured, lively; and I never saw such happy manners!—so much ease, with such perfect good breeding!'

> 'He is also handsome', replied Elizabeth, 'which a young man ought likewise to be, if he possibly can. His character is thereby complete'.

Willoughby and Marianne Dashwood are also attracted to one another at first sight; they discover in their first conversation that 'The same books, the same passages were idolized by each—or if any difference appeared, any objection arose, it lasted no longer than till the force of her arguments and the brightness of her eyes could be displayed'. . . .

Such attentions lead, however, to the more complicated forms of sexuality in Austen's novels—flirtation, infatuation and the mentor relation, all of which may precede but need not necessarily lead to courtship. Of these, flirtation is by far the most complex. As Austen treats it, flirtation is often indistinguishable from courtship. In the beginning, the same behaviour—attention, admiration, teasing, flattery, even professions of devotion—may be appropriate to both. But the two cannot be confused in the end, for courtship 'means' something—marriage—and flirtation nothing. . . .

Austen is capable of a number of attitudes toward flirtation. As practised by Frank Churchill at first with Emma or by Henry Crawford with Maria Bertram, flirtation is dangerous: one character, who is no fool, is deliberately fooling another. In such cases Austen's moral judgement is adverse; but as a rule she delights in flirtation as a form of sexuality, for example when she describes Elizabeth Bennet dressing for a ball 'with more than usual care', preparing 'in the highest spirits for the conquest of all that remained unsubdued of [Wickham's] heart, trusting that it was not more than might be won in the course of the evening'.

Flirtation shades easily into infatuation, and distinctions can be difficult: is Elizabeth flirting with Wickham or infatuated? Although she is deceived in him, Elizabeth's interest in Wickham is never strong enough to be labelled infatuation. . . .

ELIZABETH AS A MODEL AUSTEN HEROINE

In Pride and Prejudice, *Elizabeth's brief conversation with Darcy after their engagement portrays the signature qualities of Austen's heroines. Elizabeth is expressive, playful, reasoned, and strong. Jan Fergus contends that Elizabeth is energized by intelligence and sexuality.*

Elizabeth's spirits soon rising to playfulness again, she wanted Mr. Darcy to account for his having ever fallen in love with her. "How could you begin?" said she. "I can comprehend your going on charmingly, when you had once made a beginning; but what could set you off in the first place?"

"I cannot fix on the hour, or the spot, or the look, or the words, which laid the foundation. It is too long ago. I was in the middle before I knew that I *had* begun."

"My beauty you had early withstood, and as for my manners—my behaviour to *you* was at least always bordering on the uncivil, and I never spoke to you without rather wishing to give you pain than not. Now be sincere; did you admire me for my impertinence?"

"For the liveliness of your mind, I did."

"You may as well call it impertinence at once. It was very little less. The fact is, that you were sick of civility, of deference, of officious attention. You were disgusted with the women who were always speaking and looking, and thinking for *your* approbation alone. I roused, and interested you, because I was so unlike *them*. Had you not been really amiable you would have hated me for it; but in spite of the pains you took to disguise yourself, your feelings were always noble and just; and in your heart, you thoroughly despised the persons who so assiduously courted you. There—I have saved you the trouble of accounting for it; and really, all things considered, I begin to think it perfectly reasonable. To be sure, you knew no actual good of me—but nobody thinks of *that* when they fall in love."

AUSTEN PORTRAYS THE ATTRACTION OF OPPOSITES

Infatuation can begin as an attraction between what seem to be either opposite or like energies. Marianne's infatuation with Willoughby arises partially because she perceives him as her counterpart. But in Austen's novels, infatuation more frequently operates through the attraction of opposed energies, that is, through the fantasy of becoming complete by association with something that one feels oneself to lack and that one (rightly or wrongly) attributes to another. It is in this sense that Emma and Harriet are mutually infatuated, Emma by Harriet's soft blonde beauty and mindless yielding, Harriet by Emma's charm, wit and social position. Austen is well aware of the sexuality inherent in the relation, for she perceives that where the senses exist, sex exists. We could label her awareness a bisexual one, but to do so would certainly be to attach more importance to it than she would; again, she takes sexuality in social life for granted.

The attraction of opposing personalities usually takes a far stronger and more complex form than is exhibited in the relation of Harriet and Emma. This form of attraction—sexual antagonism—is most clearly dramatised in *Pride and Prejudice*. Undercurrents of sexual attraction and challenge accompany the antagonism expressed in the early exchanges between Darcy and Elizabeth, an antagonism based on differences in manner and style. Just as flirtation tries to make sex a game, antagonism makes it a combat, a contest, a power play. . . .

Although Austen does not endorse the drive for conquest that is at work in this form of sexuality, neither does she dismiss sexual antagonism as a means of making characters known to one another. Darcy and Elizabeth come to know each other despite (and partly because of) early misjudgement and conflict. One reason Darcy is attracted to Elizabeth is that she is always teasing or challenging him, not flattering him like Miss Bingley. Darcy and Elizabeth's conflicts are resolved because both can move from misjudgement, testing and conflicts of will to those fundamental likenesses in principle and perception that so often give rise, paradoxically enough, to antagonism.

It is in knowledge and intimacy, however, that Austen prefers to locate the most enduring sexual responses; she trusts sexual attraction to last only when it is based on knowledge. . . . In Austen's novels, however, sex, love and knowledge reinforce one another. All the novels are structured to move toward knowledge through testing and misjudgement. . . .

ANNE ELLIOT'S RECOVERY IN *PERSUASION*

Austen's most profound studies of sexuality occur, as one might expect, in *Mansfield Park*, *Emma* and *Persuasion*. These novels may be misread by readers insensitive to Austen's interest in sex in social life. Much will be missed, for example, by the reader of *Persuasion* who fails to recognise that the plot turns in part on Anne Elliot's recovery of her own sexuality. When the novel opens, she is 'faded and thin', for 'her bloom had vanished early'. Her broken engagement to Captain Wentworth has been the cause: 'Her attachment and regrets had, for a long time, clouded every enjoyment of youth; and an early loss of bloom and spirits had been their lasting effect'. In this state of lowered spirits or depression, Anne is forced to encounter Captain Wentworth again, a conjunction that deeply stirs her, reawakening feelings of attraction and loss that she has suppressed for years. When she goes to Lyme,[5] then, she has been to some extent reanimated by being made to feel pain, regret, attraction and jealousy. At Lyme, although she has to 'struggle against a great tendency to lowness' at the thought that the Harvilles would have been her friends, although she has grown 'so much more hardened to being in Captain Wentworth's company than she had at first imagined could ever be', that is, although she is still generally in a state of reduced or depressed feeling, Anne is able to interest herself in Captain Benwick, drawing him out and giving relief to 'feelings glad to burst their usual restraints'. On the next day, she is looked at by William Elliot 'with a degree of earnest admiration, which she could not be insensible of'. And Captain Wentworth too looks at her, giving her 'a glance of brightness, which seemed to say, "That man is struck with you—and even I, at this moment, see something like Anne Elliot again"'. Much is expressed in this novel by blushes and looks. A little later, Mr Elliot shows once more by his 'looks, that he thought hers very lovely', and Anne responds: 'Anne felt that she should like to know who he was'. Similarly, when Anne learns that Captain Benwick apparently wishes to visit her after she has left Lyme, she 'boldly acknowledged

5. Lyme Regis, a town on the southern coast of England; Jane Austen's favorite resort

herself flattered'—and she, like Lady Russell, thinks of his coming. Anne undergoes, then, a kind of sexual reawakening, feeling herself once again a sexually attractive woman.

What is remarkable in *Persuasion* is Austen's willingness to depict a heroine decidedly revived by a stranger's admiration, so revived that she takes an interest in him and in another admirer, even though she is in love with yet another man. The extreme openness of all these events is equally remarkable and (with the partial exception of *Mansfield Park*) typical of the novels. Sexual attraction always occurs in public, it is always scrutinised and speculated on, it is always a part of social life. Thus, Captain Wentworth witnesses Mr Elliot's and Captain Benwick's interest in Anne. Captain Harville praises Anne for her attentions to Captain Benwick. Mary and Charles Musgrove—himself once Anne's suitor—debate the degree of Benwick's interest in Anne before her and Lady Russell. Even more astonishing here and elsewhere in the novels than the publicity of sexual attraction is its sheer fluidity, almost promiscuousness. Captain Benwick, having lost Fanny Harville, is attracted to Anne, then to Louisa Musgrove; Captain Wentworth, having lost and rejected Anne, is pleased by Henrietta and Louisa's attentions, then seeks Anne once again; Mr Elliot admires and then loves Anne, but elopes with Mrs Clay; and Anne herself briefly fantasises marriage to William Elliot at a time when she is in love with Captain Wentworth.

In *Persuasion*, then, social life can readily accommodate the fluid and pervasive sexuality that Austen takes for granted in all her novels. . . .

SEXUAL ENERGY IN *EMMA*

In *Emma*, sex is . . . equally pervasive. The sexuality of Emma and particularly of Mr Knightley has often been denied. He is thought too stuffy, she too father-fond (to use Lovelace's term) for sexuality to flourish. But only wilful misreading can ignore the sheer vitality of both characters or can overlook passages like Mr Knightley's early description of Emma, full of open and unconscious sexual response: he praises Emma's looks, saying 'I have seldom seen a face or figure more pleasing to me than her's' and then, much more powerfully, 'I love to look at her'. Sexuality is as fluid in *Emma* as are Harriet's infatuations. An awareness of sexual energy is forced on the reader in nearly every page by

Mr Knightley's jealousy, Emma's jealousy, Jane Fairfax's jealousy, Emma's delight in matching wills with Mr Knightley, her sexual game with Frank Churchill, and his with her and Jane. This sexual energy is channelled into social forms but not contained by them, and during the famous climactic scene at Box Hill all the teased, frustrated sexuality of the various characters explodes at last. Emma's much-cited insult to Miss Bates is buried in far more obviously ugly interaction, notably Frank Churchill's declaration to Emma that when he returns from abroad, 'I shall come to you for my wife'. This flirtatious remark is designed to torment Jane Fairfax, but torments Mr Knightley with equal success; both take it as serious courtship of Emma while Emma detects a 'commission' to groom Harriet for the post.

Hereafter, of course, the novel moves quickly from frustration and misjudgement to satisfaction in every sense. Every page of Austen's novels is charged with emotional, moral and social as well as sexual conflicts, and all are resolved in the end. What distinguishes Austen's treatment of sex in social life distinguishes all her concerns equally: she gives us resolutions in which sexuality is as tested and satisfied as is morality or any other aspect of character. Between major characters, the mentor relation, sexual antagonism, flirtation and infatuation give way to or even lead to full knowledge and intimacy between equals. Though separate sexual roles are certainly adopted by Austen's married couples, her conclusions tend to disregard (without denying) the social conventions that make wives submissive to husbands. Instead, the endings celebrate an equality as complete as differences between the characters themselves allow. A witness to and model for this equality is the compromise that resolves *Emma*: out of respect for the conditions of Emma's life, Mr Knightley gives up his own home to live at Hartfield.

SEXUALITY IN EVERYDAY LIFE

The social roles and activities Austen explores are the modes of sexuality in daily life, and they pervade the emotional, moral and intellectual lives of Austen's characters perhaps even more than they do our own; in this sense, her novels may have too much sex rather than too little. Austen's rendering of everyday sexuality takes for granted in ways unthinkable to her contemporaries and often ignored by moderns that every relationship can carry a sexual charge. Sexual response and excitement are, in Austen's novels, so much a part of ordinary social life that in significant ways social intercourse is sexual intercourse. By dramatising the interplay of character and sex in ordinary life, then, Austen gives us the unavoidable and complicated sex of our social lives, seen with a persuasiveness and wit that ought not to surprise us, knowing Austen, and with a relentlessness that does not surprise us, if we do know her.

Humor in Austen's Novels

A.C. Bradley

In a lecture before a gathering of Austen admirers, A.C. Bradley informally addresses each of Austen's novels with an eye on her skill as a humorist. As a Shakespearean scholar, Bradley is attuned to characters and scenes which lend themselves to the comic stage. Bradley concludes that Austen may have written with more emotion and more poetry had she lived longer. A.C. Bradley was a renowned Shakespearean scholar in the early twentieth century. He taught literature and poetry at University College in Liverpool, Glasgow University, and Oxford University. He is the author of *Shakespearean Tragedy: Hamlet, Othello, King Lear, Macbeth* and a book on Tennyson.

Jane Austen's favourite attitude, we may ever say her instinctive attitude, is, of course, that of the humorist. And this is not all. The foibles, illusions, self-contradictions, of human nature are a joy to her for their own sakes, but also because through action they lead to consequences which may be serious but may also be comic. In that case they produce sometimes matter fit for a comedy, a play in which people's lives fall into an entanglement of errors, misunderstandings, and cross-purposes, from which they are rescued, not by their own wisdom or skill, but by the kindness of Fortune or some Providence with a weakness for lovers. This point of view, the point of view not merely of humour but of comedy, is so marked in Jane Austen's novels as to suggest that she was a good deal influenced by the drama. . . .

ELEMENTS OF COMEDY IN AUSTEN'S NOVELS

There are not a few dialogues in her works which, one imagines, might be transferred with scarcely any change to

From "Jane Austen" by A.C. Bradley, in *Essays and Studies by Members of the English Association*, Cambridge, 1911.

the stage. Some scenes that are open to criticism as parts of a novel would be quite in place in a drama. For instance, Mr. Collins's proposal to Elizabeth, delightful as it is, suggests farce. . . . Mary, again, the third of the Bennet sisters, appears always in the same attitude, like a comedy stock-figure. And where no such criticisms can be maintained, it will still be found that many scenes, as well as persons like Mr. Bennet and Sir Walter Elliot, seem almost to be made for the theatre.

But the resemblance to comedy goes further: it extends to the whole story. In all her novels, though in varying degrees, Jane Austen regards the characters, good and bad alike, with ironical amusement, because they never see the situation as it really is and as she sees it. This is the deeper source of our unbroken pleasure in reading her. We constantly share her point of view, and are aware of the amusing difference between the fact and its appearance to the actors. . . .

A cynic or a mere satirist may be intellectually pleased by human absurdities and illusions, but he does not feel them to be good. But to Jane Austen, so far as they are not seriously harmful, they are altogether pleasant, because they are both ridiculous and right. It is amusing, for example, that Knightley, who is almost a model of good sense, right feeling, and just action, should be unjust to Frank Churchill because, though he does not know it, he himself is in love with Emma. . . .

CATHERINE'S NAÏVETÉ IN *NORTHANGER ABBEY*

Of her novels perhaps *Pride and Prejudice* makes us laugh most, but *Northanger Abbey* and *Emma* are the two in which this comedy point of view is most predominant. In *Pride and Prejudice* the sources of mirth lie chiefly in the minor characters, and the main subject is not, on the whole, treated humorously. But the comic contrast of reality with Catherine Morland's illusions is the nerve of the whole story. Primarily, of course, it concerns the ideas which she has imbibed from Mrs. Radcliffe's novels, and which induce her, when she finds herself in an abbey, to look for the record of some thrilling mystery in what turns out to be a washing-bill. . . .

It culminates in the contrast between the romantic horror of General Tilney's imaginary behaviour to Mrs. Tilney, and the actual and exceedingly prosaic horror of his treatment of Catherine herself. But this theme is embroidered by perpetual minor illusions on the part of Catherine, who, for example, when she sees that shameless flirt, Captain Tilney, amusing himself with Isabella, is deeply concerned to think what he will suffer on finding that Isabella is already engaged, and interprets his very late appearance at breakfast as the consequence of a night of sleepless mental agony. *Northanger Abbey*, one of the youthful works and the most light-hearted of all, is one of the most enjoyable, and the heroine is a triumph. For her extreme simple-mindedness is always felt to be engaging and even lovable, and never suggests, like that of Harriet Smith, imbecility of mind or want of personality. Henry Tilney, too, is much the most agreeable of the clerical heroes. . . .

THE CONTRAST OF REALITY AND ILLUSION IN *EMMA*

Emma is a far more mature piece of work. It is the most vivacious of the later novels, and with some readers the first favourite. In plot-interest it is probably the strongest of the six,[1] and, not to speak of the more prominent persons, it contains, in Mr. Woodhouse and Miss Bates, two minor characters who resemble one another in being the object equally of our laughter and our unqualified respect and affection. Jane Austen, who is said to be a Shakespearian, never reminds us of Shakespeare, I think, in her full-dress portraits, but she does so in such characters as Miss Bates and Mrs. Allen. As for Mr. Woodhouse, whose most famous sentences hang like texts in frames on the four walls of our memories, he is, next to Don Quixote, perhaps the most perfect gentleman in fiction; and under outrageous provocation he remains so. This, I believe, is the severest thing he says in the story; it was said of Frank Churchill to the young man's stepmother:

> That young man (speaking lower) is very thoughtless. Do not tell his father, but that young man is not quite the thing. He has been opening the doors very often this evening, and keeping them open very inconsiderately. He does not think of the draught. I do not mean to set you against him, but indeed he is not quite the thing.

. . . Most of the characters are involved in the contrast of reality and illusion, but it is concentrated on Emma. This young lady, who is always surpassingly confident of being right, is always surpassingly wrong. She is reputed very clever, and she *is* clever; and she never sees the fact and

1. Bradley does not discuss Austen's long-unpublished *Lady Susan.*

never understands herself. A spoiled child, with a good disposition and more will than most of the people in her little world, she begins to put this world to rights. She chooses for a friend, not Jane Fairfax her equal, but the amiable, soft, stupid, and adoring Harriet Smith. Her motive, which she supposes to be kindness, is the pleasure of patronage and management. She detaches Harriet's affections from a suitable lover, and fastens them on a person wholly unsuitable and perfectly indifferent. . . .

Discovering to her dismay that she has led Harriet to raise her eyes to Knightley, and to raise them, in Harriet's opinion, not in vain, she also discovers, to her still greater dismay, that she loves Knightley herself, and then, to her delight, that she is beloved by him. She has reached a fact at last, but only by the benevolence of Fortune, who crowns her kindness by taking the heart of Harriet and flinging it, like a piece of putty, at her original lover. . . .

HUMOROUS MINOR CHARACTERS IN *SENSE AND SENSIBILITY*

Sense and Sensibility is allied on one side to *Northanger Abbey*, and there is something of the effect of that novel in the serious aspect of the story of Marianne. At seventeen she is even more convinced than of old that she will never see a man whom she can really love. Within a month or two she meets her ideal, and is brought to death's door by its behaviour to her. And at nineteen she contentedly marries a man of thirty-five who wears a flannel waistcoat, and whom, in virtue of his advanced age, she had considered as necessarily dead to "all acuteness of feeling and every exquisite form of enjoyment." Then there are scenes and minor characters worthy of Jane Austen at her best. The scene in which Mr. John Dashwood, the heir, with the help of his wife, and without any conscious insincerity, lowers his obligation to his sisters by degrees from £3,000 to occasional neighbourly acts which he never performs, is unsurpassed in all the novels, and excellently suited to the stage. It is characteristic that it comes in the second chapter. . . .

And there is dear, vulgar, warm-hearted Mrs. Jennings, who, in her pity for the love-lorn Marianne, remembers how nothing comforted her poor husband, when he had a touch of his old cholicky gout, like a glass of her finest old Constantia wine; offers it as a cordial for a broken heart; and, returning to her natural hilarity, consoles herself for Willoughby's rejection of Marianne with the design of spiriting up Colonel Brandon to take his place, on the principle that one shoulder of mutton, you know, drives another down. Shakespeare has the same thought, though he puts it differently:

As fire drives out fire, so pity pity;

and he would have loved Mrs. Jennings.

And there is her daughter, Mrs. Palmer, the ever-laughing Mrs. Palmer, who finds it so droll that Mr. Palmer is always out of humour, and so droll that her geraniums are nipped by the frost, and her chickens stolen by the fox. She and her husband, I confess, remind one of a farce more than of Shakespeare, but I should like to see that farce. And there is Lady Middleton, whose children were even worse spoilt than Mary Musgrove's, and who made friends with Mrs. John Dashwood the moment they met. "There was a kind of cold-hearted selfishness on both sides which mutually attracted them; and they sympathized with each other in an insipid propriety of demeanour and a general want of understanding."

PRIDE AND PREJUDICE VERSUS MANSFIELD PARK

Pride and Prejudice, I imagine, is the most popular of all the novels, and many of its champions seem hardly to understand why *Mansfield Park* should be much admired. The friends of *Mansfield Park* are a more select body, and they quite understand the admiration of *Pride and Prejudice....*

Mansfield Park allows less scope to Jane Austen's humour than most, perhaps than any, of her other novels.... There is often ironic humour in the presentment of the story and in the exhibition of Edmund's feelings. Both the Crawfords have themselves a pleasant vein of humour. We smile at Dr. Grant, at Mrs. Rushworth and her son; broadly at Mr. Yates, with wry faces at Mrs. Norris. But we "burst out laughing" only when we meet Lady Bertram. This again may be inevitable, and, because in keeping, may even be alleged as a merit; but is it not difficult to describe as Jane Austen's "best novel" one in which, for however good a reason, Jane Austen's humour fails to have full play?

Lastly, I will ask a question: Is there anybody in *Mansfield Park* for whom we care much, not as a study, but as a person? ... I know ... from the whole tone of the narrative, what I am expected to feel for Fanny, and though I try to feel it, I make but a moderate success of the business. I pity, approve, respect, and admire her, but I neither desire her company nor am greatly concerned about her destiny, and she makes me impatient at moments when I doubt if she was meant to.... In reading of Elizabeth Bennet, on the other hand, it is impossible for me to doubt either the author's intentions or my own feelings. I was meant to fall in love with her, and I do....

Jane Austen's feeling for Elizabeth, which appears in the letters as well as in the novel, was of a very special kind. She had a tenderness, we saw, for Fanny Price. So she had, one feels as one reads, for Anne Elliot. Yet she wrote to a niece who was eager to see *Persuasion*: "You will not like it, so you need not be impatient. You may, perhaps, like the heroine, as she is almost too good for me." Of Emma she said: "I am going to take a heroine whom no one but myself will much like." But she wrote of Elizabeth—not in the glow of her first creation, but long after, in 1813, when the novel was about to appear: "I must confess that I think her as delightful a creature as ever appeared in print, and how I shall be able to tolerate those who do not like *her* at least I do not know."...

BALANCE OF HUMOUR AND LOVE-STORY IN *PERSUASION*

Persuasion, written when Jane Austen's health had already begun to fail, was the last of the novels, and the mellowest. It is not equal to *Mansfield Park* or *Emma* on the sides where they are strongest.... Nor is *Persuasion* so entertaining as *Pride and Prejudice* and *Northanger Abbey*. But, to say nothing for the moment of its peculiar attraction, it seems to me to stand first for the balance of the humorous element and the interest of the love-story.

Admiral Croft is an instance of the value given to a novel by a person at once comical and lovable. Who has not blessed him for his praise of the Misses Musgrove: "And very nice young ladies they are; I hardly know one from another"? In her youth Jane Austen might have pushed into caricature the character of Sir Walter Elliot, with his family pride and personal vanity, and his incomparable criticisms on the hair and complexions of his relatives and acquaintances; but in *Persuasion* he is no less credible than original. His daughter Mary, whose "sore throats, you know, were always worse than anybody's," is another triumph.

If Jane Austen ever suspected herself of growing sentimental over Anne, she took her revenge in the portrait of Mrs. Musgrove senior, with "her large fat sighings over the destiny of a son whom alive nobody had cared for,"[2] and her "extraordinary burst of mind" in remembering that he had served under Captain Wentworth. And the touch of comic irony falls on the most serious characters.

The heroine herself does not escape. Lady Russell, who prides herself on her discernment of men, misjudges Captain Wentworth first, and Mr. Elliot, far more grossly, afterwards, and is left with nothing else to do "than to admit that she had been pretty completely wrong, and take up a new set of opinions and of hopes." And then there is Captain Benwick, who supposes himself doomed to eternal melancholy by the death of his *fiancée*, and who, we perceive, would certainly fall in love with Anne within a week, and, because the week is wanting, falls in love with Louisa. . . .

But humorous as *Persuasion* is, its special and distinctive charm lies elsewhere. . . . There are two sources of this effect. The heroine is treated with much sympathy and even with tenderness. This is true also of Fanny Price; but, in addition, the love-story is handled much more decidedly than in the other novels as a romance. . . .

At nineteen Anne Elliot (I quote the novelist's expressions because they are unusual with her) fell "rapidly and deeply in love," and experienced "a short period of exquisite felicity"; and though she was persuaded to renounce her lover, her love could never be renounced or transferred. It could only wither the bloom of her beauty and the joy in her heart. And Jane Austen allowed herself to portray freely and, one may even say, poetically, both Anne's suffering and the vicissitudes of its passage into hope and the re-birth of youth and bliss. . . .

I do not think she has anywhere earlier such a sentence as the second of these: "Prettier musings of high-wrought love and eternal constancy could never have passed along the streets of Bath than Anne was sporting with from Camden Place to Westgate Buildings. It was almost enough to spread purification and perfume all the way." And those speeches of Anne's in her conversation with Captain Harville, the overhearing of which produces the *dénouement*,[3] form the only passage in Jane Austen's works which I

---

2. This fact is emphasized. If we do not notice it, the passage, which has been censured, will certainly appear cruel.   3. the final unraveling of the plot

could honestly describe as "moving"—moving from the mingled sense of pathos and beauty.

This sweetest grace was added to all her other gifts but a year before her death; and in *Persuasion* too, as, some years earlier, in *Mansfield Park*, she disclosed without reserve that love of nature which was really one of her strongest feelings. She had been, I think, a little too much held in check by her keen sense of the absurdities of affectation and mere sentiment. If she had lived longer the fundamental character of her mind would not have changed, but we should have known it more fully and perhaps have seen that she was nearer to the poets of her time than she now appears.

Austen Portrays a Small World with Humor and Detachment

J.B. Priestley

J.B. Priestley argues that Austen is a great novelist who deserves enduring respect. After portraying Austen's England as a land of wars and shifting social classes, Priestley praises Austen for setting a limited goal in her writing and achieving it successfully. Priestley argues that Austen focuses on a small segment of changing social life and without overstatement captures the snobbery and pettiness of people whose lives are in flux. According to Priestley, Austen applies her critical pen with irony and a classic attitude of balance, moderation, and detachment. Though Austen's characters display the manners of early-nineteenth-century England, beneath the surface they have universal qualities. J.B. Priestley wrote novels, essays, and plays. He is the author of *The Good Companions, Delight, Dangerous Corner,* and *Literature and Western Man.*

Pride and Prejudice was first begun as early as 1796, when Jane Austen was only 21, and was then called *First Impressions.* In this form it was refused by the publisher, and afterward it was considerably revised, being published in its present form in 1813. It is worth remembering that at this time, Napoleon was still master of most of Western Europe, and that the England of Jane Austen was still engaged in a life-and-death struggle with him. The fact that her novel completely ignores all this is significant. Jane Austen was a great artist, and she knew very well that her fiction could only be effective if it were kept within certain definite limits. It is all a question of proportion and scale. If we are made aware of the fact that nations are at war and thousands of men dying

From "Afterword" by J.B. Priestley, in *Four English Novels,* edited by J.B. Priestley and O.B. Davis (New York: Harcourt, Brace, 1960). Reprinted by permission of Harcourt Brace & Company.

on battlefields, then we cannot bring ourselves to take any interest, for example, in one silly young girl's elopement. So Jane Austen, who knew exactly what she was doing, deliberately left out of her picture nine-tenths of life—war and politics and commerce and violent deaths and madness and terrible illnesses and ruin and starvation—and made all her characters reasonably cosy and comfortable, in a tiny world in which a cancelled dinner-party or a shower of rain is an important event, so that we could attend to and enjoy her delicate and subtle comedy. It is, I repeat, all quite deliberate. She was, above all else, a highly self-conscious artist, who knew exactly what she was doing.

THE ENGLISH SOCIAL WORLD
TREATED WITH A BALANCED VIEW

Now the social world she described so minutely was that of the Regency, a period, partly in the 18th, partly in the 19th century, that had its own particular characteristics. It was a time when the rigid class system of the earlier 18th century in England was breaking down, especially in the middle, between the top ruling class of the wealthy and influential land-owning aristocrats and the working classes. Now when you have a rigid class system, with everybody more or less fixed on one social level or another, there is very little snobbery, just because people know exactly where they are and it is no use pretending. It is precisely when the system is breaking down, without completely disappearing, that there is most snobbery, most pretense of social importance and grandeur. So it is not surprising that the novels of Jane Austen, a member of the middle class during this period, should be, among other things, comedies of snobbery, social pretense and prejudice. Because these attitudes existed, because they continually influenced people, Jane Austen dealt with them largely, and with infinite irony, in her novels, as we can see from *Pride and Prejudice*, in which nine-tenths of the action is really concerned with snobbery and social climbing and their various by-products. But notice that she herself is quite detached from them, though she takes for granted a social system far removed from the social democracy that America has, to some extent, achieved. But before we decide that the little world she shows us is absurdly antiquated, we had better take a good look at the social life we know, which still contains plenty of snobbery, pretense, and

Austen's Subtle Criticism

In Chapter 1 of Pride and Prejudice, *Austen captures the characters of Mr. and Mrs. Bennet in a brief dialogue and a narrator's comment. Austen's irony reveals her good-humored criticism of the couple.*

"I must throw in a good word for my little Lizzy" [Mr. Bennet begins].

"I desire you will do no such thing. Lizzy is not a bit better than the others; and I am sure she is not half so handsome as Jane, nor half so good humoured as Lydia. But you are always giving *her* the preference."

"They have none of them much to recommend them," replied he; "they are all silly and ignorant like other girls; but Lizzy has something more of quickness than her sisters."

"Mr. Bennet, how can you abuse your own children in such a way? You take delight in vexing me. You have no compassion on my poor nerves."

"You mistake me, my dear. I have a high respect for your nerves. They are my old friends. I have heard you mention them with consideration these twenty years at least."

"Ah! you do not know what I suffer."

"But I hope you will get over it, and live to see many young men of four thousand a year come into the neighbourhood."

"It will be no use to us, if twenty such should come since you will not visit them."

"Depend upon it, my dear, that when there are twenty, I will visit them all."

Mr. Bennet was so odd a mixture of quick parts, sarcastic humour, reserve, and caprice, that the experience of three and twenty years had been insufficient to make his wife understand his character. *Her* mind was less difficult to develop. She was a woman of mean understanding, little information, and uncertain temper. When she was discontented she fancied herself nervous. The business of her life was to get her daughters married; its solace was visiting and news.

prejudice. We all know people who violently condemn the local Country Club because, in fact, they have not been asked to join it. And if you are no longer snobbish about titles and estates, you can be snobbish about automobiles. Superficially, in *Pride and Prejudice*, Jane Austen is describing a world that has vanished. Go below the surface, however, and she is coming close to people, with their absurd hopes and fears, their little meannesses and acts of generosity, as they still are today. Consider carefully Mr. and Mrs. Bennet, Elizabeth, Jane and Lydia, Darcy and Bingley and Wickham, Lady Catherine and Mr. Collins, and you will soon discover people not unlike them all round you. . . .

Unlike so many later women novelists, Jane Austen was not a romantic. What does that mean? It means chiefly that she did not believe that it is worthwhile sacrificing everything for the sake of one tremendous passion. Her attitude toward life was essentially the classical one, holding a balance, not asking for too much of anything, insisting upon moderation. This attitude is of immense help to the writer of ironic comedy. It provides a sort of measuring rod of common sense, with which to test the motives, actions, and pretensions, of his or her characters. Jane Austen never stops using this measuring rod. So as soon as we begin reading *Pride and Prejudice*, we know that Mrs. Bennet, a rather foolish, amiable woman, is too eager and anxious to marry off her daughters, while Mr. Bennet, an intelligent but rather lazy and selfish man, is really not sufficiently concerned about his daughters' futures. Mrs. Bennet goes too far one way, Mr. Bennet too far the other way. And throughout the whole tangle of events that follow, the motives, actions, and pretensions of the characters are always being judged. But this does not result in heavy moralizing on the part of the author, as it was to do later, for example, in the novels of Thackeray. Jane Austen does not keep digging us in the ribs. She directs on people and events a keen but quick light glance, and, following her, we have to have our wits about us, or we are liable to miss point after point, flashing stroke after stroke. If we can appreciate to the full all these points, these tiny but effective strokes, the result can be exhilarating, like listening to a brilliant conversationalist. But we must remember that her favorite weapon is irony. This irony is there in the very first sentence of *Pride and Prejudice*: "It is a truth universally acknowledged, that a single man in possession of good fortune must be in want of a wife." Read this sentence aloud, and immediately you catch the undertone of irony. It tells us at once that we are about to meet an anxious matchmaking mother and some girls longing to get married.

SOCIAL BORES MADE COMIC: ELIZABETH MADE REAL

In real life the kind of people Jane Austen writes about, and the sort of existence they lead, so uneventful that an invita-

tion to a ball may be discussed for a month, would bore us
to desperation. But only stupid readers will be bored by her
account of such people and their existence. By selection, emphasis, and the constant sparkle of her own mind, she brings
about a magical transformation. Boring types, from whom
we would run in real life, are transformed into enchanting
comic characters. A wonderful example in this novel—and
there are plenty in her other novels—is Mr. Collins, whose
idiotic solemnity and snobbery and naïve conceit of himself
would make him unbearable as a real acquaintance,
whereas in these pages we have just enough of him to enjoy
him as a monumental ass. Not that Jane Austen is equally
good with everybody. No novelist can be. Obviously she
knows a great deal more about her young women than she
does about her young men. Characters like Darcy and Bingley and Wickham are not falsely drawn—and in places are
very shrewdly observed—but they are always seen against a
feminine background, not a masculine one; and we cannot
help feeling that Jane Austen has little idea how they talk
and behave when they are away from the ladies. Nevertheless, though Darcy is seen rather girlishly, all very imposing
and splendid, the thoughtless selfishness of such a spoilt
young man, as he himself finally has to confess, is brought
out into the open. Jane Austen never loses her head over
anybody. That cool though sparkling glance of hers always
reveals the truth.

But of course the key figure in *Pride and Prejudice* is its
heroine, Elizabeth Bennet, into whom Jane Austen undoubtedly put a great deal of herself. She is, to my mind, one of the
most delightful girls in the whole wide range of English fiction. Oddly enough—for we never associate Jane Austen with
Shakespeare, and superficially no two writers could be less
alike—Elizabeth has much in common with Shakespeare's
heroines, not the ultraromantic misses like Juliet and Desde-
mona and Ophelia but the heroines of the comedies, like
Rosalind and Viola and Beatrice. Like them—and unlike
nearly all the heroines of fiction and drama between Shakespeare and Jane Austen—she is lively and sensible, practical
and affectionate, humorous and independent-minded. She is
a real girl, a person in her own right, with a will of her own,
instead of the beautiful dummy that so many romantic men
writers bring into their fiction. Literature is crowded with
mere dream figures we are asked to accept as heroines. But

real women are much better, altogether more satisfying, than dream figures; and Elizabeth Bennet is one of the first and best of them in fiction, not only English but all fiction. And she comes closest, in motive and action, tone and style, not only of the characters in this novel but perhaps in all of Jane Austen's works, to representing Jane Austen's own attitude of mind and point of view. Even so, however, though her creator's sympathy with and affection for Elizabeth are obvious, Jane Austen still does not entirely lose her detachment.

LASTING QUALITIES IN AUSTEN'S ART

It is this detachment, together with her power of selection and emphasis and her constant unforced social and moral criticism, that makes Jane Austen a great novelist. That she was a great novelist, and remains one, there can be no doubt whatever. She is not great in the sense of being huge, expansive, overwhelming, as novelists like Tolstoy and Dickens and Balzac are. She created for her own use, as we have seen, a tiny world of her own, but no novelist before or since has succeeded better than she did in bringing close to perfection what she set out to do. While her characters may be merely gossiping and chattering about some small social event, their creator is coolly and exquisitely presenting us with her version of the perpetual human comedy, in which we all have to play our parts. And to watch her making one delicate but sure stroke after another is a most engrossing and rewarding pastime, and one that, so long as we begin to appreciate it, we shall enjoy all the more the older and wiser we are. Jane Austen is in fact one of the most lasting of English novelists: she "wears well," as they say in England. Make friends with this quiet but brilliant woman, this superb artist in fiction, and you have made a friend for life.

CHAPTER 3

Techniques and Devices in Jane Austen's Novels

READINGS ON
JANE AUSTEN

Stylistic Devices That Create Irony

Andrew H. Wright

Andrew H. Wright analyzes irony in Austen's novels and the stylistic devices she uses to create it. Wright says that Austen uses pompous words and overelaborate sentence structure to signal false and shallow meaning. She uses understatement in the form of litotes; that is, affirming statements by negating the opposite, as in This is no small problem. Austen also uses antiphrasis, a device in which a word takes on a meaning opposite from the usual; for example, if a bully has taunted children cruelly, a form of antiphrasis might admire his assertiveness. In other instances, Austen exposes illogic not directly but by blandly connecting ideas or emotions that have no logical connection. Wright also notes that Austen uses few metaphors except in specific situations when immoral and foolish characters speak in trite metaphors and clichés. According to Wright, these devices are what gives Austen's work its ironic tone. American scholar Andrew H. Wright has taught English literature at Ohio State University and the University of California at San Diego. He is the author of *Henry Fielding: Mask and Feast* and a book on William Blake.

Few students have failed to observe [Austen's] great indebtedness to her 'dear Dr. Johnson'.[1] Indeed, in examining Jane Austen's style we must remember that, for her, Johnsonian diction and syntax are the standard. The principal significance of this fact is indicated by Mary Lascelles:[2] 'To us Jane Austen appears like one who inherits a prosperous and well-

1. Austen's reference to Dr. Samuel Johnson, who published *Dictionary of the English Language* in 1755 2. in *Jane Austen and Her Art*

From *Jane Austen's Novels: A Study in Structure* by Andrew H. Wright (New York: Oxford University Press, 1953). Reprinted by permission of the author and Oxford University Press.

ordered estate—the heritage of a prose style in which neither generalization nor abstraction need signify vagueness,
because there was close enough agreement as to the scope
and significance of such terms'. Thus she can write, without
the least suspicion of irony, the following remarks about
John Willoughby:[3]

> The world had made him extravagant and vain—Extrava-
> gance and vanity had made him cold-hearted and selfish.
> Vanity, while seeking its own guilty triumph at the expense of
> another, had involved him in a real attachment, which ex-
> travagance, or at least its offspring, necessity, had required to
> be sacrificed.

That is, she can use abstractions freely, her sentences can be
carefully balanced, she can employ rhetorical repetition—
all, as it were, naturally: it is her tradition. And in fact it is by
virtue of this tradition that the irony of Jane Austen's style
derives much of its sharpness and point. For of course, like
all great writers, she goes beyond her literary heritage—
takes it, employs it, but changes it.

IRONY USED TO FOCUS AND POKE FUN

Jane Austen . . . often uses irony as a stylistic device and for
quite unironic purposes—to flay, to poke fun, to underline a
decided judgment—when there is no real contradiction involved. Thus, she wholly condemns (to incorrigible inanity)
the Reverend William Collins, whose famous orotund[4] letters are meant to be read with an eye to the unconscious
ridicule which they contain. But more often these apparently plain rhetorical displays are related to the larger ironic
themes of the novels themselves. . . .

[Austen's] diction is only slightly orotund, her overelaborate syntax never aspires to the mock-heroic. Thus,
Marianne Dashwood is both the target of her comedy and, as
we have seen, the subject of her irony. Marianne

> was *reasonable* enough to allow that a man of five and thirty
> might well have outlived *all* acuteness of feeling and *every* ex-
> quisite power of enjoyment. She was perfectly disposed to
> make *every* allowance for the colonel's *advanced* state of life
> which humanity required.[5]

The reader's first impression may be that it is Jane Austen
who is describing Marianne as 'reasonable' here, but the

---

3. in *Sense and Sensibility* 4. pompous and bombastic 5. in *Sense and Sensibility*.
Italics in this and subsequent quotations are Andrew H. Wright's.

very over-statement—'*all* acuteness of feeling', '*every* exquisite power'—throws such an assumption in doubt; and confirmation comes from the use of the word 'humanity', applying to the 'advanced state of life' of a man thirty-five years old. After being attracted to Willoughby:

> Marianne began now to perceive that the *desperation* which had *seized* her at sixteen and a half, of ever seeing a man who could satisfy her ideas of perfection, had been rash and unjustifiable.

Here . . . is the use of language too heavy for the structure it must support—and so the diction casts the shadow of suspicion on the validity of the thought. . . .

DISPLAYS OF HIGH-POWERED DICTION SUGGEST CRITICISM

By the same device Jane Austen discloses her sharply critical attitude toward the Bingley sisters.[6] Because they think Jane Bennet 'sweet':

> Miss Bennet was therefore *established* as a sweet girl, and their brother felt *authorised* by such *commendation* to think of her as he chose.

When Caroline Bingley writes to Jane, she says: 'If you are not so *compassionate* as to dine today with Louisa and me, we shall be in danger of *hating* each other for the rest of our lives'. Behind the diction we see Caroline Bingley and Mrs. Hurst as they really are—snobbish, domineering, self-consequential. And Mary Bennet's remarks are loaded with heavy words:

> While I can have my mornings to myself . . . it is enough.—I think it no *sacrifice* to join occasionally in evening engagements. Society *has claims on* us all; and I *profess* myself one of those who consider intervals of *recreation and amusement* as desirable for every body.

Her sisters have only asked her to go walking to Meryton— and this is her way of saying 'yes'.

Again—and perhaps even more obvious—is William Collins's proposal to Elizabeth: 'Believe me, my dear Miss Elizabeth, that your modesty, so far from doing you any *disservice*, rather adds to your other *perfections*'. Later: 'And now nothing remains for me but to assure you in the *most animated language* of the *violence* of my affection'. . . . Jane Austen is not afraid, when she wishes to present a character

6. in *Pride and Prejudice*

(like William Collins) in a particularly unfavourable light, to stack heavy words together.

This orotundity, as contained in the passages just cited, cannot be misunderstood by the experienced reader: the contradiction between statement and meaning does not have further reference to any ambivalent intention. Marianne is plainly a moon-struck adolescent, William Collins clearly an ass. . . .

EXCESSIVELY ELABORATE SENTENCES

In her later works she develops a variation on this technique; she constructs sentences 'too elaborate', as Mary Lascelles says, 'for . . . [the] powers' of her 'tiresome talkers'. . . . One thinks, in this connection, of Miss Bates, whose conversation is far from meaningless. She has, as Lascelles points out, two subtle idiosyncrasies in speech; she 'seldom completes a sentence' and 'each sentence flies off at a tangent from the last, but so characteristic are the trains of thought that, when need is, every sentence elucidates its curtailed predecessor'. Thus Miss Bates says to Emma, '. . . upon my word, Miss Woodhouse, you do look—how do you like Jane's hair?'

UNDERSTATEMENT AND NEGATIVES

Understatement is of course a main aspect of irony; the device used is almost always that of negation—the *New English Dictionary* cites as its example of litotes,[7] 'a citizen of no mean city'. In Jane Austen's works there are hundreds of instances of this kind of irony.

> Mrs. Jennings was a widow, with an ample jointure. She had only two daughters, both of whom she had lived to see respectably married, and she had now therefore nothing to do but to marry all the rest of the world.[8]

The sentence reads 'straight' until the last phrase, which brings the reader up short, makes him ponder (and transform) the meaning of the word 'nothing' here—and thus get a glimpse of the triviality of Mrs. Jennings's existence in a way that would not be possible were the author to state the facts unironically. The reversal, however, is deceptively simple, for in essence Mrs. Jennings is a character ironically perceived: she is a woman who leads a trivial existence, her gossipy curiosity is positively painful, her failure of intelligence leads to a too facile approbation of Willoughby. But

---

7. an understatement in which an affirmative is expressed by negating its opposite
8. in *Sense and Sensibility*

her heart is unfailingly kind, and her instinctive generosity stands in clear contrast to the calculating Lucy Steele—even, in fact, to the coldly selfish Lady Middleton. So the reader must be wary of taking ironic remarks and merely holding them up to a mirror.

In dialogue or in letters the people of whom Jane Austen disapproves sometimes have a penchant for multiple negatives.... General Tilney remarks to Catherine: '... no endeavours shall be wanting on our side to make Northanger Abbey not wholly disagreeable'. And William Collins writes: 'I cannot be otherwise than concerned at being the means of injuring your amiable daughters ...'. Neither of these people is saved by any extenuating characteristic; both are unconscious of the ironies which they so often utter. In the case of the general, this postscript to his invitation to Catherine is but a subtle forewarning of the kind of man he will turn out to be: he is a villain, much more terrifyingly the villain of the piece than John Thorpe, for General Tilney is the agent of Catherine's realization that common sense, of which she is gradually learning the value, is itself limited. And William Collins, while he provides delight not only to Mr. Bennet and Elizabeth but to every reader of *Pride and Prejudice*, serves (as we have seen) as the straw which breaks the back of whatever morality Charlotte Lucas possesses....

In fact, as one moves from the early works into the complexities of *Mansfield Park* and the two succeeding novels, one observes a deepening of Jane Austen's stylistic use of understatement.... Henry Crawford who, however attractive, is always intended by the author as a villain, betrays his own trifling character when he confides in his sister his ambition with regard to Fanny:[9]

> I only want her to look kindly on me, to give me smiles as well as blushes, to keep a chair for me by herself wherever we are, and be all animation when I take it and talk to her; to think as I think, be interested in all my possessions and pleasures, try to keep me longer at Mansfield, and feel when I go away that she shall never be happy again. I want nothing more.

CONTRADICTION IN MEANING AND LOGIC

... Without further multiplying examples of understatement, we shall turn to another stylistic device of irony, antiphrasis—that is, use of words in a sense opposite to their

9. in *Mansfield Park*

proper meaning. The sign of antiphrasis is not negation, as in litotes, but of reasonable contradiction in meaning.... Mrs. Ferrars is described with venom:[10]

> ... her features [were] small, without beauty, and naturally without expression; but a *lucky* contraction of the brow had *rescued* her countenance from the *disgrace of insipidity*, by giving it the strong characters of pride and ill nature.

If the reader wonders why he gets such a strong impression of Mrs. Ferrars's 'pride and ill nature', he need only reexamine the antiphrasis by which Jane Austen prepares us for these descriptive words. By forcing the words to stand self-contradicted, the author enjoins our attention to a passage which might otherwise be skipped over as conventional description....

The device of what Lascelles calls 'counterfeit connexion'—'the deliciously bland appearance of logical connexion'—is an important facet of Jane Austen's style.... But this technique does, it seems to me, do more than evoke our laughter; it demonstrates convincingly Jane Austen's awareness of the limitations of common sense: there is always the implied criticism of bad logic, but so is there the emphatic indication that human beings, as they do not judge rationally, cannot be totally grasped by reason alone. Marianne Dashwood has the following impression of John Willoughby:

> His name was good, his residence was in their favourite village, and she soon found out that of all manly dresses a shooting-jacket was the most becoming.

It may not be logical for Marianne to approve Willoughby on account of his shooting jacket (or perhaps to approve shooting-jackets because he wears one)—but this is a natural reaction and cannot be merely laughed off. After the marriage of Edward and Elinor, the young couple 'had in fact nothing to wish for, but the marriage of Colonel Brandon and Marianne, and rather better pasturage for their cows'. Reason cannot yoke these two ideas together; it is rather the unreason of new happiness—and the reduction in perspective it brings—that reduces all wishes to the same level....

SYNTACTICAL ANTI-CLIMAX

Syntactical anti-climax is no new thing in Jane Austen. ... There are many echoes and variations of this device in Jane Austen's novels. John Dashwood 'was not an ill-disposed

---

10. in *Sense and Sensibility*

young man, unless to be rather cold hearted, and rather selfish, is to be ill-disposed'. Thus she indicates by anticlimax the
vapidity of the young man. Isabella Thorpe writes to Catherine Morland as follows:[11]

> I am quite uneasy about your dear brother, not having heard
> from him since he went to Oxford; and am fearful of some
> misunderstanding. Your kind offices will set all right:—he is
> the only man I ever did or could love, and I trust you will con-
> vince him of it. The spring fashions are partly down; and the
> hats the most frightful you can imagine.

Here the anti-climax is unintentional on the part of the
writer of the letter; and the juxtaposition of her reassertion
of love for James with her remarks on the spring fashions
only shows that she puts both on the same level, and cannot
be quite serious about Catherine's brother. . . .

METAPHORS AND CLICHÉS

One of the most interesting facts about Jane Austen's style is
that it is almost entirely unmetaphorical, except when more
or less adverse criticism is meant. . . . A look at Jane Austen's
novels will convince the reader that any figurative expression is suspect. Sir John Middleton tells Marianne:

> Poor Brandon! he is quite smitten already, and he is very well
> worth *setting your cap* at, I can tell you, in spite of all this
> tumbling about and spraining of ancles.

The baronet's mode of expression is rather vulgar; he is a
rather vulgar man—a good and decent neighbour but so un-
perceptive as to approve Willoughby because the young man
rides and shoots well. Intelligence is not his strong suit, and
the point is made (in part) by his use of cliché. . . .

Mr. Collins is, of course, full of figures. He says in his letter to Mr. Bennet that he hopes the latter will not 'reject the
offered olive branch', a cliché which even Mary discovers to
be 'not wholly new'. And writing to Mr. Bennet after hearing
of Lydia's elopement, he says:

> Let me advise you . . . to console yourself as much as possible,
> to *throw off* your unworthy child from your affection for ever,
> and leave her to *reap the fruits* of her own heinous offence.

Mary Bennet's reaction is quite as frightening:

> This is a most unfortunate affair; and will probably be much
> talked of. But we must *stem the tide* of malice, and *pour into* the
> *wounded bosoms* of each other, the *balm* of sisterly consolation.

11. in *Northanger Abbey*

Here the effect—or perhaps the cause—of fossilized thinking takes a nasty turn. . . .

AUSTEN'S OVERALL STYLE

'I doubt', says R.W. Chapman, 'if J.A. was conscious of having a style of her own. Outside her dialogue it is not highly individual; it is just the ordinary correct English that, as Johnson had said, "everyone now writes".' I believe he underrates her on this point. It seems to me fully apparent that Jane Austen is as thoroughly original . . . in her style as she is in the other aspects of her work. . . .

Jane Austen's irony is much more pervasive than the usual rhetorical categories will allow. Understatement and antiphrasis by no means account for all the ironies in her diction and syntax. . . . Style, more perhaps than any other aspect of a novel, is a finally indissoluble unity, a fabric which cannot be cut up without destroying the harmony of the whole. It is because of this fact that such difficult but useful words as 'tone' and 'texture' are so often applied to style. And, however difficult it may be to analyse the whole style of a lyric poem, the task is plainly impossible in a novel—unless one is willing to read perhaps a thousand pages of explication; and this is no doubt more trouble than it is worth. One recourse, and it is a pleasant one, is to read the novels themselves.

Games as a Device in Austen's Novels

Alistair M. Duckworth

Alistair M. Duckworth argues that ordinary social games of the early 1800s represent serious themes in Austen's novels. Duckworth supports his assertion by quoting from Austen's letters. In *Sense and Sensibility*, Austen associates games, especially card playing, with selfish, mindless characters who lack moral substance. Game players in *Pride and Prejudice* represent two extremes.

According to Duckworth, *Mansfield Park* represents a more complex use of games. In *Persuasion*, Anne Elliot, who represents morality, has become completely severed from society while other characters indulge themselves in entertainment. Finally, Duckworth concludes that in *Emma*, Austen portrays a transformed society, demanding high moral standards of its members while allowing them games as trivial recreation. Alistair Duckworth has taught at the University of Virginia, at the State University of New York in Buffalo, and at the University of Florida. He is the author of *The Improvement of the Estate: A Study of Jane Austen's Novels*.

Games of skill, games of chance, games with words were familiar features of Jane Austen's life from first to last. A few months before her death in 1817 she wrote to her niece, Fanny Knight, asking her to tell her brother William that "I often play at *Nines* and think of him."[1] She might have recalled other games, battledore and shuttlecock, for example, or bilbocatch (at which she was an acknowledged expert) or spillikins (which she considered "a very valuable part of our Household furniture"), or such card games as whist, com-

---

1. Austen's personal comments are taken from her letters, edited by R.W. Chapman and published by Oxford University Press.

Adapted, with the author's permission, from "'Spillikins, Paper Ships, Riddles, Conundrums, and Cards': Games in Jane Austen's Life and Fiction" by Alistair M. Duckworth, in *Jane Austen: Bicentenary Essays*, edited by John Halperin. Copyright ©1975 by Cambridge University Press. Reprinted by permission of the author and Cambridge University Press.

merce, casino, loo, cribbage and especially speculation, whose usurpation by brag at Godmersham during Christmastide 1808–9 "mortified" her, because "Speculation was under my patronage."[2]

Equally, she could have recalled word games, including riddles, acrostics, and charades, that not only provided "intervals of recreation and amusement . . . desirable for every body," as Mary Bennet sententiously concedes in *Pride and Prejudice*, but were an integral part of Austen family life. When her sister-in-law, Elizabeth Bridges Knight, died in 1808, Jane Austen took care of the two eldest boys. Her care comprised games as well as Psalms, Lessons, and a sermon at home. "We do not want amusement," she wrote to her sister Cassandra: "bilbocatch, at which George is indefatigable, spillikins, paper ships, riddles, conundrums, and cards."

GAMES HAVE NEGATIVE SIGNIFICANCE IN AUSTEN'S NOVELS

Given the delight in recreation of all kinds that is manifest in the letters, we may be unprepared for the negative uses to which Jane Austen puts games in her fiction. Seldom are games unambiguously ratified in the novels. One thinks of the "merry evening games," reminiscent of those in Goldsmith's *The Vicar of Wakefield*, that Harriet plays at the Martins' until Emma teaches her to play a new and more dangerous sport. In *Emma*, too, the geriatric amusement Mrs Bates and Mrs Goddard get from playing picquet and quadrille with Emma's father at Hartfield seems harmless enough. Like age, youth may be exempt from serious criticism. Catherine Morland's preference, in *Northanger Abbey*, for "cricket, base ball, riding on horseback, and running about the country at the age of fourteen" is perfectly suited to her unheroic debut, the carefree childhood prelude to more dubious recreational involvement with Gothic fiction. Such positive uses are slight, however, compared with Austen's normal mode. Lovers of games in the novels, or of field sports, an outside and exclusively masculine form of games, are more often than not selfish, irresponsible or empty-headed characters whose pursuit of a favorite pastime labels them in various ways as morally or socially deficient.

Card games, especially, are suspect, becoming emblems of a vacuous and despicable society, as in the following de-

2. The games cited in this essay are common family games in Austen's day.

scription of a typical evening at Lady Middleton's house in *Sense and Sensibility*:

> They met for the sake of eating, drinking, and laughing together, playing at cards, or consequences, or any other game that was sufficiently noisy.... The insipidity of the meeting was exactly such as Elinor had expected; it produced not one novelty of thought or expression.

Not surprisingly the anti-social Marianne Dashwood detests cards: while Lady Middleton and others play at the table, and Elinor Dashwood and Lucy Steele exchange information over the work basket, Marianne is at the pianoforte, "wrapt up in her own music and her own thoughts."...

SUBTLE DIFFERENCES IN THE MEANING OF GAME PLAYING

In some ways the society of *Persuasion* reminds us of that in *Sense and Sensibility*, but the heroines are significantly different. Unlike Marianne, whose refusal to play card games was at least in part selfish repudiation, Anne Elliot is the most perfect of Jane Austen's heroines, always in search of a useful social role following her expulsion from her home, Kellynch Hall, as a result of her father's extravagance and vanity. That Anne should be "no card-player," should find that "the usual character" of evening parties has "nothing" for her, becomes a severe indictment of the society manifest in the last novel. The same indictment could only have been served in *Sense and Sensibility* if Elinor as well as Marianne had refused to play the game....

At the end of *Persuasion* the separation of morality from its basis in society is marked when Anne, secretly happy in her engagement to Wentworth, attends a social gathering in Bath: "It was but a card-party, it was but a mixture of those who had never met before, and those who met too often—a common-place business, too numerous for intimacy, too small for variety."...

The game-playing societies in *Sense and Sensibility* and *Persuasion*, which reveal "no poverty of any kind, except of conversation," may remind us that Jane Austen did not always endorse games in the letters. Like Elizabeth Bennet in *Pride and Prejudice*, she had a distrust of "playing high":

> We found ourselves tricked into a thorough party at Mrs. Maitland's.... There were two pools at Commerce, but I would not play more than one, for the Stake was three

shillings, & I cannot afford to lose that, twice in an evening.

She could go beyond Elinor Dashwood's recognition of social mediocrity to something like Marianne's misanthropy, as when she wrote to Cassandra from Bath in May 1801 about "another stupid party":

> There were only just enough to make one card table, with six people to look on, & talk nonsense to each other. . . . I cannot anyhow continue to find people agreable. . . . Miss Langley is like any other short girl with a broad nose & wide mouth, fashionable dress, & exposed bosom.

. . . And in other letters, her attitude to card-playing, as well as to field sports, could be severe.

When such passages in the letters are set against the novels, it is possible to argue for a continuity of ironic criticism directed against sterile social settings, to talk of a discharge of aggression against social conventions that is often overt in the letters and ineffectively disguised in the novels. . . . Both as sister, or aunt, in the letters, and as author, she separates family (the unit of meaning in which games have value) from society outside (the discredited arena in which games become the expression of inconsequential or repugnant behavior). Such an argument carries a measure of truth, but it fails to acknowledge the crucial generic difference between letters and novels or to recognize how games are used in the novels for ultimately positive ends.

GAMES REPRESENT OPPOSITE EXTREMES IN *PRIDE AND PREJUDICE*

In *Pride and Prejudice* card games, like the motifs of piano-playing, letters, and books, are deftly integrated into the novel's antithetical structure so as to expose extremes of social conformity and individual freedom and to define a normative marriage of the moral self to a worthy society. Thus, balanced against the "nice comfortable noisy game of lottery tickets, and a little bit of hot supper afterwards" promised by Mrs Philips, there is the "superlatively stupid" evening of quadrille and casino at Rosings, during which "scarcely a syllable was uttered that did not relate to the game." Not only are the particular games chosen fitted to the families that play them, but noise is appropriate to the underbred vulgarity of Mrs Philips as silence is to the sterile formality of Lady Catherine. Between vulgar trade and arrogant aristocracy the social-climbing Bingleys at Netherfield play games that recall their origin in trade and announce their social aspirations: commerce, picquet, loo, vingt-un. Even Mr Collins sees cards as his entrée to better prospects, proud to be sent for by Lady Catherine to "make up her pool of quadrille in the evening" but equally willing, when the card tables are placed at Mrs Philips', to sit down to whist. . . .

Significantly, neither Elizabeth nor Darcy is a noted card-player. Elizabeth has no Puritanical objection to cards but declines to gamble at loo while staying at Netherfield. Her refusal causes Mr Hurst, "an indolent man, who lived only to eat, drink, and play at cards," to think her "singular," and Miss Bingley to insinuate that she is a blue-stocking who "despises cards." When Mr Hurst reminds Miss Bingley of the card table a little later, it is of no avail: "She had obtained private intelligence that Mr Darcy did not wish for cards.". . .

In the perfectly articulated plot of *Pride and Prejudice* Jane Austen uses card games to expose obnoxious behavior much in the way she does in her letters, but she also creates a fictional world of her own—a far superior version, it might be suggested, of the word games she and her family enjoyed—in which the skilful deployment of various motifs gives aesthetic and moral shape to her experience. . . .

PLAYERS IN *MANSFIELD PARK* THREATEN CULTURE AND COUNTRYSIDE

The whole debate [over sermon delivery] exists within the larger metaphor of estate improvements. . . . Henry Crawford, the "pre-eminent" card-player and "capital improver" not only finds fault with commonplace biblical texts and "redundancies" in the liturgy, but with the structure of houses and the dispositions of landscapes. . . . The recreational "systems" of Henry and his sister—their play-acting, card-playing, landscape "improvements" and other "manoeuvres against common sense"—carry subversive cultural implications. . . .

In *Mansfield Park* "speculation," like "improvement" of a radical kind, is kept under control, even as its social threat is revealed. The relevant scene is in chapter vii of the second volume, precisely at the center of the work, where the "round" game of Speculation not only serves as a synecdoche[3] of the novel's characterization and themes but per-

3. a rhetorical term in which the part signifies the whole

mits Jane Austen, in distinguishing between good and bad players, to suggest, inversely, a distinction between socially responsible and irresponsible individuals. It is a subtle and complex chapter in which the motif of card-playing is more fully integrated into the fictional fabric than ever before. . . . What the evening of cards does show, in brief compass, is the ambivalence surrounding Sir Thomas Bertram, a man theoretically committed to worthy concepts of stewardship who, under the pressures of a failing West Indian venture and an extravagant elder son, compromises his principles and gives way to venal speculation. He wins his "game" when his daughter Maria marries the very rich but stupid Rushworth, but loses it when Maria, carrying the stage role she plays in *Lovers' Vows* into real life, runs off with Henry Crawford, bringing disgrace on herself and her family.

Mansfield Park is saved from his "grievous mismanagement" not by Sir Thomas's children but by his adopted niece, Fanny Price. It is therefore appropriate that Fanny "had never played the game [of Speculation] nor seen it played in her life." Opposed to the play-acting, which endangers the physical and moral fabric of the Mansfield house, and to Crawford's proposed improvements at Rushworth's house and grounds at Sotherton, she has no desire to play or win at cards. The only "speculation" she allows herself during the card game is of her midshipman brother William's future as an Admiral. Fanny's real antagonist is Henry Crawford, "pre-eminent in all the lively turns, quick resources, and playful impudence that could do honour to the game." Even while helping her bid ("the game will be yours," he says), he engages in an imaginative play of the mind which, no less than his views on sermon delivery, reveals to Fanny the cultural threat he poses. His speculation takes the form of detailed plans for the "improvement" of Edward Bertram's future parsonage at Thornton Lacey. . . .

The association of cards with the speculators and false improvers in *Mansfield Park* is a major shift in emphasis. True, cards may still serve to expose stupidity and indolence. Thus Lady Bertram will complain: "Fanny, you must do something to keep me awake. I cannot work. Fetch the cards,—I feel so very stupid." But more often than not cards are connected with active manipulators of people and situations. . . . Only when the active speculators and improvers are expelled from Mansfield, and Fanny marries Edmund, can the right mediation between "nothing doing" and "bustle," "yawns" and "restlessness," old-fashioned Sotherton and "completely altered" Compton be achieved. . . .

GAMES TRANSFORMED IN *EMMA*

In *Emma*, so different in tone from *Mansfield Park*, there is, if not the same ostracism, still a serious qualification of the vitality that takes on a manipulative character. By transforming rather than eradicating false wit, however, Jane Austen makes *Emma* a far more palatable affirmation of culture.

There is a curious split in *Emma* between card games such as whist, picquet and quadrille, whose function seems to be to provide harmless and trivial amusement for the superannuated and valteudinarian characters, and the word games such as riddles, charades, enigmas, conundrums, anagrams, and acrostics, which involve the youthful and lively Emma in dubious relations with Harriet, the Eltons, and Frank Churchill.

Complete with "a vast deal of chat and backgammon," evenings at Hartfield define the second childhood of Emma's father, his abrogation of all connection with progress or generation, his wish to live cosseted from draughts, marriages, and time itself, supported by his diet of thin gruel and endless "rounds" of cards. On one level, cards suggest that society and identity alike are endlessly repetitive, not subject to dynamic change or the decay that leads to death. . . .

Card games serve in other ways in *Emma*: to permit an evaluation and comparison of Mr Weston's "gregarious, indiscriminate bonhomie" and John Knightley's "strong domestic habits," for example, or to expose Mrs Elton's parvenu[4] ambitions, or to emphasize Mr Knightley's strong sense of social responsibility, as on the occasion of the ball at the Crown inn. There Emma, seeing Mr Knightley among the standers-by, feels that "he ought to be dancing,—not classing himself with the husbands, and fathers, and whist-players, who were pretending to feel interest in the dance till their rubbers were made up." This is a resonant scene, which not only reveals Emma's unconscious love of Mr Knightley, but sets "cards" against "dancing" as emblems of qualitatively different social orders. Mr Knightley ought in-

4. newly rich or powerful

deed to be dancing, that is, to be participating fully in High-bury society. . . .

FAMILY GAMES

In a letter to her sister Cassandra dated October 24, 1808, Jane Austen mentions the family games played during the visit of her nephews George and Edward Austen, whose mother had recently died in childbirth. The letter is included in Penelope Hughes-Hallett's collected correspondence of Austen, My Dear Cassandra.

My dear Cassandra

Edward and George came to us soon after seven on Satur-day, very well, but very cold, having by choice travelled on the outside, and with no great coat but what Mr. Wise, the coachman, good-naturedly spared them of his. . . .

They behave extremely well in every respect, showing quite as much feeling as one wishes to see, and on every oc-casion speaking of their father with the liveliest affection. His letter was read over by each of them yesterday, and with many tears; George sobbed aloud, Edward's tears do not flow so easily; but as far as I can judge they are both very properly impressed by what has happened. . . .

We do not want amusement: bilbocatch, at which George is indefatigable, spillikins, paper ships, riddles, conun-drums, and cards, with watching the flow and ebb of the river, and now and then a stroll out, keep us well employed; and we mean to avail ourselves of our kind papa's consider-ation, by not returning to Winchester till quite the evening of Wednesday. . . .

While I write now, George is most industriously making and naming paper ships, at which he afterwards shoots with horsechestnuts, brought from Steventon on purpose; and Edward equally intent over the 'Lake of Killarney,' twisting himself about in one of our great chairs. . . .

We have just had two hampers of apples from Kintbury, and the floor of our little garret is almost covered. Love to all.

Yours very affectionately, *J. A.*

Even more than cards and dancing, word games have an important function in *Emma.* Lovers of word games may be simply childish like Mr Woodhouse who cannot remember beyond the first stanza of the riddle "Kitty, a fair but frozen maid," or Harriet whose only "mental provision . . . for the evening of life, was the collecting and transcribing all the riddles of every sort that she could meet with." But word games do more in *Emma* than expose childish triviality; they reveal a threat to social community. In the first volume the misunderstood charade leads to the fiasco of Elton's proposal and the failure of Emma's first matrimonial scheme; in the third volume the anagrams at Hartfield mark the wide separation, physical as well as moral, between Emma and Knightley, Frank and Jane, at this juncture; and in between the first crisis and the climax on Box Hill various games involving puzzles and secrets occur. Often these games are more or less complex riddles involving personal identity. Who is the charade really addressed to? Who is the donor of Jane Fairfax's piano? Who sent Churchill news of Perry's "plan of setting up his carriage"? What two letters express perfection? . . .

A curious but instructive reversal has occurred: in real life, where names should be known, gifts acknowledged, and engagements made public, there is secrecy, whereas in children's games "proper names" (Miss Woodhouse, Dixon, Perry, Emma) keep appearing. Given the confusion between games and life, it is not perhaps surprising that Jane Fairfax should be "a riddle, quite a riddle" to Emma, or that Jane's willingness to endure "the mortification of Mrs Elton's notice and the penury of her conversation" should appear as a "puzzle.". . .

Churchill, of course, is the games player, *par excellence*. It is he who introduces into Highbury "guesses," "surprises," "tricks" far in excess of his need to set up a "blind to conceal his real situation" with Jane Fairfax. . . . Emma, no doubt comically exaggerating in her annoyance at being duped, accuses him of "a system of hypocrisy and deceit-espionage, and treachery." Mr Knightley, analyzing his letter of apology to Mrs Weston, sees that Churchill was "playing a most dangerous game" and exclaims: "Mystery, Finesse—how they pervert the understanding! My Emma, does not every thing serve to prove more and more the beauty of truth and sincerity in all our dealings with each other." Knightley stands against Churchill throughout as a plain and "open" man. He "does nothing mysteriously," he feels that "surprises are foolish things." In his behavior, unlike Churchill's, community and communicator are correspondent terms. . . .

Yet Churchill is not ostracized at the end of *Emma,* nor is
Emma's vitality subdued. When Mrs Weston gives birth to a
girl, Emma's first thought, only half suppressed, is to make
"a match for her, hereafter, with either of Isabella's sons."
Now morally detached from Churchill, however, her love of
games is ratified, as when she sympathetically imagines Mr
Weston's "fireside enlivened by the sports and nonsense, the
freaks and fancies of a child never banished from home," or,
"laughing and blushing," composes a last riddle as she
promises to call Mr Knightley once by his Christian name
"in the building in which N. takes M. for better, or worse."
Such games are very different from those played on Box Hill,
where "Perfection" came too soon. Only Mrs Elton could
wish for a replay of that game, though Churchill in his last
meeting with Emma tries to start up the "Dixon" and "Perry"
games again. Emma no longer plays with him, however, her
sympathies, as distinguished from her behavior on Box Hill,
being with Jane. For Emma, games are no longer a threat.
Married to Knightley and living at Hartfield with him and
her father, she will participate in "a vast deal of chat and
backgammon," not to mention "Candour & Comfort & Cof-
fee & Cribbage." The triumph of Emma, in the end, is that it
can require society to be the noblest game of all, exacting the
most demanding of moral performances, and yet give space
within this play for recreation in its most trivial guises. In
Emma Jane Austen described not only a family but a society
in which the Miss Austen of the *Letters* could feel at home.

CHAPTER 4

Jane Austen's Early Novels

READINGS ON
JANE AUSTEN

Satire and Realism in *Northanger Abbey*

Norman Sherry

Norman Sherry analyzes the plot and the heroine of *Northanger Abbey*, discussing the novel as a work in two halves. According to Sherry, in the first part, Austen satirizes popular novels of her day. She constructs events like those in romantic stories, but her heroine, Catherine Morland, entirely lacks the beauty, intelligence, and mystery of the typical heroines in popular books. Sherry goes on to show how, in the second half of the novel, Austen charts Catherine's education in the realities of ordinary life. Having been deceived by her friend Isabella, Catherine takes less at face value and profits from her past mistakes. Norman Sherry was educated at the University of Durham in England, and lectured in English at the Universities of Singapore, Liverpool, and Lancaster. He is the author of *Conrad's Eastern World*, *Conrad's Western World*, *Charlotte and Emily Brontë*, and *Thomas Hardy: A Reassessment*.

Northanger Abbey derives most obviously from Jane Austen's reaction to the popular novel of her time, and in this is most closely related to her earliest writing. It was begun in 1797 or 1798, was then known as *Susan* and was sold in 1803 to Crosby the publisher. But it obviously underwent a great deal of revision after it was bought back from him and is, therefore, a book which was being written during most of her adult life.

It apparently began as a burlesque[1] of the contemporary novel of horror and of sentiment, and much of the story still depends on this—there is a great deal of parody[2] and bur-

1. an art form made comic by ridiculous exaggeration   2. imitation of another work for comic or ridiculous effect

From *Jane Austen* by Norman Sherry (London: Evans Bros., 1966). Copyright ©1966 by Norman Sherry. Reprinted by permission of the author.

lesque still there. But the novel moves from this concern with literature to a concern with life, and so it follows Jane Austen's own development as a writer.

THEMES AND STRUCTURE: CATHERINE AS ANTIHEROINE

There are two themes which determine the novel's structure, and Catherine Morland, the heroine, is central to both. Catherine has first to learn to distinguish between literature and life, and then has to learn the difficulties of ordinary life. The two themes are clearly announced. Chapter I begins: 'No one who had ever seen Catherine Morland in her infancy, would have supposed her born to be an heroine'; and when Catherine is disabused of her romantic fancies, the second theme is announced: 'The anxieties of common life began soon to succeed to the alarms of romance'.

Catherine is the antiheroine in that, although she is to be the heroine of this novel, she has none of the characteristics of the conventional fictional heroine—no beauty, intellect, mysterious background—not even a lover. If we compare her with Emmeline, the heroine of the currently popular *Orphan of the Castle*, we find how conspicuously Catherine lacks the attainments necessary for a heroine.

Emmeline formed correct literary tastes in a ruined library and had 'of every useful ornamental feminine employment . . . long since made herself mistress without any instruction'. But Catherine Morland 'never could learn or understand any thing before she was taught; and sometimes not even then, for she was often inattentive, and occasionally stupid'. Emmeline learnt to play the harp only by listening to someone else receiving instruction in that instrument, and with no more instruction in drawing could execute a perfect portrait of her lover, leaving it on the pianoforte for him to find. Catherine, on the other hand, only progressed so far in musical appreciation as to be able to 'listen to other people's performance with very little fatigue', and 'Her greatest deficiency was in the pencil—she had no notion of drawing—not enough even to attempt a sketch of her lover's profile, that she might be detected in the design'. . . .

Yet in spite of her disadvantages, Catherine is destined to be a heroine—a heroine in terms of common life.

The first part of the novel is conceived of in terms of the opposition between fact and fiction. The structure here is, therefore, determined by the structure of the contemporary novel. Like Fanny Burney's Evelina, Catherine must be introduced into society—in this case, the sophistication of Bath.[3] Like Evelina, her ignorance and innocence cause her some embarrassments and troubles. She meets the hero, Henry Tilney, who constantly makes fun of the conventions of the popular novel to her, and of the correct behaviour for a heroine:

> 'I see what you think of me,' said he gravely—'I shall make but a poor figure in your journal tomorrow.... Friday, went to the Lower Rooms; wore my sprigged muslin robe with blue trimmings—plain black shoes—appeared to much advantage; but was strangely harassed by a queer, half-witted man, who would make me dance with him, and distressed me by his nonsense.'

At Bath, she also finds the friend and confidante necessary to a sentimental heroine in Isabella Thorpe, who helps her extend her reading in Gothic fiction by providing her with a reading list of the most popular novels:

> The progress of the friendship between Catherine and Isabella was quick as its beginning had been warm, and they passed so rapidly through every gradation of increasing tenderness, that there was shortly no fresh proof of it to be given to their friends or themselves. They called each other by their Christian name, were always arm in arm when they walked, pinned up each other's train for the dance, and were not to be divided in the set.

John Thorpe, Isabella's brother, and James Morland, Catherine's brother, who are friends at university (though Catherine had not known of this previously) arrive in Bath together. The behaviour of the Thorpes causes some embarrassment to Catherine where Henry Tilney and his sister are concerned, but Isabella's engagement to James gives her great happiness.

Unknown to Catherine, General Tilney, Henry's father, has been told by John Thorpe that Catherine is an heiress, and as a result Catherine is invited by the Tilneys to stay with them at their home, Northanger Abbey:

> Her passion for ancient edifices was next in degree to her passion for Henry Tilney—and castles and abbies made usually the charm of those reveries which his image did not fill. ... With all the chances against her of house, hall, place, park, court, and cottage, Northanger turned up an abbey, and she was to be its inhabitant. Its long, damp passages, its nar-

3. a resort city in the west of England

row cells and ruined chapel, were to be within her daily reach, and she could not entirely subdue the hope of some traditional legends, some awful memorials of an injured and ill-fated nun.

Before she leaves Bath, Catherine is aware of a change in Isabella's attitude to James—some unkind behaviour, and a weakness for flirting with Captain Tilney—which disturbs her for her brother's sake.

Up to this point, Catherine has undergone many of the trials of the sentimental heroine, but always in a realistic and probable fashion. She has been prevented from dancing by John Thorpe, teased into riding with him when she ought to have been walking with the Tilneys, and generally led into small mistakes of courtesy. But none of them are serious, and many possible troubles she misses entirely because she is too simple and honest to see them.

During the drive to the Abbey, Henry continues his satire on the horror novel by telling her what she, as a heroine, might expect on her arrival: 'And are you prepared to encounter all the horrors that a building such as "what one reads about" may produce?—Have you a stout heart?—Nerves fit for sliding panels and tapestry?'. He goes on to talk of a remote and gloomy chamber in which she is to sleep, of 'a ponderous chest', and of 'Dorothy the ancient housekeeper'.

After this, it is a set piece of irony on Jane Austen's part that the Abbey should be modern:

> An abbey!—yes, it was delightful to be really in an abbey!— but she doubted, as she looked round the room, whether any thing within her observation, would have given her the consciousness. The furniture was in all the profusion and elegance of modern taste. The fire-place . . . was contracted to a Rumford, with slabs of plain though handsome marble, and ornaments over it of the prettiest English china.

Yet it is not surprising that Catherine's imagination is allowed full play, and that she sees mysteries where none exist. General Tilney, suspected by her of murdering his wife or at least of having locked her up somewhere in the house, takes on 'the air and attitude of a Montoni', the sinister owner of the Castle of Udolpho in Mrs. Radcliffe's novel. The burlesque here is all intended to reveal to Catherine that she is imaginatively at fault. In each instance where her imagination has transformed an object or incident into an aspect of a horror novel, she is eventually shown that the object or incident is commonplace, or, if it has a significance which is unpleasant, it is unpleasant in terms of common life. Thus General Tilney may not be a wife-murderer, but he is a selfishly ambitious man.

CATHERINE'S INNER JOURNEY

In an excerpt from Jane Austen, *critic June Dwyer explains the significances of Catherine Morland's experiences. Catherine's trip to Bath and to Northanger Abbey parallels an inner journey in which she learns the realities and complexities of adult life.*

The plot centers around seventeen-year-old Catherine Morland's trip to Bath in the company of her neighbors, the Allens. There she makes the acquaintance of two very different families, the vulgar Thorpes and the more reserved and well-bred Tilneys. Each family represents a possible model for her own life: one is superficial and excessive; the other, refined and measured. Catherine's venture to Bath and then on to the Tilneys' estate of Northanger Abbey is paralleled by the inner journey that she makes as she crosses over from the world of youth and fantasy to that of complex, adult life.

This inner journey constitutes something of a triumph for Catherine, for many women in Jane Austen's novels never mature; they remain childlike and dependent, preoccupied with little-girl games like tea parties and dress-up. Catherine's neighbor and chaperone, Mrs. Allen, is just such a child-woman. She has a limited set of interests and little if any moral sense. . . . *Northanger Abbey* explores the kind of guidance a young woman growing up in the confines of parochial nineteenth-century English society has available.

It is Henry who eventually disabuses Catherine of her confusion of literature with life—'Remember the country and the age in which we live. Remember that we are English, that we are Christians. Consult your own understanding, your own sense of the probable'.

The burlesquing of literature ends with Volume II, Chapter X (Chapter 25 in other editions), when Catherine is finally awakened to the dangers of confusing life with literature—'The visions of romance were over'. And in the same chapter the second theme is taken up more strongly and forms the basis of the rest of the book. This is the theme of education into real life—into human nature and human behaviour. It has been part of the earlier chapters also, but it comes out strongly again with James' letter telling Catherine that he has been jilted by Isabella. The difficulties of real life increase when the General, who has now learnt that Catherine is not an heiress, expels her from his house and she is consequently separated from Henry.

THE EDUCATION OF CATHERINE

These two themes are linked in that they centre on Catherine and the educative process which is to mature her. She learns not to be deceived by literature, and not to be deceived by life. Catherine is inadequate as a fictional heroine, missing opportunity after opportunity to suffer, to act, to confide in the way of the sentimental heroines of the age. She refuses to be persuaded into love by Isabella:

'But you should not persuade me that I think so very much about Mr. Tilney, for perhaps I may never see him again.'
'Not see him again! My dearest creature, do not talk of it. I am sure you would be miserable if you thought so.'
'No, indeed, I should not.'

She is blind to the idea of Isabella being in love with her brother, in spite of her friend's hints:

'Well, my taste is different. I prefer light eyes; and as to complexion—do you know—I like a sallow better than any other. You must not betray me, if you should ever meet with one of your acquaintance answering that description.'
'Betray you!—What do you mean?'
'Nay, do not distress me. I believe I have said too much. Let us drop the subject.'

Isabella, who apes the sentimental heroine in her speech and manners, can impose on Catherine's simplicity for a time:

'Had I the command of millions, were I mistress of the whole world, your brother would be my only choice.'
This charming sentiment, recommended as much by sense as novelty, gave Catherine a most pleasing remembrance of all the heroines of her acquaintance.

Catherine is gullible because of her nature. She is 'Open, candid, artless, guileless, with affections strong but simple, forming no pretensions, and knowing no disguise'. But her natural simplicity and directness is not always taken in by Isabella, John Thorpe, or General Tilney, and her insight into character is not always mistaken.

However, it is necessary for her to be more perceptive, to be educated so that she can no longer be imposed upon by literature or life. She is educated into a love of beauty by Miss Tilney, and into understanding of character by Henry. She learns not to take at its face value what people say and do, but to look beneath at character and motive. Thus, Isabella's final letter to her can no longer deceive:

> 'I see what she has been about. She is a vain coquette, and her tricks have not answered. I do not believe she had ever any regard either for James or for me, and I wish I had never known her. . . . There is but one thing that I cannot understand. I see that she has had designs on Captain Tilney, which have not succeeded; but I do not understand what Captain Tilney has been about all this time. Why should he pay her such attentions as to make her quarrel with my brother, and then fly off himself?'
>
> 'I have very little to say for Frederick's motives, such as I believe them to have been. He has his vanities as well as Miss Thorpe, and the chief difference is, that, having a stronger head, they have not yet injured himself. If the *effect* of his behaviour does not justify him with you, we had better not seek after the cause.'
>
> 'Then you do not suppose he ever really cared about her?'
> 'I am persuaded that he never did.'
> 'And only made believe to do so for mischief's sake?'
> Henry bowed his assent.
> 'Well, then, I must say that I do not like him at all.'

Catherine is Jane Austen's most innocent heroine. She has none of the certainty of Elizabeth Bennet, none of the gentler perception of Anne Elliot, none of the righteousness of Fanny Price. She is closer in nature to Harriet Smith. But she is like Emma Woodhouse in that her ignorance catches her up in mistakes and misjudgements, so that the reader is always ahead of her in perception. From this derives, as in *Emma,* much of the irony of plot. . . .

TYPICAL METHODS

Two techniques which are typical of Jane Austen appear in this novel. The first is the use of the letter to communicate a *dénouement.*[4] Catherine is withdrawn from the scene of the subplot when she leaves Bath for Northanger Abbey, and she must therefore receive the news of her brother's broken engagement and Isabella's attempt to re-instate herself with the Morlands, by letter. Elizabeth Bennet, in *Pride and Prejudice*, is similarly situated—she learns of Lydia's elopement by letter, and later of how Wickham was persuaded to marry

4. the final unraveling of the plot

her, by the same means. Fanny Price is also away from the main action, and receives intelligence by a newspaper report and by letter.

The second technique is Jane Austen's ironic withdrawal from her characters once the story reaches its conclusion. She clears up outstanding issues by an ironic and swift disclosure of the future, which distances everything and puts the characters firmly within the covers of a book:

> The anxiety, which in this state of their attachment must be the portion of Henry and Catherine, and of all who loved either, as to its final event, can hardly extend, I fear, to the bosom of my readers, who will see in the tell-tale compression of the pages before them, that we are all hastening together to perfect felicity.

This seems to reflect her impatience with the conventions of the novel which demand always such 'felicity' at the end. For her the interest of the novel seems to lie in the delineation and play of character according to what she conceives of as probable. She will bring this out even to the detriment of her heroine:

> Though Henry was now sincerely attached to her ... I must confess that his affection originated in nothing better than gratitude.... It is a new circumstance in romance, I acknowledge, and dreadfully derogatory of an heroine's dignity; but if it be as new in common life, the credit of a wild imagination will at least be all my own.

In *Northanger Abbey* Jane Austen satirises the more exaggerated conventions and excesses of the Gothic and sentimental novel, but although she here makes her stand on realism, she could not throw off entirely the conventions of romance. Hero and heroine must come together in happiness, and while she adapted the framework to her own ends, her impatience with it does at times show through.

Sense and Sensibility Has Little Irony

John Odmark

John Odmark argues that while irony is fundamental to Austen's novels, in *Sense and Sensibility* Austen's narrative is least ironic. Here, Odmark suggests, Austen clearly indicates that Elinor's reasoned compliance with society's rules is superior to Marianne's emotionalism, an opinion that reflects her own point of view. Only in the few instances when the reader's knowledge exceeds Elinor's does irony exist, according to Odmark. In addition to his study of Jane Austen, John Odmark edited a collection of criticism, *Language, Literature, and Meaning.*

The basis of Jane Austen's irony is usually shown to be the conflicting systems of norms and values in the world portrayed, the contrast between the author's values and those in the little country village of her setting, or a combination of these possibilities. . . . As a rule *irony* in Jane Austen's fiction has been defined primarily in terms of content. What I want to draw attention to is the fact that *irony* is above all a structuring principle that determines the shape of all the novels. . . .

A distinction is made between what I term 'local' irony and 'structural' irony. The first refers to those ironies readily perceived by the reader from his perspective of superior knowledge. . . . Those ironies that are central to the plot—the 'structural ironies'—are dependent on the reader's changing perceptions of character and situation. The limits of change occur at that point in the narrative where the reader's knowledge finally approaches that of the omniscient narrator.[1] . . .

1. the storyteller, who knows the thoughts and feelings of all the characters

CLEAR CONTRASTS IN *SENSE AND SENSIBILITY*

With *Sense and Sensibility* Jane Austen moves . . . to a serious treatment of moral and social themes. Such themes are not absent from *Northanger Abbey*, but they are not central to the development of the plot. *Sense and Sensibility* is quite different and more ambitious. It is a contrast novel, didactic[2] in intent. As the title suggests, two alternatives to similar situations are presented. One of them is shown to be prudent and correct, the other a violation of what is socially and morally acceptable, and, in addition, inherently dangerous to the well-being of the individual who chooses it.

In some respects Jane Austen's technique represents an advance over *Northanger Abbey*. There are no awkward shifts in the point of view, and some of her scenes are developed in a more complex and subtle manner. Nevertheless, *Sense and Sensibility* has been generally acknowledged to be the least satisfactory of all the novels. Probably, the weaknesses are due in part to the novel's origin as a novel in letters, and in part to the author's commitment to relating two parallel stories. This commitment leads to a lack of economy in the narration. Moreover, it encourages a schematic presentation of character. There is a tendency for characters to be categorized according to an absolute set of moral values, and to act predictably thereafter. Finally, much of the story is told from Elinor's point of view. This angle of vision reduces the possibilities for irony, since Elinor's views are essentially the same as the narrator's.

It would be an oversimplification to suggest that Elinor embodies *sense* and Marianne *sensibility*, for Marianne is also capable of rational judgement just as her sister is capable of responding emotionally; nevertheless, throughout most of the novel the sisters are diametrically opposed to one another—Marianne allowing her feelings to govern her behaviour, and Elinor refusing to give in to such impulses. The reader is never left in any doubt as to how he should judge their behaviour. They are introduced as follows:

> Elinor, this eldest daughter whose advice was so effectual, possessed a strength of understanding and coolness of judgment, which qualified her, though only nineteen, to be the counsellor of her mother, and enabled her frequently to counteract, to the advantage of them all, that eagerness of

2. morally instructive

114 Readings on Jane Austen

mind in Mrs Dashwood which must generally have led to imprudence. She had an excellent heart;—her disposition was affectionate, and her feelings were strong; but she knew how to govern them: it was a knowledge which her mother had yet to learn, and which one of her sisters had resolved never to be taught.

Marianne's abilities were, in many respects, quite equal to Elinor's. She was sensible and clever; but eager in every thing; her sorrows, her joys, could have no moderation. She was generous, amiable, interesting: she was every thing but prudent. The resemblance between her and her mother was strikingly great.

This introductory description places the sisters for the reader, and in the course of the narrative he is never given any reason to doubt the objective validity of these characterizations. The introduction of all the characters who are not immediately given the opportunity to reveal themselves through their behaviour and conversation is similar. The introduction of a new character is one of the few instances in which it is necessary for the narrator to intrude into the novel.

Events Seen Through Elinor's Eyes

For the most part past events are related from Elinor's point of view. There is little reason for the additional perspective of a reliable narrator, for Elinor does not allow her emotions to distort her judgement of characters and situations. Her values are the narrator's. Her judgements and actions are based on the assumption that the conventional rules of propriety are identical with the external manifestation of true propriety. The organization of the plot and the means employed to render character suggest that the author shares Elinor's understanding of propriety and its implications. It is therefore hardly surprising that irony is seldom directed at Elinor, and that it is only directed at her sister before the effects of Marianne's foolish behaviour become known.

Elinor is placed in an ironic light only on those few occasions when the course of events takes a turn that she is unaware of. Even in such instances, however, the irony does not affect Elinor's image as an individual who is always conscious of what conduct is proper under any given circumstances. Nevertheless, it would be an oversimplification to suggest that, whenever alternatives are presented, Elinor's choice is inevitably correct and Marianne's wrong. In the long run, Elinor's alternatives prove to be the better means for maintaining the social order and surviving within it; but at times Marianne's choices seem more acceptable even though they threaten the social order, for they are motivated by deeply felt emotions, which should not at all costs be suppressed completely.

THE NOVEL LACKS CHARACTERS WITH INNER STRUGGLES

The conflicts in *Sense and Sensibility* do not exist in the consciousness of one individual as they do, for example, in Elizabeth Bennet or Emma Woodhouse. In part the conflicts arise from the differences of opinion between the sisters, and in part from external circumstances over which they have little or no control. The secret agreement between Lucy Steele and Edward Ferrars, for instance, appears until the next to the last chapter an insurmountable obstacle to Elinor's happiness. She knows her own feelings, but her actions are governed by reason. When Colonel Brandon asks her to inform Edward that he will be given a living, Elinor assumes this will be very welcome news, for it will finally make it possible for Edward and Lucy to marry. Despite this knowledge or, more likely, because of it, Elinor sees it as her duty to carry out this task and accept what she assumes will be the conse-

SYMBOLIC IRONY

In Jane Austen's Novels: A Study of Structure, *Andrew H. Wright says that* Sense and Sensibility *is ironic because Elinor and Marianne change positions in the course of the novel. This exchange elevates them from allegorical figures to ironic symbols, Wright argues.*

From a narrowly moralistic point of view the lesson of *Sense and Sensibility* can be stated as follows: it is wise to behave sensibly, and foolish—even dangerous—to expose oneself to the excesses of sensibility. But on a higher level the book contains the germs of a divided vision: Elinor and Marianne are in fact twin heroines, each embodying a mode of existence which is desirable, but each of which contradicts the other. And the grand irony is that Elinor and Marianne virtually interchange their positions (though there are many modifications along the way): Marianne, it is quite clear, does gradually acquire sense; but it is also true that Elinor becomes increasingly sensitive as the book progresses. So the two elder Dashwood sisters function not as mere allegorical figures but as ironic symbols.

quences. Such behaviour leaves little room for irony.

Elinor seems at times more like a principle than an individual. Her speeches tend to be long and didactic even at moments of stress, which suggests that they are remnants of letters dating from an earlier version of the novel. Marianne is more clearly individualized, but her thoughts and feelings are viewed for the most part from Elinor's perspective, so that even in those situations where Marianne has a viable alternative to one of her sister's proposals, it is presented in an unfavourable light. The reader has no alternative to Elinor's clear-sighted and rational observations, though in retrospect he may feel that she was not always as clear-sighted as she assumes.

Because of the reader's closeness to Elinor's perspective, he is led to accept Marianne's decision to marry Colonel Brandon, although the Colonel embodies those social and moral values for which Marianne has had little use. The reader is informed at the beginning that Marianne has her portion of *sense* as well as *sensibility*, but her decision to marry Colonel Brandon remains unconvincing. It is unconvincing because the reader has experienced so little of Marianne's mental life and has therefore little cause to think she has changed so fundamentally in her attitudes as to be willing to accept this boring, colourless alternative. Like the other contrived developments in the plot, it corresponds to the author's didactic intent and Elinor's sense of what is correct, but it seems inconsistent with Marianne's character.

To summarize, Jane Austen's handling of point of view in *Sense and Sensibility* is once again problematical. The views of the narrator, Elinor and presumably the author coalesce to such an extent that it is difficult for the reader to find the basis for an opinion which differs from Elinor's. His knowledge is only incidentally and not consistently superior to Elinor's. Earlier I suggested that irony is the structuring principle of all Jane Austen's novels. In respect to *Sense and Sensibility*, however, this observation must be qualified. The overall conception of the novel is clearly defined; however, it is not based on an ironic view of Elinor or Marianne. It is based on Elinor's concept of proper moral and social behaviour, and presented from her point of view. As a result, the reader has little opportunity to weigh her opinions against those of others. The exigencies of the plot require a broader perspective. The development of the plot, and above all the revolution, seem forced.

Minor Characters Reflect the Theme of *Sense and Sensibility*

Howard S. Babb

Howard S. Babb asserts that Austen carries the antithesis of sense and feeling into all elements of *Sense
and Sensibility*, including the minor characters. Babb
argues that the novel's minor characters range from
the extremely emotional to the extremely sensible,
and none of them succeeds in moving beyond narrow self-interest. To clarify his point, Babb classifies
the minor characters into four categories: those who
talk excessively and most lack sense, those who are
inclined toward sensibility but do have kindhearted
natures, those who manipulate while playing the
emotional-victim role, and those who represent
sense while disguising their selfishness. Though
Babb acknowledges that *Sense and Sensibility* may be
flawed, he implies that the novel's artistic symmetry
compensates for any faults it may have. Howard S.
Babb was a scholar, educator, editor, and writer. He
taught English at Ohio State University at Columbus
and at the University of California at Irvine. He is the
author of *Novels of William Golding*.

Everyone would agree that *Sense and Sensibility* creates the
impression of being extremely rigid. The title itself an-
nounces the main antithesis, yet it can hardly suggest how
diligently Jane Austen distinguishes between the mode of
sense and the mode of feeling in the novel's plot, style, and
theme. To review these quickly, before we look into the linguistic habits of the characters, may remind us how uncom-
promising *Sense and Sensibility* is, and how insistently it resolves—though readers sometimes overlook this—the initial
antithesis.

From *Jane Austen's Novels: The Fabric of Dialogue* by Howard S. Babb. Copyright ©1962
by the Ohio State University Press. Reprinted courtesy of Estate of Howard S. Babb.

In its broadest outlines, the plot sets up a series of comparable situations in which we are to watch the sense of Elinor Dashwood and the sensibility of Marianne, her younger sister, at work. The novel's first phase opposes the restrained courtship of Elinor by a despondent Edward Ferrars to Willoughby's ebullient relationship with Marianne, and, more important, contrasts Elinor's relative composure during Edward's long absences with Marianne's distraction at being separated from Willoughby. In the second stage, when both attachments seem impossible because of Edward's engagement to Lucy Steele and Willoughby's sudden marriage, Elinor's stoicism is reckoned against Marianne's wild despair. By the end of the novel, though, these extremes approach each other: the sisters agree in judging Willoughby's character, and Elinor, after suffering through Marianne's illness, Willoughby's self-vindication, and what appears to be Edward's marriage to Lucy, is finally united with Edward, while Marianne subdues herself to the point of accepting the warmhearted Colonel Brandon. . . .

The minor characters fill out the theme by taking positions along a line stretching from the extreme of emotion to the extreme of sense, either limit marking a complete self-interest. The novel proposes, we remember, that one ought to mediate between the claims of the rival camps, sense determining one's adjustment to society and unselfish feeling animating it. What the minor characters reveal, each in his different way, is a series of failures in mediation, therefore a variety of uncreative social adjustments, some less serious, some more. It is unfair to them as individuals to categorize them roughly in four groups, but perhaps such an arrangement will throw the dominant motifs of the novel into higher relief.

TALK WITHOUT SENSE

At one extreme is a cluster of figures whose feelings perpetually run riot in their talk, divorcing it from sense. Charlotte Palmer's exclamatory bursts flatten all she mentions to the dead level of the superlative, obliterating any distinction between the particular and the general, thus annihilating rationality. Her absolutism has driven Mr. Palmer to one just as drastic, though the reverse of hers in that he invariably voices his disgust. And if Miss Steele's grammatical errors seem a rather nasty insistence on the part of the author that Anne is underbred, still her vocabulary implies that she is almost as witlessly intense as Mrs. Palmer: everything is "monstrous," "plaguing," "vast," the energetic counters proving, so Anne hopes, that she belongs to the fashionable world.

GOOD-HEARTED CHARACTERS

The three characters in the second group are somewhat more subdued, and the novel presents them as essentially good-hearted, even though their conversation usually shows sense at the mercy of warmly private feeling. The talk of Sir John Middleton brims with generalizations, all of them based on his own pleasure, whether in hunting or in getting up a party to gratify himself and others. The vigorous emotions of Mrs. Jennings often confuse her thinking—witness her many false inductions—and sometimes make her as careless with her words, as in her indecorous reference to Colonel Brandon's "love child"; but when faced with the reality of Marianne's rejection by Willoughby and subsequent illness, Mrs. Jennings shows herself wholeheartedly sympathetic.

With the last member of this group, Mrs. Dashwood, we approach Marianne's position on the scale, for the mother has an active sensibility of her own; though it tempts Mrs. Dashwood into a number of false inductions, still her sensibility is triggered by her unselfish love for her daughters. Lucy Steele has a post all to herself, out beyond Elinor's and not yet at the limit of sense: as we shall see in a moment, she almost always calculates her relation to society shrewdly, but her calculations do not square with her real feelings. As for the John Dashwoods and Robert Ferrars, who are placed at the extreme of sense, they brandish their reason in everything they say, but their version of reason consists of the ugliest self-interest.

Most of these minor characters reveal themselves so transparently in their remarks that they need not detain us. Yet we might linger briefly with Lucy Steele and then the John Dashwoods, for they are playing a deeper linguistic game. Lucy is convinced in her heart that she is the equal of anyone and jealously guards her success with Edward as a token of her value. But she also recognizes that society regards her as an inferior. In much of the novel she turns this fact to her advantage, playing the role of the inferior for all it is worth. However, the conflict between the role she assumes and her real self breaks into the open toward the end of her two long talks with Elinor.

LUCY STEELE THE MANIPULATOR

Throughout them Lucy is warning Elinor to leave Edward alone, most of the time with her usual astuteness. For instance, she parades her inferiority by drawing attention to her indecorums, thus in effect neutralizing her opponent by

THE PALMERS AS PAIRED OPPOSITES

In Sense and Sensibility, *Jane Austen describes the Palmers as they call on the Dashwoods. On a subsequent visit, Mr. Palmer insults his mother-in-law, Mrs. Jennings, who is also present. These excerpts illustrate Austen's skill at pairing opposites.*

[Mrs. Palmer] was short and plump, had a very pretty face, and the finest expression of good humour in it that could possibly be. . . . [Mr. Palmer] entered the room with a look of self-consequence, slightly bowed to the ladies, without speaking a word, and, after briefly surveying them and their apartments, took up a newspaper from the table and continued to read it as long as he staid.

*   *   *   *   *

"Then you would be very ill-bred," cried Mr. Palmer.

"My love, you contradict every body,"—said his wife with her usual laugh. "Do you know that you are quite rude?"

"I did not know I contradicted any body in calling your mother ill-bred."

"Aye, you may abuse me as you please," said the good-natured old lady, "you have taken Charlotte off my hands, and cannot give her back again. So there I have the whip hand of you."

Charlotte laughed heartily to think that her husband could not get rid of her; and exultingly said, she did not care how cross he was to her, as they must live together. It was impossible for any one to be more thoroughly good-natured, or more determined to be happy than Mrs. Palmer. The studied indifference, insolence, and discontent of her husband gave her no pain: and when he scolded or abused her, she was highly diverted.

"Mr. Palmer is so droll!" said she, in a whisper, to Elinor. "He is always out of humour."

Elinor was not inclined after a little observation, to give him credit for being so genuinely and unaffectedly ill-natured or ill-bred as he wished to appear. His temper might perhaps be a little soured by finding, like many others of his sex, that through some unaccountable bias in favour of beauty, he was the husband of a very silly woman.

making Elinor over into a social arbiter (although of course the maneuver also serves Lucy by implying that she feels delicately enough to know her breaches for what they are). At the same time, she alleges a special fondness for Elinor, thus tying her rival's hands. Moreover, Lucy proclaims her passion for Edward at every turn, which automatically entitles her to the pity of the world for lovers in difficulties. These facets of Lucy's role are caught together in a speech near the end of her first encounter with Elinor:

> I was afraid you would think I was taking a great liberty with you . . . in telling you all this. . . but . . . as soon as I saw you, I felt almost as if you was an old acquaintance. Besides . . . I am so unfortunate, that I have not a creature whose advice I can ask. . . . I only wonder that I am alive after what I have suffered for Edward's sake these last four years.

With ammunition like this, Lucy wins the first battle hands down.

But her tone changes, as does Elinor's, after they meet again. Elinor is under a special obligation to preserve the forms of decorum because she has been cast as the social superior; yet she has also been personally attacked by Lucy and can return the fire only by manipulating those forms so obviously that Lucy will understand her. Thus Elinor resorts, quite uncharacteristically, to generalizations loaded with ambiguity, such as "If the strength of your reciprocal attachment had failed, as between many people and under many circumstances it naturally would during a four years' engagement, your situation would have been pitiable indeed." And Lucy, fully alive to Elinor's implication that the "attachment" may have "failed," feels driven to speak out herself—not at all in the manner that her role demands—when she replies with a generalization that authoritatively measures her power as a person: "I can safely say that he has never gave me one moment's alarm on that account from the first." By the end of their talk Lucy may again convert Elinor into a judge, but now the strain on her temper shows through her sentences:

> "'Tis because you are an indifferent person," said Lucy, with some pique, and laying a particular stress on those words, "that your judgment might justly have such weight with me. If you could be supposed to be biassed in any respect by your own feelings, your opinion would not be worth having."

The personal venom here, however obliquely she may express it, and her assumption of equality, even superiority, in judging Elinor make it plain that Lucy's private sense of herself is wholly at odds with her normal public pose as the docile social inferior. Evidently Jane Austen wants us to make no mistake about this, for her own words strain, in the previous passage and throughout the two conversations, to fix Lucy's unpleasantness for us.

JOHN AND FANNY'S SEEMING REASON

In treating the John Dashwoods, though, Jane Austen stands at a greater distance, trusting her irony and their dialogue to interpret them for us. They differ from most of the other minor characters in being perfectly aware that it is improper to generalize on the basis of personal feeling alone; thus, though they always do so, they scrupulously insist that they are not acting out of private prejudice but in an enlightened way, according to a community of opinion.

Their behavior is outlined at the opening of their first talk, which dramatizes their allegiance to society, but to an utterly private version of it. The conversation begins with John reminding Fanny that he has promised his dying father to "assist" Mrs. Dashwood and her daughters, John himself having settled on an amount of three thousand pounds. This prospect irritates Fanny because she is entirely selfish, but of course she cannot admit such an indecorous motive. So she sets about erecting a supposedly reasonable standard of behavior, first by assuming that the father was insane, although she propitiates her husband with "I dare say," then by citing the probability of "ten to one" to justify her assumption: "He did not know what he was talking of, I dare say; ten to one but he was light-headed at the time. Had he been in his right senses, he could not have thought of such a thing as begging you to give away half your fortune from your own child." A norm so patently rational, Fanny presumes, should appeal automatically to John. Still, she refuses to take any chances, pushing on to color her father-in-law's departure from the norm by the emotive "begging." Her husband hesitates momentarily: though admitting his father's aberration, "He could hardly suppose I should neglect them," John yet sees himself as a man of honor who must behave according to the letter of decorum's law, "The promise, therefore, was given, and must be performed." But a way out begins to glimmer in the generalization with which he closes: "Something must be done for them whenever they leave Norland and settle in a new home." It sounds pompous and authoritative enough to satisfy propriety, yet is unparticular enough to evade any rashly concrete promises.

Fanny, however, is still not content. She takes over his generalization to avoid provoking him, but she feels impelled to qualify it, even at the risk of mentioning the specific sum, though she minimizes this breach of decorum by keeping her phrasing as impersonal as possible: "Well, then, *let* something be done for them; but *that* something need not be three thousand pounds. Consider . . . that when the money is once parted with, it never can return." And she immediately fortifies her position by calling up the maxim about "money . . . once parted with."

By the end of her speech she is seeking additional support in another emotive reminder of "our poor little boy," but she hardly needs it, for her husband has already caught sight of the grounds on which he can turn against the Dashwoods. Though acknowledging that his boy may some day "regret" the giving up of "so large a sum," John can make out what appears a much more objective case by following up Fanny's maxim with an appeal of his own to a community of opinion: "If he should have a numerous family . . . it would be a very convenient addition." Now safely allied with a public attitude, John can pronounce on the particular case, and of course start cutting down the amount of his assistance: "Five hundred pounds would be a prodigious increase to their fortunes!" His "prodigious" is wonderfully hypocritical, less congratulating him on his own kindness than expressing what he takes to be a normal public view of the Dashwoods' situation. And this hypocrisy typifies his character as well as Fanny's throughout the novel. Both subscribe to a presumably enlightened community of opinion, but it is one that utterly perverts social value because it twists reason into the service of merely selfish feeling. Thus, they provide the sharpest ironic statement of *Sense and Sensibility*'s theme.

CHAPTER 5

Pride and Prejudice

The Best Qualities of *Pride and Prejudice*

W. Somerset Maugham

W. Somerset Maugham, English novelist born a century after Austen, chose *Pride and Prejudice* as one of the ten greatest novels ever written. Maugham cites other critics to highlight the reasons for his choice, which include its exceptional presentation of ordinary life, its humor and wit, and above all its readability, the engagement that makes the reader eager to turn each page. After preparing for a medical career, W. Somerset Maugham decided to devote his life to writing. Between 1900 and 1910, Maugham was a successful playwright. His first major work, *Of Human Bondage* (1915), explores adolescence and brought recognition of his literary talent. Maugham's genius lies in his ability to catch the essence of a character. He is also the author of *The Razor's Edge, The Moon and Sixpence, Cakes and Ale*, and many short stories.

In 1809, in which year [Jane Austen] settled with her mother and sister in the quiet of Chawton, she set about revising her old manuscripts, and in 1811 *Sense and Sensibility* at last appeared. By then it was no longer outrageous for a woman to write. . . . *Pride and Prejudice* was published in 1813. Jane Austen sold the copyright for £10.

AUSTEN'S LIMITED WORLD

Besides [these novels and *Northanger Abbey*] she wrote three more, *Mansfield Park, Emma* and *Persuasion*. On these few books her fame rests, and her fame is secure. She had to wait a long time to get a book published, but she no sooner did than her charming gifts were recognized. Since then the most eminent persons have agreed to praise her. I will only quote what Sir Walter Scott had to say; it is characteristically

From "Jane Austen and *Pride and Prejudice*" by W. Somerset Maugham, in *Pride and Prejudice* by Jane Austen, edited by W. Somerset Maugham. Copyright ©1949 by W. Somerset Maugham. Reprinted by permission of A.P. Watt Ltd. on behalf of The Royal Literary Fund.

generous: "That young lady had a talent for describing the involvements, feelings and characters of ordinary life which is to me the most wonderful I have ever met with. The big bow-wow I can do myself like anyone going; but the exquisite touch which renders commonplace things and characters interesting from the truth of the description and the sentiment is denied to me."

It is odd that Scott should have omitted to make mention of the young lady's most precious talent: her observation was searching and her sentiment edifying, but it was her humor that gave point to her observation and a kind of prim liveliness to her sentiment. Her range was narrow. She wrote very much the same sort of story in all her books, and there is no great variety in her characters. They are very much the same persons seen from a somewhat different point of view. She had common sense in a high degree, and no one knew better than she her limitations. Her experience of life was confined to a small circle of provincial society, and that is what she was content to deal with.

She wrote only of what she knew; and it has been noticed that she never attempted to reproduce a conversation of men when by themselves, which in the nature of things she could never have heard.

She shared the opinions common in her day and, so far as one can tell from her books and letters, was quite satisfied with the conditions that prevailed. She had no doubt that social distinctions were important, and she found it natural that there should be rich and poor. A gentleman's younger son was properly provided for by taking orders and being given a fat family living; young men obtained advancement in the service of the King by the influence of powerful relations; a woman's business was to marry, for love certainly, but in satisfactory financial circumstances. All this was in the order of things, and there is no sign that Miss Austen saw anything objectionable in it. Her family was connected with the clergy and the landed gentry, and her novels are concerned with no other class.

It is difficult to decide which is the best of them because they are all so good, and each one has its devoted, and even fanatic, admirers. Macaulay thought *Mansfield Park* her greatest achievement; other critics, equally illustrious, have preferred *Emma*; Disraeli read *Pride and Prejudice* seventeen times; today many look upon *Persuasion* as her most exquisite and finished work. The great mass of readers, I believe, has accepted *Pride and Prejudice* as her masterpiece, and in such a case I think it well to accept their judgment. What makes a classic is not that it is praised by critics, expounded by professors and studied in college classes, but that the great mass of readers, generation after generation, have found pleasure and spiritual profit in reading it.

ANOTHER CRITIC QUALIFIES SCOTT'S PRAISE

In the 1859 publication of Blackwood's Magazine, *critic George Henry Lewes refers to Sir Walter Scott's praise of Austen's description of ordinary life and, like Maugham, says Scott misses the point. In the excerpt, Lewes claims that Austen does not "describe" anything; her skill is the art of dramatic presentation, more difficult than mere description.*

Scott felt, but did not define, the excellence of Miss Austen. The very word "describing" is altogether misplaced and misleading. She seldom describes anything, and is not felicitous when she attempts it. But instead of *description,* the common and easy resource of novelists, she has the rare and difficult art of *dramatic presentation*: instead of telling us what her characters are, and what they feel, she presents the people, and they reveal themselves. In this she has never perhaps been surpassed not even by Shakespeare himself. If ever living beings can be said to have moved across the page of fiction, as they lived, speaking as they spoke, and feeling as they felt, they do so in *Pride and Prejudice, Emma,* and *Mansfield Park.* What incomparable noodles she exhibits for our astonishment and laughter! What silly, good-natured women! What softly-selfish men! What lively, amiable, honest men and women, whom one would rejoice to have known!

My own opinion, for what it is worth, is that *Pride and Prejudice* is on the whole the most satisfactory of all the novels. *Emma* offends me by the snobbishness of the heroine; she is really too patronizing to the persons she looks upon as her social inferiors, and I can take no particular interest in the love affair of Frank Churchill and Jane Fairfax. It is the only one of Miss Austen's novels that I find long-winded. In *Mansfield Park* the hero and heroine, Fanny and Edmund, are intolerable prigs, and all my sympathies go out to the unscrupulous, sprightly and charming Henry and Mary Craw-

ford. *Persuasion* has a rare charm, and except for the incident on the Cobb at Lyme Regis I should be forced to look
upon it as the most perfect of the six. . . .

AUSTEN AS STORYTELLER

Professor Garrod, a learned and witty critic, has said that
Jane Austen was incapable of writing a story, by which, he
explains, he means a sequence of happenings, either romantic or uncommon. But that is not what Jane Austen had
a talent for, and not what she tried to do. She had too much
common sense and too sprightly a humor to be romantic,
and she was not interested in the uncommon, but in the
common. She made it uncommon by the keenness of her observation, her irony and her playful wit. By a story most of
us mean a connected and coherent narrative with a beginning, a middle and an end. *Pride and Prejudice* begins in the
right place, with the arrival on the scene of the two young
men whose love for Elizabeth Bennet and her sister Jane is
the main theme of the novel, and it ends in the right place
with their marriage. It is the traditional happy ending.

This sort of ending has excited the scorn of the sophisti-
cated, and of course it is true that many, perhaps most, marriages are not happy, and further, that marriage concludes
nothing; it is merely an entry upon another order of experience. Many authors have in consequence started their novels with marriage and dealt with its outcome. It is their right.
But I have a notion that there is something to be said for the
simple people who look upon marriage as a satisfactory
conclusion to a work of fiction. I think they do so because
they have a deep, instinctive feeling that by mating, a man
and a woman have fulfilled their biological function; the interest which it is natural to feel in the steps that have led to
this consummation, the birth of love, the obstacles, the misunderstandings, the avowals, now yields to its result, their
issue, which is the generation that will succeed them. To nature each couple is but a link in a chain, and the only importance of the link is that another link may be added to it.
This is the novelist's justification for the happy ending. In
Jane Austen's books the reader's satisfaction is considerably
enhanced by the knowledge that the bridegroom has a substantial income from real estate and will take his bride to a
fine house, surrounded by a park, and furnished throughout
with expensive and elegant furniture.

THE CHARACTERS IN *PRIDE AND PREJUDICE*

Pride and Prejudice seems to me a very well-constructed book. The incidents follow one another naturally, and one's sense of probability is nowhere outraged. It is, perhaps, odd that Elizabeth and Jane should be so well-bred and well-behaved, whereas their mother and three younger sisters should be so ordinary; but that this should be so was essential to the story Miss Austen had to tell. I have allowed myself to wonder why she did not avoid this stumbling-block by making Elizabeth and Jane the daughters of a first marriage of Mr. Bennet and making the Mrs. Bennet of the novel his second wife and the mother of the three younger daughters. Jane Austen liked Elizabeth best of all her heroines. "I must confess," she wrote, "that I think her as delightful a creature as ever appeared in print." If, as some have thought, she was herself the original for her portrait of Elizabeth; and she has certainly given her her own gaiety, high spirit and courage, wit and readiness, good sense and right feeling; it is perhaps not rash to suppose that when she drew the placid, kindly and beautiful Jane Bennet she had in mind her sister Cassandra.

Darcy has been generally regarded as a fearful cad. His first offense was his refusal to dance with people he didn't know and didn't want to know at a public ball to which he had gone with a party. Not a very heinous one. It is true that when he proposes to Elizabeth it is with an unpardonable insolence, but pride, pride of birth and wealth, was the predominant trait of his character, and without it there would have been no story to tell. The manner of his proposal, moreover, gave Jane Austen opportunity for the most dramatic scene in the book; it is conceivable that with the experience she gained later she might have been able to indicate Darcy's feelings in such a way as to antagonize Elizabeth without putting into his mouth speeches so improbable as to shock the reader.

There is perhaps some exaggeration in the drawing of Lady Catherine and Mr. Collins, but to my mind little more than comedy allows. Comedy sees life in a light more sparkling, but colder than that of common day, and a touch of exaggeration, that is of farce, is often no disadvantage. A discreet admixture of farce, like a sprinkle of sugar on strawberries, may well make comedy more palatable. With regard to Lady Catherine one must remember that in Jane Austen's day rank gave its possessors a sense of immense superiority over persons of inferior station, and not only expected to be treated by them with the utmost deference, but were. If Lady Catherine looked upon Elizabeth as so much white trash, let us not forget that Elizabeth looked upon her Aunt Phillips, because she was the wife of an attorney, as very little better. In my own youth, a hundred years after Jane Austen wrote, I knew great ladies whose sense of importance, though not quite so blatant, was not far removed from Lady Catherine's. And as for Mr. Collins, who has not known even today men with that combination of pomposity and sycophancy?

THE STYLE AND READABILITY OF *PRIDE AND PREJUDICE*

No one has ever looked upon Jane Austen as a great stylist. Her spelling was peculiar and her grammar often shaky, but she had a good ear. I think the influence of Dr. Johnson can be discerned in the structure of her sentences. She is apt to use the word of Latin origin rather than the plain English one, the abstract rather than the concrete. It gives her phrase a slight formality which is far from unpleasant; indeed it often adds point to a witty remark and a demure savor to a malicious one. Her dialogue is probably as natural as dialogue can ever be. To set down on paper speech as it is spoken would be very tedious, and some arrangement of it is necessary. Since so many of the speeches are worded exactly as they would be today we must suppose that at the end of the eighteenth century young girls in conversation did express themselves in a manner which would now seem stilted. Jane Bennet, speaking of her lover's sisters, remarks: "They were certainly no friends to his acquaintance with me, which I cannot wonder at, since he might have chosen so much more advantageously in many respects." I am willing to believe that this is just how she put it, but I admit, it requires an effort.

I have said nothing yet of what to my mind is the greatest merit of this charming book: it is wonderfully readable—more readable than some greater and more famous novels. As Scott said, Miss Austen deals with commonplace things, the involvements, feelings and characters of ordinary life; nothing very much happens and yet when you reach the bottom of a page you eagerly turn it in order to know what will happen next; nothing very much does and again you turn the page with the same eagerness.

Clashes and Compromises in *Pride and Prejudice*

Laura G. Mooneyham

Laura G. Mooneyham argues that the key to the popularity of Austen's *Pride and Prejudice* is the equality of its main characters, Elizabeth and Darcy. She then argues that their equality controls the structure of the novel. According to Mooneyham, the flaws of both Elizabeth and Darcy stem from the same source, self-love, but the fault manifests itself differently in each. Elizabeth's prejudice is revealed in her dogmatic opinions expressed with ironic wit. Darcy's pride is indicated by his superior attitude, expressed in formal, detached language. Through the first half of the book, the couple's clashes escalate to outright verbal battle at the midpoint, with Darcy's first proposal. In the second half of the novel, both learn about each other, acknowledge their own errors, and find ways to compromise. Mooneyham attributes Elizabeth and Darcy's success at resolution and their achievement of a satisfying marriage to their mutual sexual attraction and the equality of their intelligence, education, and independence. Laura G. Mooneyham teaches English at Trinity University in Texas.

The secret of *Pride and Prejudice*'s popularity lies in the dynamics between its hero and heroine. The spark of their relationship depends on their equality of intelligence and perception, for Elizabeth and Darcy are more fully equal in this sense than any other of Austen's protagonists. Each is both protagonist and antagonist; that is, their struggle is as much against each other as it is against the pressures of society or family. The novel presents a balance of power not only between two characters but between two conflicting modes of

From *Romance, Language, and Education in Jane Austen's Novels* by Laura G. Mooneyham. Copyright ©1988 by Laura G. Mooneyham. Reprinted with permission of St. Martin's Press, Inc.

judgment, and, by extension, between two conflicting systems of language which both reflect and shape these judgments. *Pride and Prejudice* resolves these conflicts in a compromise; Darcy and Elizabeth both change, though in different directions. . . .

THE STRUCTURE OF *PRIDE AND PREJUDICE*

In *Pride and Prejudice*, the structure is a product of the relationship between Elizabeth and Darcy. The novel's pace is characterized by a rising intensity when Elizabeth and Darcy are together, and a lull, a sense of intermission, when they are apart. Since the structure results from the dynamics of attraction and antagonism between hero and heroine, it is appropriate that Darcy's first proposal to Elizabeth marks almost the exact centre of the novel. Thus *Pride and Prejudice* in its first half chronicles the growing consequences of those vices in Darcy and Elizabeth which form its title, moves at its centre to the open expression of pride and prejudice in a love scene gone desperately sour, and in its second half traces the resolution of this disunion, the compromises made in the name of love.

The structural stability of *Pride and Prejudice* also relies on the treatment of language. The first half of the novel displays the growing linguistic divisions between Elizabeth and Darcy as each perceives reality according to his or her own habit of speech—Elizabeth through wit and its attendant blindness, Darcy through the language of reserve and privilege. When, at midpoint in the novel Darcy proposes, these two systems of language and thought clash openly for the first time. Neither Elizabeth nor Darcy hold anything back in this scene, for in the heat of anger reticence evaporates. The many months of prior misunderstanding on either side are swept away in accusation and counter-accusation. Darcy's letter, which follows the next day, supplies all missing information but does so in the rhetoric of injured pride.

From this central point of aired grievances and angry honesty, Elizabeth and Darcy reconstitute a language, building their romance in the process. Darcy must discard much of his stiffness and reserve; he must recognize that others beside himself have the right to be proud. . . . Elizabeth learns to temper her wit by a more careful internal evaluation of her own feelings. The precise articulation of each stage in her changing feelings for Darcy is crucial for Elizabeth's emotional and linguistic maturation because it betokens her new respect for language as a mode of judgment. Darcy too has benefited from an enforced period of meditation, for at the end of the novel we find that his period of reevaluation, analysis and regret has run parallel to Elizabeth's own. . . .

THE LANGUAGES OF PRIDE AND OF PREJUDICE

In this period of mutual education, Elizabeth relinquishes the language of prejudice, Darcy, the language of pride. Each of these languages expresses the same flaw—love of self. . . . Pride and prejudice are forms of the same sin; therefore the structure of the novel depends less on the clash of mutually exclusive properties than it does on a chiastic[1] pattern of balance; as Darcy and Elizabeth discard both pride and prejudice in order to find each other; they rehabilitate their patterns of speech and thought, and grow to share a less selfish rhetoric.

Though both pride and prejudice manifest the sin of self-love, each has its own characteristic linguistic expression. The antagonism between Elizabeth and Darcy is thus as much a war of words as of ideas. Pride nourishes itself through isolation and elevation; therefore the language of pride is reserved and authoritative. Prejudice is an inordinate love of one's own perceptions; hence the language of prejudice is one which manipulates that which it perceives into the mould of prior opinions. The language of prejudice must therefore be both fluid and dogmatic. . . .

Darcy's language is formal, precise, stolid. Even with his social equals—Bingley and his sisters; Lady Catherine—Darcy speaks with a detachment born of his intellectual superiority. Such language is not suited to intimacy but to the exercise of authority. Though sometimes ironic, it is not witty and never jocular. Elizabeth's language, on the other hand, is dominated by a prevailing sense of irony and the wit such an ironic viewpoint generates. In respect to Darcy, Elizabeth's language is subversive; that is, she seeks to undermine his authority, both temporal and linguistic, through verbal aggression.

The comic conflict of the first half of the novel is in con-

---

1. the balance of inversely related syntactic elements in which change in one element parallels an opposite change in the other

sequence a result of a double misinterpretation of language. On the one hand, Darcy errs in his criticism of Elizabeth's language—not in the substance of that criticism, but in its implications about his own use of words. Darcy accuses Elizabeth of inaccuracy and inconsistency: 'You expect me to account for opinions which you chuse to call mine, but which I have never acknowledged'. Likewise, at Rosings, Darcy tells Elizabeth: 'I . . . know, that you find great enjoyment in occasionally professing opinions which in fact are not your own'. . . .

Darcy is right in his assumption that Elizabeth's language is not an absolute, not consistent; he errs in his assumption that his own is—that it is not an appropriate subject for the witty sallies of others. And this implicit assumption of the self-evident propriety and rightness of his own words is what Elizabeth attacks: 'Mr. Darcy is not to be laught at!'. . .

ELIZABETH IS ATTRACTED TO DARCY

At the end of the novel, Darcy admits to Elizabeth that he thought she returned his affection before the first proposal. . . . Darcy is right that Elizabeth's punishing speeches indicate her attraction to him, but he is wrong to suppose that Elizabeth herself is aware of this attraction. . . .

That Elizabeth is attracted to Darcy and cares for him without knowing it before the proposal, is evident from a variety of signs. When Pemberley is mentioned at the Netherfield card table, Elizabeth's interest is caught and she lays down her book to hear more about Darcy's estate. Though she tells herself that she wishes to hurt Darcy, she checks her laugh at one point when she perceives that he is offended by one of Bingley's jests, just as later, newly engaged, she will check a laugh against Darcy because 'he had yet to learn to be laught at'. Moreover, Darcy forms a large part of Elizabeth's musings in Volume I; though she dislikes him, she is unable to drive him from her thoughts. . . . Darcy is more a part of Elizabeth's consciousness than she knows. Elizabeth's misreading of her own feelings is linked to her misreading of Darcy. . . . As Elizabeth later acknowledges to Darcy, in the early stages of their relationship she spoke wishing only to cause him pain. But Elizabeth's role as verbal aggressor has an unsought consequence: Darcy's admiration and regard. Darcy is piqued by Elizabeth's resistance, and finds her a challenge. As the wiser Elizabeth of the third volume can see, her animosity in part caused Darcy's love: 'you [Darcy] were sick of civility, of deference, of officious attention. You were disgusted with the women who were always speaking and looking, and thinking for *your* approbation alone. I roused, and interested you, because I was so unlike them'. Antagonism breeds conflict; conflict in turn breeds attraction. . . .

ELIZABETH MISJUDGES DARCY

Elizabeth's propensity to underestimate the consequences of her own wit is equalled by her proclivity to overestimate Darcy's ill-will. His every act and statement Elizabeth interprets as evidence of malice and scorn. In doing so, she demonstrates another characteristic of prejudice—the projection onto others of one's own way of judging. Because Elizabeth's speeches to Darcy are antagonistic, she assumes his are equally so. She cannot, will not, see that, after her visit to Netherfield, his interest in her is romantic, not adversarial. . . .

Elizabeth challenges Darcy again and again to insult her, to repay her intended rudeness with some of his own. At Netherfield, she accuses him of 'premeditated contempt'— an exact definition of her own attitude towards him—and challenges him, 'despise me if you dare'. Darcy's gallant reply—'Indeed I do not dare'—only amazes Elizabeth without affecting her entrenched opinion of him. At the Netherfield ball, this principle of projection works in reverse when Elizabeth accuses herself in Darcy's presence of thinking and speaking as she presumes Darcy does:

> 'I have always seen a great similarity in the turn of our minds.—We are each of an unsocial, taciturn disposition, unwilling to speak, unless we expect to say something that will amaze the whole room, and be handed down to posterity with all the eclat of a proverb'.

> 'This is no very striking resemblance of your own character . . .' said he. 'How near it may be to *mine*, I cannot pretend to say.—*You* think it a faithful portrait undoubtedly'.

Darcy's response strikes at the heart of Elizabeth's misjudgment: he is not what she says he is. . . .

THE THEME OF READING, WRITING, AND EDUCATION

Their almost total rhetorical division in the first half of the novel is revealed through Austen's carefully worked theme of reading and writing. Since Elizabeth and Darcy cannot be united until they share a common language, a common mode of perceiving the world, their early disunion is under-scored by the treatment given to books and letters. For in-stance, as we have seen before, Elizabeth's attention is first engaged at the Netherfield card table by the mention of Pemberley; she lays down her book to hear more. But more revealing is the fact that the particular aspect of Pemberley under discussion is its library. Miss Bingley draws a com-parison between the relatively scanty stock of Netherfield's books and the 'delightful' library of Pemberley. Darcy's reply—'It ought to be good . . . it has been the work of many generations'—underscores both the difference between the *nouveau riche*[2] Bingley and the established wealth of Darcy as well as the connection between Darcy's heritage and his use of language. Bingley's wealth is of relatively recent ori-gin, and his library in consequence is the product of only one generation's bibliophilic pretensions.

But the Pemberley library is an emblem for Darcy's long line of cultured and literate forebears. When Darcy goes on to say, 'I cannot comprehend the neglect of a family library in such days as these', we see that he regards himself as a guardian of his ancestral inheritance and views the present age as particularly threatening to the transmission of liter-ary and hereditary values. He is therefore a conservative, and his language expresses his conviction that he is a warder of the past. Darcy's style of writing demonstrates this conservatism. His is a painstaking and formal rhetoric; as Bingley says, '[Darcy] does *not* write with ease [but] studies too much for words of four syllables'. Our one example of Darcy's writing style bears Bingley out, for in his letter to Elizabeth the vocabulary is formal, even legalistic; the sen-tence structures are complex and laboriously balanced; and there are ninety-nine words of four syllables or more. . . .

Elizabeth's education, her own history with books and their effect on her character, is . . . an issue in the novel. Like most young ladies of her day, Elizabeth has received no for-mal education. What information she has, she has garnered during her own researches in her father's library. Like Austen herself, Elizabeth is largely self-taught. . . .

Elizabeth's education is an achievement of the individual will; Darcy's, more a result of the pressures of tradition.

2. newly rich

Their opposition is thus partly a consequence of the age-old clash between the eclectic[3] and the scholastic. How appropriate a signal it is, therefore, that on Elizabeth's last day at Netherfield, Darcy chooses to demonstrate his aristocratic indifference to her charms by 'adher[ing] most conscientiously to his book'. The chasm of words between them is at its broadest when, a few days later at the ball, Elizabeth tells Darcy that not only do they not read the same books nor with the same feelings, but that the comparison of their different opinions on books which he proposes is impossible. . . .

It is not until after the open display of angry honesty in the proposal scene that a reconciliation of these two rhetorics is prepared for. In Darcy's and Elizabeth's last scene together, after the two lovers have achieved a linguistic rehabilitation and have accepted each other's declarations, we see a reunion of language: Darcy and Elizabeth writing letters, side by side, neither intruding on the other, but penning the news of their engagement to their respective aunts in an equable and friendly silence. . . .

One last element of *Pride and Prejudice* which illustrates the linguistic component of Elizabeth's and Darcy's errors and education is the theme of the formal introduction. . . . Elizabeth and Darcy are never formally introduced; they never enjoy that first essential act of accommodation. The central conflict of the novel derives from Darcy's refusing to be introduced to Elizabeth at the first ball. . . .

THE ISSUE OF SEXUALITY

The theme of introductions becomes doubly important when we remember that Darcy's refusal to be introduced to Elizabeth denies not only her social but also her sexual presence. What Elizabeth overhears Darcy say is this: 'She is tolerable; but not handsome enough to tempt *me*'. . . . Only in *Pride and Prejudice* is sexuality an explicit issue between the heroine and hero. . . .

Elizabeth never has a mere placid prettiness; her unconventional beauty sparks sexual interest. We are not bound exclusively to Elizabeth's narrative perspective until after she and Jane have left Netherfield in order to allow the reader to see Darcy's changing views on Elizabeth's physical appeal. We know from his conversation with Miss Bingley

---

3. selected for individual interests as opposed to prescribed by an academy

that he thinks Elizabeth has 'fine eyes'....

As the novel unfolds, Darcy becomes increasingly disturbed by his attraction to Elizabeth. Elizabeth's attractiveness, like her use of language, has a subversive quality; it pleases outside the formal rules of aesthetics. Darcy recognizes this property of Elizabeth's beauty early: 'No sooner had he made it clear to himself and his friends that she had hardly a good feature in her face, that he began to find it was rendered uncommonly intelligent by the beautiful expression of her dark eyes [and] though he had detected with a critical eye more than one failure of perfect symmetry in her form, he was forced to acknowledge her figure to be light and pleasing'. So Elizabeth's appeal is not conventional. When she bursts into the Netherfield drawing room, flushed and muddy, Darcy's reaction is divided between admiration for her looks and disapproval for her vaguely improper actions. Where else in Austen's novels do we see a heroine's petticoats, muddied or clean? Elizabeth has a physical presence which draws Darcy along with his appreciation for her keen mind. This element of sexuality in the relationship between Elizabeth and Darcy is essential to an understanding of their war of words....

If Elizabeth's attractiveness is in part a function of her freedom and independence, Darcy's is a function of his position as lord of the manor. Darcy represents the virtuous and responsible exercise of power; part of his attractiveness derives from the same source. He is an emblem of the landed gentry at its best. When Elizabeth falls in love with him, she does so not merely because he is Darcy the individual personality but also because he is Darcy of Pemberley.... For as she sees Pemberley, its tasteful landscaping, architecture and appointments, she is seeing the expression of Darcy's character and heritage....

RESOLUTION OF ELIZABETH'S PREJUDICE AND DARCY'S PRIDE

Elizabeth's former frankness is replaced by restraint because Elizabeth is now denied the idiom of absolute certainty. Unlike her earlier self who had proclaimed that 'one knows exactly what to think', Elizabeth can no longer trust her opinions. She now knows that her opinions are subject to change, that her own are in fact changing daily as she grows more and more to love her former enemy. Darcy too participates in a period of tempered speech, but the element of his language which must be restrained is pride, not the rashness of wit. . . .

In this period, Elizabeth and Darcy obviate the dangers of speech by keeping to a mutual silence. Since both are silent, both must play a part in ending that silence. So when their love is proclaimed at last, when the romantic resolution is achieved, we find that both Darcy and Elizabeth are responsible for propelling into being the moment of mutually declared love. Darcy must dare to propose again, must reopen the subject of the previous spring. Elizabeth contributes to his renewed addresses in two ways. First, Elizabeth's staunch resistance to Lady Catherine's demands leads to her ladyship to relay to Darcy Elizabeth's intransigence,[4] information which assures Darcy of Elizabeth's open heart. Secondly, Elizabeth's thanks to Darcy for his aid to Lydia smooths the way for his resumed wooing. . . .

Fluency is restored to Darcy and Elizabeth only after a final period of education and penance. There are still consequences of their earlier errors to bear. Darcy must endure the attentions of Mrs. Bennet and the rest of Meryton society. Elizabeth's travails are even more substantial, because she must undo the effects of her earlier harsh words about Darcy. One of the lessons Elizabeth learns when she must acknowledge her engagement to her family is that her duty is made all the more difficult because of her earlier speeches. Prejudiced views, once uttered, take on a strength of their own; words cannot be easily disallowed. . . .

Only after the consequences of earlier errors have been fully atoned for can Elizabeth and Darcy be at full verbal liberty with each other. We see enough into their married life to know that they have achieved that liberty, for Darcy is now willing to be laughed at. The unspoken corollary of Darcy's new acceptance of Elizabeth's sportiveness is that she is now able to use her wit responsibly. Removed to the 'comfort and elegance of their family party at Pemberley', Elizabeth and Darcy now speak in related and compatible idioms: wit tempered by wisdom and wisdom tempered by wit.

4. refusal to change a position

The Significance of Pictures in *Pride and Prejudice*

Tony Tanner

Besides noting the importance of pictures as mental images, Tony Tanner argues that portraits are significant props in *Pride and Prejudice*. He uses Austen's letters describing her trips to art galleries, documenting her preference for the most individualistic portrait subjects and her delight in finding portraits that look just like the fictional subjects in her mind's eye. Tanner then traces Elizabeth's visit to Pemberley from the outer grounds to the general rooms to the central room, where Darcy's portrait hangs. According to Tanner, it is there that Elizabeth comes to full realization of Darcy's true worth. Tony Tanner has taught English at King's College, Cambridge. Besides authoring books on Joseph Conrad and Saul Bellow and studies of American literature, he has edited the Penguin editions of *Sense and Sensibility* and *Mansfield Park*.

Just what constitutes a person's 'real character' is one of the concerns of [*Pride and Prejudice*]: the phrase occurs more than once, usually with the added idea that it is something that can be 'exposed' (and thus, by the same token, concealed). In particular, Darcy in his letter writes that whatever Elizabeth may feel about Wickham it 'shall not prevent me from unfolding his real character,' just as later in the letter he narrates Wickham's attempt to seduce Georgiana, 'a circumstance ... which no obligation less than the present should induce me to unfold to any human being.' Cordelia's last words before being banished are:

From the Introduction by Tony Tanner to *Pride and Prejudice* by Jane Austen (London: Penguin Classics, 1972). Introduction copyright ©1972 by Tony Tanner. Reprinted by permission of Penguin UK.

Time shall unfold what plighted cunning hides
Who covers faults, at last shame them derides.[1]

'Unfolding' a hidden reality is of course replacing mere appearance with substance. The fact that reality can get folded up and hidden away—because we are so built that we are forced to work from first impressions which can be cynically manipulated—means that it is very important to be careful about what we regard as convincing evidence. It is the mistake of both Lear and Othello that they ask for the wrong kind of evidence, thus making themselves vulnerable to those who are willing to fabricate a set of false appearances. But in Shakespearean tragedy, as also in *Pride and Prejudice*, the 'real character' of both the good and the bad—of Cordelia and Iago, of Darcy and Wickham—is 'unfolded.' The cost and process of the unfolding are of course very different in each case. But the perennial theme is common to both.

At this point we may ask if Elizabeth has any more than calligraphic evidence for her new belief as to the relative merits of Darcy and Wickham. Obviously something more is required to give 'substance' to what could be mere 'assertion.' There is of course the magnanimous part he plays in the crisis precipitated by the elopement of Lydia and Wickham, but Elizabeth's improved vision has already by then 'learned to detect' the boring affectation in Wickham's manner, and appreciate the solid merit of Darcy.

The education of her vision, if we may call it so, starts with Darcy's letter but it is not complete until she has penetrated his house and confronted his portrait. This occurs on her visit to Derbyshire when the Gardiners persuade her to join them in looking round Pemberley, Darcy's fine house and its beautiful grounds. This physical penetration of the interior of Pemberley, which is both an analogue[2] and an aid for her perceptual penetration of the interior quality of its owner, occurs at the beginning of Book Three, and after the proposal-letter episode I regard it as the most important scene in the book and wish to consider it in some detail.

Austen's Use of 'Picture'

The word 'picture' occurs frequently in the novel, often in the sense of people 'picturing' something—a ball, a married couple, a desired situation—to themselves. One important exam-

1. from Shakespeare's *King Lear*   2. analogous, or similar to

ple of this is the following. 'Had Elizabeth's opinion been all drawn from her own family, she could not have formed a very pleasing picture of conjugal felicity or domestic comfort.' These pictures, then, are mental images, either derived from impressions or conjured up by imagination. (It is of course a particular quality of Elizabeth's that she is able to think outside the reality picture offered to her by her own family.) There are also more literal references to pictures—as when Miss Bingley suggests to Darcy, by way of a spiteful joke, that he should hang portraits of some of Elizabeth's socially inferior (to Darcy) relatives at Pemberley, adding 'As for your Elizabeth's picture, you must not attempt to have it taken, for what painter could do justice to those beautiful eyes?'

The relation between actual portraits and mental pictures is suggested when Darcy is dancing with Elizabeth. She has teased him with a witty description of their common characteristics. '"This is not a very striking resemblance of your own character, I am sure," said he. "How near it may be to *mine*, I cannot pretend to say. *You* think it a faithful portrait undoubtedly."' Later in the same dance he says 'I could wish, Miss Bennet, that you were not to sketch my character at the present moment, as there is reason to fear that the performance would reflect no credit on either.' Her answer is: 'But if I do not take your likeness now, I may never have another opportunity.' This is more than mere banter because, since we cannot literally internalize another person, it is at all times extremely important what particular picture or portrait of that person we carry with us. The portrait metaphor allows one to suggest that the picture should be done with some care in order that the gallery of the mind should not be hung with a series of unjust unlikenesses.

AUSTEN AS GALLERY VISITOR

We know that Jane Austen herself went to art galleries when she could. Thus in a letter to Cassandra in 1811:

> Mary & I, after disposing of her Father & Mother, went to the Liverpool Museum, & the British Gallery, & I had some amusement at each, tho' my preference for Men & Women, always inclines me to attend more to the company than the sight.

And in 1813 it is clear that when she went to a portrait gallery she had her own fictional portraits in mind. Again the letter is to Cassandra:

> Henry and I went to the Exhibition in Spring Gardens. It is

not thought a good collection, but I was very well pleased—
particularly (pray tell Fanny) with a small portrait of Mrs
Bingley, excessively like her. I went in hopes of finding one of
her Sister, but there was no Mrs Darcy;—perhaps however, I
may find her in the Great Exhibition which we shall go to, if
we have time;—I have no chance of her in the collection of Sir
Joshua Reynolds's Paintings which is now shewing in Pall
Mall, & which we are also to visit.—Mrs Bingley's is exactly
herself, size, shaped face, features & sweetness; there never
was a greater likeness. She is dressed in a white gown, with
green ornaments, which convinces me of what I had always
supposed, that green was a favourite colour with her. I dare
say Mrs D. will be in Yellow.

Later in the letter she adds:

We have been both to the Exhibition & Sir J. Reynolds',—and
I am disappointed, for there was nothing like Mrs D. at either.
I can only imagine that Mr D. prizes any Picture of her too
much to like it should be exposed to the public eye.—I can
imagine he wd have that sort of feeling—that mixture of Love,
Pride & Delicacy.—Setting aside this disappointment, I had
great amusement among the Pictures.

It is worth noting that she does not expect to find a recog-
nizable portrait of Elizabeth in Sir Joshua Reynolds's collection. For Reynolds, the artist, including the portraitist, 'ac-
quires a just idea of beautiful forms; he corrects nature by
her self, her imperfect state by her more perfect.'

GENERAL VERSUS INDIVIDUAL QUALITIES

In his *Discourses* Reynolds laid typical neo-classical stress
on 'central forms,' and generalized figures which are not
'the representation of an individual, but of a class.' This neo-
classic approach tended to minimize the individuating qualities of a person or thing in favour of more generic attributes
or in deference to classical models. But for Jane Austen, the
novelist and admirer of Richardson, it was precisely the individuating qualities, which sharply differentiated even the
sisters in the same family, which held most interest.

Elizabeth is not a type; indeed she has that kind of independent energy which is most calculated to disturb a typo-
logical attitude to people. She wants recognizing for what
she is and not what she might represent (Mr Collins's regard
for her as for Charlotte, is, she knows, wholly 'imaginary'—
he sees her only as a suitable wife-figure, and is dismissed
according to his deserts.) She is fortunate in attracting the
discerning eye of Darcy—he is always staring at her, as if

ELIZABETH SEES DARCY'S PORTRAIT

At the beginning of Volume III of Pride and Prejudice, *Mrs. Reynolds, the housekeeper at Pemberley, guides Elizabeth and the Gardiners on a tour of the house, all the while praising the owner. After showing them the miniatures on the main floor, she leads them to the upstairs gallery to see the portrait of Darcy. In this excerpt, Austen describes Elizabeth's reaction.*

In the gallery there were many family portraits, but they could have little to fix the attention of a stranger. Elizabeth walked on in quest of the only face whose features would be known to her. At last it arrested her—and she beheld a striking resemblance of Mr. Darcy, with such a smile over the face, as she remembered to have sometimes seen, when he looked at her. She stood several minutes before the picture in earnest contemplation, and returned to it again before they quitted the gallery. Mrs. Reynolds informed them, that it had been taken in his father's life time.

There was certainly at this moment, in Elizabeth's mind, a more gentle sensation towards the original, than she had ever felt in the height of their acquaintance. The commendation bestowed on him by Mrs. Reynolds was of no trifling nature. What praise is more valuable than the praise of an intelligent servant? As a brother, a landlord, a master, she considered how many people's happiness were in his guardianship!—How much of pleasure or pain it was in his power to bestow!—How much of good or evil must be done by him! Every idea that had been brought forward by the housekeeper was favourable to his character, and as she stood before the canvas, on which he was represented, and fixed his eyes upon herself, she thought of his regard with a deeper sentiment of gratitude than it had ever raised before; she remembered its warmth, and softened its impropriety of expression.

---

trying to read her fully, or capture the most complete likeness for his memory—for he alone of the men in the book is equipped to do justice to all her real qualities. It is thus only right that she should be brought to a full recognition of *his* real qualities. And this finally happens at Pemberley.

ELIZABETH'S VISIT TO PEMBERLEY

As they drive through the grounds Elizabeth admires the unobtrusive good taste in evidence—'neither formal nor falsely adorned'—and 'at that moment she felt that to be mistress of

Pemberley might be something!' Then they are led through the house where again the elegance and genuine taste—'neither gaudy nor uselessly fine'—awakens her admiration, and she again reverts to what she regards as her lost opportunity. '"And of this place," thought she, "I might have been mistress!"' Showing them round the house is Mrs Reynolds, a sort of cicerone[3] who may be guilty of 'family prejudice' but whose testimony concerning the youthful qualities of Darcy and Wickham has authority for Elizabeth. She is a voice from *within* the house and thus acquainted with Darcy from his origins, and is not, as Elizabeth necessarily is, a purely social acquaintance. She shows them some miniatures, including one of Darcy ('"the best landlord, and the best master"') and invites Elizabeth to go and look at a larger portrait of Darcy upstairs in the picture-gallery. Elizabeth walks among the portraits. . . . One can almost detect the unformulated thought—'and of this man I might have been the wife.' It is a thought which explicitly occurs to her in due course.

Standing in the middle of the house, contemplating the qualities in the face in the portrait (qualities imparted and corroborated to some extent by the housekeeper), Elizabeth completes the act of recognition which started with the reading of Darcy's letter. Notice the fact that the truest portrait is the large one in the more private part of the house upstairs; downstairs Darcy is only visible in 'miniature.' We can imagine that the further a man goes from the house in which he is truly known, the more liable he is both to misrepresentation and non-recognition.

SEEING DARCY'S PORTRAIT: ELIZABETH'S TURNING POINT

Standing before the large and true image of the real Darcy, Elizabeth has in effect completed her journey. When she next meets the original, outside in the grounds, she is no longer in any doubt as to his true worth. The rest of the book is, indeed, for the most part concerned with externalities—the mere melodrama of Wickham's elopement with Lydia which gives Darcy a chance to reveal his qualities in action. But all this is only delay, not advance, in terms of the novel. For the most important action is complete when Elizabeth has finished the contemplation of the portrait. In answer to Jane's ques-

3. a guide for sightseers

tion concerning when Elizabeth first realized she was in love with Darcy, Elizabeth replies: 'I believe it must date from my first seeing his beautiful grounds at Pemberley.'

This is not wholly a joke, nor should it be taken to indicate that at heart Elizabeth is just another materialist in what is shown to be a distinctly materialistic society. In this case the grounds, the house, the portrait, all bespeak the real man—they represent a visible extension of his inner qualities, his true style. And if Pemberley represents an ordering of natural, social, and domestic space which is everything that the Bennet household is not, who shall blame Elizabeth for recognizing that she would be more truly at home there. However, it is true that such a remark could only be made in the context of a society which shared certain basic agreements about the importance and significance of objects, domiciles, and possessions.

Good Manners Mirror Good Morals in *Pride and Prejudice*

Jane Nardin

Jane Nardin argues that *Pride and Prejudice* exam-
ines the assumption that manners reveal character.
Nardin contends that Austen uses Elizabeth to define two principles that underlie standards of propriety and to persuade the reader of their merit. Elizabeth's principles include rule one, that individuals
ought to respect rules as a means of maintaining
order and decency in society and rule two, that
moral judgment supersedes slavish compliance with
any rule. Nardin cites numerous examples in which
characters either misinterpret or violate both social
and moral rules and, in so doing, reveal their moral
and intellectual flaws. Nardin concludes that by
carefully establishing each character's manners
when he or she first appears, Austen gives the
reader a dependable measure with which to judge
the subsequent behavior of the character. Jane
Nardin has taught English at the University of Wis-
consin in Milwaukee. She is the author of *He Knew
She Was Right: The Independent Woman in the Novels
of Anthony Trollope.*

In *Pride and Prejudice,* Jane Austen makes the basic assumption that a person's outward manners mirror his moral
character. If, in this novel, a man or woman always displays
good manners, it is perfectly safe for the reader to assume
that his character is truly good. The characters in the novel
continually try to evaluate one another's manners and the
moral worth to which they are a clue. Often these evalua-
tions are wrong, but it is important to note that they are
never wrong because the manners of the individual in ques-

Reprinted from *Those Elegant Decorums: The Concept of Propriety in Jane Austen's
Novels* by Jane Nardin by permission of the State University of New York Press. Copyright ©1973 State University of New York.

tion have lied about his character. If an attempt to judge character from manners backfires in the world of *Pride and Prejudice*, it is invariably either because the judging individual has misperceived the nature of the manners of the individual he is judging, or because the standard of propriety according to which the judgment is being made is a mistaken one. The problem of judgment in *Pride and Prejudice* is not, as it is in *Persuasion*, for example, primarily a question of penetrating behind the facade of the manners to the reality of moral character; rather it is a question of perceiving and estimating the nature of an individual's manners with a reasonable degree of accuracy.

ELIZABETH PERSUADES READERS TO ACCEPT STANDARDS OF PROPRIETY

In a novel where a person's public manners are assumed to be an accurate clue to his private character, the definition of what truly proper manners actually are has an extraordinary importance. The reader must be convinced that the standard of propriety in question is one to which intelligent people of good feeling can give their wholehearted adherence. Jane Austen, it seems to me, achieves this aim in *Pride and Prejudice*. Elizabeth Bennet's standards of decorous behavior do not grate upon the reader's sensibilities as, for example, Elinor Dashwood's excessively rigid and stoical conception of propriety sometimes does. Yet Elizabeth's standards of propriety, at least at the close of the novel, are being presented as identical to the best standards of proper behavior held by her society, as well as identical to the standards of the novel as a whole—and so conformist an ethic might be expected to offend modern readers.

Jane Austen manages to get her readers—even most of her twentieth-century readers—to approve Elizabeth's adherence to a socially acceptable standard of propriety by employing a variety of subtly concealed persuasive techniques. The definition of true propriety which *Pride and Prejudice* offers—to anticipate somewhat—is simply a healthy respect for the conventional rules of social behavior, modified by an understanding that those forms are important, not as ends in themselves, but as means of regulating social intercourse, and that therefore they need not always be followed slavishly. . . .

The first aspect of this definition of propriety—that individuals ought generally to respect the conventional rules of

social behavior, especially where those rules have a significant moral element—is a tacit assumption in *Pride and Prejudice.* Jane Austen does not state this idea overtly, perhaps
because she senses that the bald statement of so conformist
a norm might alienate some readers and, at any rate, could
hardly be found novel or intriguing, but she enforces it vig-
orously, nonetheless, by using all her charm as a humorous
writer to lure her readers into participating in her censure
of *all* those characters who fail to respect the conventional
forms of decorum. *Pride and Prejudice* contains no character, like Mrs. Jennings or Admiral Croft, whose impropriety
of behavior is actually a clue to internal worth. . . .

MR. COLLINS EXCEEDS GOOD MANNERS

*Mr. Collins fails in propriety by thanking, praising, and apol-
ogizing to excess. In excerpts from* Pride and Prejudice,
*Austen describes the flaws he exhibits at a party given by
Lady Catherine.*

As Mrs. Collins had settled it with her husband that the
office of introduction should be hers, it was performed in a
proper manner, without any of those apologies and thanks
which he would have thought necessary. . . .

He took his seat at the bottom of the table, by her ladyship's desire, and looked as if he felt that life could furnish
nothing greater.—He carved, and ate, and praised with de-
lighted alacrity; and every dish was commended. . . .

When the gentlemen had joined them, and tea was over,
the card tables were placed. . . . Mr. Collins was employed in
agreeing to every thing her Ladyship said, thanking her for
every fish he won, and apologising if he thought he won too
many. . . .

They were summoned by the arrival of the coach, and
with many speeches of thankfulness on Mr. Collins's side.

Indeed, Jane Austen is very careful, in *Pride and Prejudice*,
to give her readers precise characterizations of the manners
of most of her important characters very close to their first appearances in the novel, and perhaps one of her reasons for following this rather uncharacteristic procedure is her desire to
make absolutely sure that her readers do not begin by making the erroneous assumption that unattractive characters
like Miss Bingley can ever have really well-bred manners. . . .

However, Jane Austen is much more explicit in defining

the second aspect of her idea of true propriety in this novel: that is, her belief that all the forms of propriety are there for a purpose (be that purpose basically moral or basically a matter of social convenience) and hence are being perverted if they are treated as ends in themselves. The incident of Elizabeth's solitary three-mile walk to Netherfield, which occurs very early in the novel, embodies the views on the purpose of the forms of decorum which the novel as a whole enforces, in a clear and unambiguous way. Jane Bennet, who has been visiting Netherfield, has fallen ill there and Elizabeth "feeling really anxious was determined to go to her, though the carriage was not to be had; and as she was no horsewoman, walking was her only alternative."

The situation here is thus set up most plainly. Elizabeth has a very valid reason for wishing to go to Netherfield (we learn later that Jane "longed for such a visit"), and walking is her only means of getting there. Readers are obviously meant to feel that the rules of propriety prohibiting solitary cross-country hikes for young ladies—rules which are concerned with the neatness of the lady's appearance and the possible danger to her consequent upon making a practice of walking long distances alone—ought rationally to be set aside in this unusual situation. In taking a three-mile walk, Elizabeth, as she is well aware, breaks no moral law.

MISINTERPRETATION OF RULES REVEALS CHARACTER FLAWS

And in fact, by their reactions to this crucial and unambiguous decision on a point of decorum, Jane Austen allows several of her characters to reveal what sort of stuff they are made of. "You will not be fit to be seen when you get there," cries Mrs. Bennet, proving once again both that she has no idea of what is really important in social behavior and that she regards her daughter as merchandise on display. "Every impulse of feeling should be guided by reason ... exertion should always be in proportion to what is required," says Mary Bennet, revealing the fact that she completely fails to understand what is required by Elizabeth's love for Jane. "We will go as far as Meryton with you," say Kitty and Lydia, uninterested in theoretical questions of propriety in the heat of their own headlong pursuit of officers. "It seems to me to show ... a most country-town indifference to decorum," says Miss Bingley, a social climber who values herself on the elegance and fashion of her own behavior, which, however, is often contemptuous and rude.

The good-natured, unpretentious Bingley is able to see that Elizabeth's walk "shows an affection for her sister that is very pleasing." And Mr. Darcy, admiring "the brilliancy which exercize had given [Elizabeth's] complexion," but doubting "the occasion's justifying her coming so far alone" reveals both a basic understanding of what good manners are and a characteristic tendency to place too much stress on preserving the forms of gentility, a tendency that results from pride in his own high social status.

Thus, the incident of Elizabeth's walk defines explicitly what might be called the functional aspect of the *Pride and Prejudice* ideal of propriety and smaller incidents of similar import later in the novel—such as the one in which Elizabeth defends the right of younger sisters to come out socially before the elder ones are married—prevent the reader from forgetting the point.

By failing to live up to the novel's ideal of propriety—a respect for the conventions of propriety modified by an understanding that those conventions are not ends in themselves—or by revealing the fact that their concept of proper behavior differs from that suggested by the novel as a whole, the characters in *Pride and Prejudice* reveal their own moral shortcomings. And it is not merely that something vaguely wrong with the manners is a clue to something vaguely wrong with the character, for in fact the flaw in the manners usually turns out to be a very precise counterpart to the moral flaw in question.

MINOR CHARACTERS REVEAL THEIR MORAL SHORTCOMINGS

A significant example of the way this concept works can be seen in the character of Charlotte Lucas. Charlotte is a sensible, well-meaning young woman, and her manners are generally polite and unaffected. In fact, Charlotte is guilty of only one real breach of propriety in the course of the novel, but this breach is very significant, for it provides an unambiguous clue to the moral flaw which will eventually cause Charlotte to marry Mr. Collins and become the sycophantic[1] dependent of Lady Catherine de Bourgh.

Charlotte arrives to visit the Bennet family immediately after Elizabeth has refused Mr. Collins's proposal of mar-

1. trying to gain favor by servile flattery of influential people

riage. As she is sitting with Mrs. Bennet and the girls, Mr. Collins enters, and on perceiving him, Mrs. Bennet says, "Now I do insist upon it that you, all of you . . . let Mr. Collins and me have a little conversation together." Elizabeth, Jane, and even Kitty "passed quietly out of the room" at this request, but Charlotte "detained at first by the civility of Mr. Collins . . . and then by a little curiosity, satisfied herself by walking to the window and pretending not to hear." In fact, Charlotte eavesdrops on the whole conversation and this tiny incident contains the key to Charlotte's character.

Elizabeth and Jane, with their delicate sense of personal honor, would consider it beneath them to eavesdrop on any conversation, however interesting. But Charlotte is perfectly willing to satisfy her curiosity (which, of course, reveals her interest in Mr. Collins) in this underhand way, for it is the fault of her character that she lacks firm principle and the sense of personal integrity that make one obey one's conscience when it dictates the sacrifice of personal advantage. Thus, by this minor act of impropriety, Charlotte reveals the traits which will later make it possible for her to violate principle in order to marry, for security, a man she does not love and to court, for advancement, a woman she cannot respect. A woman who marries Mr. Collins, says Elizabeth, "cannot have a proper way of thinking . . . though it is Charlotte Lucas!" and it is precisely her improper way of thinking that Charlotte's improper manners would have demonstrated to Elizabeth, had Elizabeth observed those manners more closely.

And as Charlotte's manners reveal her character flaw so precisely, so do the manners of virtually all the other characters in the novel. Sir William Lucas and Mr. Collins are both, in different ways, so enamored of the forms of civility that the purpose of those forms has largely been forgotten. Sir William occupies "himself solely in being civil to all the world," hardly a worthy lifetime occupation. Mr. Collins has fallen deeply in love with two of the commonest forms of politeness—the apology and the thank you—and has completely failed to understand that those forms have definite functions in social intercourse. Thus, he bestows his thanks liberally on people who have absolutely no claim to his gratitude—as when he thanks Lady Catherine "for every fish he won" from her at cards. And, by the same token, he apologizes when he cannot possibly have offended—at cards again "apologizing" to Lady Catherine "if he thought he won too many [fish]." The fact that both these characters are so concerned with empty forms of propriety reveals both their empty heads and their purposeless lives.

Another group of characters misunderstand or ignore the forms of politeness in various ways. Mrs. Bennet addresses those who please her "with a degree of civility which made her two daughters ashamed," but is frankly rude to anyone who crosses her, and this inconsistency of manners is just one more example of Mrs. Bennet's characteristic tendency to judge and react to things entirely as they affect her as an individual, completely disregarding any function they may serve in the world as a whole. "I do think it is the hardest thing in the world that your estate should be entailed away from your own children; and I am sure if I had been you I should have tried long ago to do something or other about it," she tells her husband.

Good manners to Mrs. Bennet are just one more way of getting what she wants, and she has failed to teach her daughters Kitty and Lydia, "always unguarded and often un-civil," anything at all about the importance or function of decorous behavior. Lydia's tendency to ignore the rules of propriety without thinking anything much about them is the clue to her more serious decision to ignore the rules of morality in living with a man who has not married her ("she was sure they would be married sometime or other and it did not much signify when"). Lydia ignores both propriety and morality in an unthinking pursuit of personal satisfaction.

Miss Bingley and Mrs. Hurst "were in the habit . . . of as-sociating with people of rank. . . . They were of a respectable family . . . a circumstance more deeply impressed on their memories than that their brother's fortune and their own had been acquired by trade." They hope to succeed with the nobility and place a good deal of stress on elegance and fashion in manners, but they reveal their lack of true gentil-ity in their willingness to be rude to social inferiors like Elizabeth. Lady Catherine's dictatorial and condescending manners toward those she considers socially inferior reveal her pride of rank as well as the fact that she is uninterested in judging people by their inherent worth.

Mr. Bennet's manners are in a class by themselves, for he is clever enough to be able to pervert the forms of polite-ness—which he, unlike the characters discussed above, thoroughly understands—into a weapon which he uses against those whom he despises. "My dear," he says to Mrs. Bennet, masking insult under the forms of courtesy, "I have two small favors to request. First, that you will allow me the free use of my understanding on the present occasion; and secondly, of my room. I shall be glad to have the library to myself as soon as may be"—an offensively polite way of saying shut up and get out. Thus Mr. Bennet makes the forms of politeness serve the purposes of his contempt for others. And in a similar manner Mr. Bennet perverts his considerable talents ("talents which rightly used, might at least have preserved the respectability of his daughters"), using them not to serve any desirable end, but merely to increase his idle amusement at the follies of a family to which he should have taught better behavior.

Many other examples could be given of the way in which manners mirror the moral character in the world of *Pride and Prejudice,* for this is true of nearly every character in the novel. And this is an important difference between *Sense and Sensibility* and *Pride and Prejudice.* In *Sense and Sensibility,* the rules of propriety are ultimately justified by their connection with the concept of duty—and true propriety consists of following them to the letter, even when they oppose personal judgment and feeling. This is a very exacting and theoretical standard of propriety and perhaps that is why Jane Austen does not assume that to fall below this high standard is invariably evidence of real immorality....

But *Pride and Prejudice*'s standard of propriety suggests that the truly proper individual must disobey the rules whenever sound common sense and good morality approve—so that only people possessing these two important attributes *can* live up to the novel's ideal of propriety, even in a purely external sense. That is why improper characters must be either immoral or stupid in *Pride and Prejudice.*

CHAPTER 6

Jane Austen's Late Novels

READINGS ON JANE AUSTEN

Portraits of People in Austen's *Emma*

Richard Church

Richard Church argues that *Emma* is Austen's most perfect novel, comparing its growth to the development of a Mozart symphony. Church praises its sustained plot and satisfying ending, but, he maintains, it is Austen's skillful portrayal of character that makes the book a masterpiece. As examples, he cites Miss Bates and her foil Mrs. Elton; Harriet, who is Emma's project; and Jane, who is Emma's foil. Though Emma is a sheltered snob, Mr. Knightley's devotion to her reflects on her better nature. Richard Church spent part of his career as a civil servant and devoted another part to literature societies. He wrote *British Authors* and *Growth of the English Novel* as well as poetry and fiction.

It is difficult to believe that there can be any controversy about *Emma*, as has been possible over *Persuasion* and *Northanger Abbey*. It is so consummate purely as a story that again the hard-worn comparison with Mozart's symphonies must be made. The tale has an organic growth, developing upon a completely sustained surmise as to the inevitable fate, and deserved retribution, of the naughty little heroine. How admirable, for example, is the seemingly artless preparation, gradually delayed, for the entry of Frank Churchill and Jane Fairfax, carried in upon a growing tide of gossip and excitement in the country houses concerned. Not a soul knows (and this includes the reader) that these two characters have met previously, and are secretly engaged; the secrecy to play a major part in the working out of the plot and the relationship of the whole *caste* in the delicious artefaction of the drama. This device, the trick of the thriller writer rather than of the novelist proper, is of course exposed to the

Introduction by Richard Church from Jane Austen's *Emma* (London: The Folio Society Ltd., 1962). Reproduced by permission of The Folio Society Ltd.

reader at a second enjoyment of the story; but the miracle is that one's pleasure and excitement are not diminished thereby. Attention is all the more concentrated on the skill with which the characters are developed, particularly that of Emma, a person who has aroused violent partisanship since her appearance in 1816, the year before Jane Austen died.

It is the clarity of portraiture in the delineation of those characters which gives the book its authority as the masterpiece of the six novels. Most readers will agree about that, though there are some who prefer *Mansfield Park*, and others who think *Persuasion* the most mature. But surely for sheer technical, literary perfection, *Emma* must bear the palm. Its flawlessness makes it elusive for the critic. It includes some autobiographical allusions, with the author interpolating herself and her problems into the story, as where Emma says to her all too pliable protegéé, Harriet Smith, 'A single woman, with a very narrow income, must be a ridiculous, disagreeable, old maid . . . but a single woman, of good fortune, is always respectable, and may be as sensible and pleasant as anybody else.' Again, Jane makes Emma's sister, Mrs John Knightley, say of Mr Weston and his son Frank Churchill, 'But how sad it is that he should not live at home with his father! There is something so shocking in a child's being taken away from his parents and natural home! I can never comprehend how Mr Weston could part with him. To give up one's child! I really never could think well of anybody who proposed such a thing to any body else.' What did Jane's handsome and generous brother Edward, and his foster parents the Knights,[1] think of this allusion, made by Jane not in irresponsible girlhood, but in the last few years of her life, long after the event? It is comparable to some of the surprising acerbities that were to sting in the pages of *Persuasion*. The venom darts out as from a snake's tongue. It formerly was a gay wit, but presumably illness was already touching that wit with poison.

MISS BATES AND HER FOIL

Not enough of it, however, appears in Emma to flavour the good humour of the book as a whole. *Emma* is a benevolent comedy. Even the portrayal of Miss Bates, who was agreed

1. Edward Austen was adopted as a boy by the rich, childless Thomas Knight; he assumed the name Austen Knight.

EMMA'S SNOBBERY

*In chapter three of Emma, Jane Austen describes Emma as
she reflects on Harriet Smith. While Harriet is the ostensible
subject, Austen actually provides insight into Emma's attitudes about class.*

Harriet Smith was the natural daughter of somebody.
Somebody had placed her, several years back, at Mrs Goddard's school, and somebody had lately raised her from the
condition of scholar to that of parlour-boarder. This was all
that was generally known of her history. She had no visible
friends but what had been acquired at Highbury, and was
now just returned from a long visit in the country to some
young ladies who had been at school there with her.

She was a very pretty girl, and her beauty happened to be
of a sort which Emma particularly admired. She was short,
plump and fair, with a fine bloom, blue eyes, light hair, reg-
ular features, and a look of great sweetness; and before the
end of the evening, Emma was as much pleased with her
manners as her person, and quite determined to continue
the acquaintance.

She was not struck by any thing remarkably clever in
Miss Smith's conversation, but she found her altogether very
engaging—not inconveniently shy, not unwilling to talk—
and yet so far from pushing, shewing so proper and becoming a deference, seeming so pleasantly grateful for being
admitted to Hartfield, and so artlessly impressed by the
appearance of every thing in so superior a style to what
she had been used to, that she must have good sense and
deserve encouragement. Encouragement should be given.
Those soft blue eyes and all those natural graces should
not be wasted on the inferior society of Highbury and its
connections.The acquaintance she had already formed
were unworthy of her. The friends from whom she had just
parted, though very good sort of people, must be doing her
harm. They were a family of the name of Martin, whom
Emma well knew by character, as renting a large farm of
Mr Knightley, . . . but they must be coarse and unpolished,
and very unfit to be the intimates of a girl who wanted only
a little more knowledge and elegance to be quite perfect.
She would notice her; she would improve her; she would
detach her from her bad acquaintance, and introduce her
into good society; she would form her opinions and her
manners. It would be an interesting, and certainly a very
kind undertaking; highly becoming her own situation in
life, her leisure, and powers.

by most of her associates to be a bore, contrives to present that aspect of her without making her one. Her famous gar-rulities,[2] though they hold up the movement of the tale (as they are intended to do) are no more than the cadenzas in a concerto, where the solo instrument is allowed to break out into a burst of bravura. Old Mr Woodhouse thinks Miss Bates 'Speaks rather too quick,' as indeed she does. But she never stumbles technically. The author must have taken some pride in these musical asides, which make the reader catch a breath, for fear that the fabric should snap. It never does. Miss Bates is triumphant in her innocent fatuousness, and always brings a drop of honey to the waiting hexagonals of the hive.

Her foil is the odious Mrs Elton, the newcomer brought into the locality by the vicar as his wife, after he has been re-fused by Emma. That couple are the *real* bores, because they are emotionally obtuse and vulgar. But they are necessary, as worldly critics of Emma's foibles. Otherwise, her naugh-tiness, induced by her over-protected life, her wealth, and the doting of her hypochondriac father, would be insipid and therefore unbearable. She gets no quarter from this malig-nant couple, and that antagonism prepares us for our in-creasing sympathy and understanding, giving her space, as it were, to prepare a site in our hearts for the author to build our acceptance of Emma's contrition at the end of the tale.

It is a necessary device, for from the start this young woman can be infuriating, and I cannot understand the reader who said that he would rather marry Emma than Elizabeth Bennett. I am still not sure, after several re-read-ings which have increased my condoning of Emma's faults, that I would not rather be domesticated with Anne Elliot than either of the two.

EMMA THE SNOB

Emma was a purse-proud snob. She began as one and was still one even after her sharp lesson over the patronage of Harriet Smith. She almost ruined that girl's life and charac-ter by her interference. Even after true-love had put things right, and Harriet's volatile heart was safely wrapped in a happy marriage with a good man from her own station in life, Emma could soliloquise (one dare not attribute this pas-

2. excessive talkativeness

sage in the book to Jane herself) that 'the event, however, was most joyful. Harriet's parentage became known. She proved to be the daughter of a tradesman, rich enough to afford her the comfortable maintenance which had ever been hers, and decent enough to have always wished for concealment. Such was the blood of gentility which Emma had formerly been so ready to vouch for! It was likely to be as untainted, perhaps, as the blood of many a gentleman: but what a connexion had she been preparing for Mr Knightley—or for the Churchills—or even for Mr Elton! The stain of illegitimacy, unbleached by nobility or wealth, would have been a stain indeed.'

There is no reason to suspect that this last reflection did not come from the very depths of Emma's nature. Even allowing for the social conventions and the caste system of that Whiggish period, and the dreadful economic acceptances which even today have not been distilled out of our welfare society, Emma's easy acceptance of such ideas and conditions does not persuade us of her sensitivity. She remains at the end, after her exposure and repentance, the same person who said at the beginning of the tale, when Harriet told her, so innocently, of young Farmer Martin's proposal, 'A young farmer, whether on horseback or on foot, is the very last sort of person to raise my curiosity. The yeomanry are precisely the order of people with whom I feel I can have nothing to do.'

That lack of curiosity, odd in so young a woman, may have accounted for her slavish submission to her doting old father's fear of draughts from the outside world. Here she lived, heiress to thirty thousand pounds, in a village sixteen miles from London (it is called Highbury, but has been located as Leatherhead); but she had never seen the sea, and until two-thirds of the way through the story, had never even been to Boxhill, eight miles away. These facts, like those of her social and economic outlook, cannot be explained away wholly as being due to the viewpoint and conditions of the age in which she lived. There must have been more enterprising and intelligent young women in those days. . . . Jane Austen called Emma 'an imaginist.' Let us leave it at that, and accept Emma as Mr Knightley so faithfully and hopefully saw her, and as she reveals her deeper self in her agony of remorse after circumstances have played their derisive part in upsetting her schemes for disposing of other people's affairs.

What a foil to this character is Jane Fairfax, the reserved, inscrutable young woman of straightened circumstances. Emma is all too positive in her assured stance. Jane by contrast is a negative element in the tale. The first word she utters when she enters the stage is 'No.' That is significant of the part she is to play throughout, at least until the very end after her secret has been revealed, and she appears in her true colours as a person of firm character who is likely to keep the somewhat unstable Frank Churchill steadily anchored in a happy marriage. Mr Knightley sagely estimated the quality of both that couple. We must therefore accept his devotion to Emma as being the true gauge of her character. It is not as though Miss Austen, in conclusion, is confessing to some remorse herself over her shrewd delineation of Emma, for Mr Knightley so estimated her from the beginning. And we know that he was not a person to be blinded by passion. There is consequently much justification for Emma being the favourite of so many readers, and the woman whom many male Janeites would prefer to marry, if they were members of that tiny universe into which the French Revolution and the machine wreckers and the convict ships never intruded.

Emma: A Heroine with Faults

Douglas Jefferson

Douglas Jefferson argues that instead of creating the stock comic heroine, popular in novels of the time, Austen portrays Emma as a complex person with faults. Jefferson says Emma is a true portrait, the first of many imperfect women characters in fiction. According to Jefferson, Emma is great because Austen risked a heroine with flaws and because Austen depicts her so artfully. Douglas Jefferson has taught English at the University of Leeds in England.

Great authors take risks, and Jane Austen's choice of heroines, and of the circumstances threatening them, often shows an artistic courage worthy of her high rank. Elizabeth Bennet,[1] for example, most admirable and most popular of heroines, is nevertheless her father's daughter, with a shade too much fondness for the ridiculous; and her position of social disadvantage presents her with too much occasion for a defiant outspokenness which sometimes approaches the limits of the tolerable. Fanny Price, on the other hand as the youngest, the least assured and the least robust member of the Mansfield Park household, with a conscience as delicate as her constitution, represents a different kind of risk and some readers feel that the dangers of such a choice were not averted. Emma presents almost the exact opposite of Fanny, with faults that continually challenge our tolerance, and Jane Austen is not afraid to show them specifically in operation, with all details. Chapter 7, in which she makes sure of Harriet's rejection of Robert Martin's proposal, putting more pressure than she wishes to admit, makes painful reading; and even after the Elton fiasco she can still act with terrible self-confidence in the equally

---

1. in *Pride and Prejudice*

From *Jane Austen's "Emma": A Landmark in English Fiction* by Douglas Jefferson (London: Chatto & Windus, 1977). Copyright ©1977 by Douglas Jefferson. Reprinted by permission of the author.

painful episode (Chapter 23) where she strictly monitors poor Harriet's visit to the Martins, restricting it to its fourteen minutes. Emma feels the suffering that this must cause, but, sure of her rightness, she cannot repent.

Lionel Trilling ... has given an excellent explanation of our sympathetic acceptance of Emma, in spite of her faults. To quote him:

> We come close to Emma because, in a strange way, she permit us to—by being very close to herself. . . . She believes she is clever, she insists that she is right, but she never says that she is good. A consciousness is always at work in her, a sense of what she ought to be and do. It is not an infallible sense, any thing but that, yet she does not need us, or the author, or Mr Knightley, to tell her, for example, that she is jealous of Jane Fairfax and acts badly to her.

Within this very impressive moral frame, Jane Austen can afford to make Emma in some respects a comic character. In places where a straight account of her attitudes is presented unobtrusive comic inflections are discernible. A good illustration may be found in Chapter 16, which follows upon the episode with Mr Elton in the coach: 'The hair was curled, and the maid sent away, and Emma sat down to think and be miserable. . . .' One passage will suffice:

> The distressing explanation she had to make to Harriet, and all that poor Harriet would be suffering, with the awkwardness of future meetings, the difficulties of continuing or discontinuing the acquaintance, of subduing feelings, concealing resentment, and avoiding eclat,[2] were enough to occupy her in most unmirthful reflections some time longer, and she went to bed at last with nothing settled but the conviction of her having blundered most dreadfully.

> To youth and natural cheerfulness like Emma's, though under temporary gloom at night, the return of day will hardly fail to bring return of spirits. The youth and cheerfulness of morning are in happy analogy, and of powerful operation; and if the distress be not poignant enough to keep the eyes unclosed, they will be sure to open to sensations of softened pain and brighter hope.

> Emma got up on the morrow more disposed for comfort than she had gone to bed, more ready to see alleviations of the evil before her, and to depend on getting tolerably out of it.

Another novelist might have noted more pointedly Emma's capacity to sleep well. The words 'if the distress [it is Harriet's distress] be not poignant enough to keep the eyes un-

2. ostentation or a dazzling effect

closed' are somehow slipped in between sentiments so innocent and harmless that they might—indeed, they do—pass unnoticed. The fact is that Emma's good health and resilience are of positive value. No good purpose would have been served by her lying awake half the night, though the decorum of sensibility might prescribe it. Jane Austen neither mocks the decorum of sensibility nor suggests that Emma is too tough. The reader may select this aspect of Emma, her indestructible buoyancy and cheerfulness, as comic, but the novelist has so embedded the comedy in the context that the total statement could appear to read as rather favourable to Emma or, at the most, neutral. . . .

EMMA'S DESIRE TO DOMINATE

In "Emma: *Point Counter Point," Joseph Wiesenfarth likens* Emma *to a fugue, a musical composition with interwoven contrapuntal themes. One of Emma's melodies is her desire to dominate, a trait that runs counter to her own well-being.*

Now this desire on Emma's part to dominate, more than anything else, threatens her well-being. She has everything at her command and is at the command of no man alive. Though she sees marriage as woman's best good, she does not see it as her own. Though she calculatingly promotes the marriages of others, she has to be surprised into her own: 'It darted through her, with the speed of an arrow, that Mr Knightley must marry no one but herself!' Emma's manipulation of Harriet is simply the primary example of her love to dominate. Harriet's portrait is an image of Emma's 'disposition to think a little too well of herself.' The creating of an elegant eligible Harriet is the comedy of Emma's narcissism. . . .

One of the inevitable delights of comedy comes from its rendering of the complexities and pitfalls of life without allowing them to overcome the order of affection and intelligence which makes life joyful. The delight of a comedy is akin to that of a complex musical form—the form of a fugue, for instance—which sets in harmony the dissonance of counterpoint as well as its melody. For all the complications that develop in the course of its rendering, we know from the form itself that the ending will resolve them brilliantly and delightfully.

The first paragraph offers a good example of the 'closeness' to Emma of which Trilling writes. It exposes Emma, perhaps, but what does it do to the reader, if he is honest? Emma gets her priorities right: 'all that Harriet would be suffering' comes first. But only a comma separates this from thoughts of social embarrassment, and we see how fertile she is in imagining different kinds of embarrassment, how very readily her mind turns to such themes. Jane Austen gives us no lead here. The sequence is uncoloured by the slightest satirical emphasis. If we wish to accuse Emma of turning too quickly from Harriet's suffering to embarrass-ments which will also affect herself, the choice lies with us, and we may decide that Jane Austen's knowledge of general human nature here is too true for comfort. We are free to ex-tract the comic point, but at our own risk. It has not been forced upon us. And like so much comedy in real life it can be viewed neutrally even by intelligent people, because not everyone focuses on the comic. Many quite competent read-ers would take the whole of this passage straight.

If Emma could be accused, in this scene, of being exces-sively tough, a most impressive passage occurs later in the novel where toughness comes into its own. The brilliant se-quence . . . which consists of chapters 46 and 47 and begins with the comedy of Mr Weston's agitation, comes to an ex-traordinary climax with Emma's sudden moment of self-realisation as she recognises the state of Harriet's hopes. Toughness comes into its own because Emma must now control feelings of surprising intensity. Here again we are very close to Emma as the various ingredients of her mental state are specified. The language may be generalised, as Emma sees how inconsiderate, how indelicate, how irra-tional and so forth her behaviour has been, and 'what blind-ness, what madness' has led her on. It is also rather for-malised in the eighteenth century way, and this is not amiss. Emma's moral sense, though genuine, would find the con-ventional, rhetorical terms sufficient. But her plight, as she sits with Harriet, is stated in language that does justice to less ideal factors than conscience and duty:

> Some portion of respect for herself, however, in spite of these demerits—some concern for her own appearance, and a strong sense of justice by Harriet—(there would be no need of *compassion* to the girl who believed herself loved by Mr Knightley—but justice required that she should not be made unhappy by any coldness now) gave Emma the resolution to sit and endure farther with calmness, with even apparent kindness.—For her own advantage indeed, it was fit that the

utmost extent of Harriet's hopes should be enquired into; and Harriet had done nothing to forfeit the regard and interest which had been so voluntarily formed and maintained—or to deserve to be slighted by the person, whose counsels had never led her right.—Rousing from reflection, therefore, and subduing her emotion, she turned to Harriet again, and, in a more inviting accent, renewed the conversation; for as to the subject which had first introduced it, the wonderful story of Jane Fairfax, that was quite sunk and lost.—Neither of them thought but of Mr Knightley and themselves.

Harriet, who had been standing in no unhappy reverie, was yet very glad to be called from it, by the now encouraging manner of such a judge, and such a friend as Miss Wood-house, and only wanted invitation, to give the history of her hopes with great, though trembling delight.—Emma's trem-blings as she asked, and as she listened, were better con-cealed than Harriet's, but they were not less. Her voice was not unsteady; but her mind was in all the perturbation that such a development of self, such a burst of threatening evil, such a confusion of sudden and perplexing emotions, must create.—She listened with much inward suffering, but with great outward patience, to Harriet's detail.—Methodical, or well arranged, or very well delivered, it could not be expected to be; but it contained, when separated from all the feeble-ness and tautology of the narration, a substance to sink her spirit—especially with the corroborating circumstances, which her own memory brought in favour of Mr Knightley's most improved opinion of Harriet.

Emma's concern for her own self-respect, the no more than 'apparent' kindness with which she endures Harriet's conversation, the development of 'self': all these are symp-toms hardly in accordance with the decorum associated with heroines, even after Jane Austen; but they have the ef-fect, not of lessening our admiration for her, but of revealing her moral strengths in their close relation to the primitive forces to which they are allied but which they must hold in check. Possessiveness, sheer will, what Jane Austen calls 'self': these, rather than sex, are the terms in which Emma's nature is here presented, and they are primitive enough. It is especially appropriate that Harriet, during this episode, should appear at her most foolish. She is day-dreaming ('in no unhappy reverie') when Emma invites her to begin. The description of her weaknesses in narration must reflect Emma's irritable state of nerves: an acute piece of psychol-ogy. At the very moment when kindness to Harriet is most called for, and most difficult to achieve, her poverty of man-ner increases the strain. Harriet's misconceptions relating to

Mr Knightley are the extreme limit of her departure from reality and common sense, and here we see her as rather spoilt, and capable of rudeness when Robert Martin's name is mentioned.

A ROUNDED CHARACTER

The goodness of Emma in this chapter may appeal to us all the more for not being an ideal goodness. It only just succeeds. Justice is done to Harriet's story, and with great effort an ugly situation avoided, and that is all. But in Emma's state of raw anguish, with so much of 'self' to contend with, and with what she recognises as her very limited natural supply of tenderness, the achievement must win our respect.

The portrait of Emma is wonderfully rounded. We see her with the novelist's humorous awareness, when Emma is unaware; but, as we have seen, Emma also achieves humorous self-awareness in the place already noted where she imagines her charming refusal of Frank Churchill; and even in one of her worst moments, at Box Hill, she sees herself almost cynically as she supposes others may see her. Frank's gallantry which, in her falsely enlivened state, she encourages, means nothing, as she knows, but

> in the judgment of most people looking on it must have had such an appearance as no English word but flirtation could very well describe. 'Mr Frank Churchill and Miss Woodhouse flirted together excessively.' They were laying themselves open to that very phrase—and to having it sent off in a letter to Maple Grove by one lady, to Ireland by another.

It would be a pleasure to be able to say that this art of rounded portraiture was inherited and developed by later English novelists; but it would be only partly true. . . .

Jane Austen's most obvious contribution in her characterisation of Emma, is the conception of a heroine with serious defects. Earlier heroines, like Clarissa,[3] had made tragic errors, but in circumstances of extreme pressure. They do not lose thereby their ideal quality. But Emma's errors are caused by ordinary uncomely faults: lack of consideration for others, a conceited opinion of her own judgment. She is the first of the distinguished line of great faulty heroines in English fiction. Perhaps hers is the best composed portrait of all.

---

3. heroine of a novel by Samuel Richardson

Mansfield Park: The Portrayal of Quiet, Complex Love

June Dwyer

June Dwyer argues that in *Mansfield Park* Austen reconsiders *Pride and Prejudice*. A shyer heroine and a more complex love supplant Elizabeth's charming wit and Elizabeth and Darcy's charged attraction for each other. Austen's later heroine, Fanny, is so shy and plain that she goes unnoticed by everyone at Mansfield Park except Edmund, who treats her with kindness. Fanny, who has been at Mansfield Park since she was ten, grew to love Edmund first as a kind friend and only later romantically. Because her devotion to Edmund is constant, she resists Henry's advances. Edmund, unaware of his feelings for Fanny, falls for Mary's flirtation and suffers when she rejects him. Then he turns to Fanny, whom he has protected and who has for years been his confidante and comforting friend. According to Dwyer, their story promotes the virtues of loyalty, duty, and affection over social sophistication and wit and presents a love stronger than that sparked in Elizabeth and Darcy. June Dwyer has been particularly interested in researching and interpreting Jane Austen's characters. She has published several scholarly articles.

Mansfield Park is best understood and appreciated if it is looked at as a rethinking of *Pride and Prejudice*. What Austen celebrated in the earlier book, she criticizes in the later one. The very qualities that made Elizabeth Bennet so appealing in *Pride and Prejudice*—her playful wit, her arch remarks, her candor—appear as weapons of deception in the hands of *Mansfield Park*'s self-absorbed and not wholly honest Mary Crawford. Darcy's fascination with Elizabeth's

Excerpted from *Jane Austen* by June Dwyer. Copyright ©1989 by June Dwyer. Reprinted with the permission of The Continuum Publishing Company.

looks and lively manner is an important spur to his continued pursuit of her and to their eventual happy union in *Pride and Prejudice*, but *Mansfield Park* sees such physical attraction as misleading. The kind of social intercourse that was so important and so necessary to the development of Elizabeth and Darcy's relationship is suddenly suspect in *Mansfield Park*, where what one says matters less than what one does. *Mansfield Park* is a book about glossy surfaces and depths that are difficult to sound. It is Jane Austen's most comprehensive exploration of those deeper attractions and feelings that cannot easily be expressed.

FANNY AS AN EXPLORATION INTO QUIET GOODNESS

The story centers around the growth and education of Fanny Price, who comes from a life of poverty and disorder to live with her wealthy uncle Sir Thomas Bertram's family at the country estate of Mansfield Park. Her transition is not easy, for Fanny's shyness and modesty result in her being either ignored or taken advantage of by the overly self-confident and sometimes self-important Bertrams. Only her cousin Edmund, Sir Thomas's second son, treats her with genuine kindness. The arrival of Mary and Henry Crawford on the Mansfield grounds throws Fanny further into the shadows, for they are worldly and outgoing, quickly captivating the Bertram household in a way that Fanny never can.

In *Mansfield Park*, however, the articulate and appealing characters are not the heroes but the villains. Henry and Mary Crawford, although they are witty and worldly, prove shallow, selfish, and weak as events unfold. In contrast, the sober Edmund and the extremely shy Fanny hold fast to their principles and gain happiness in the end without losing their integrity. Instead of elevating the showy qualities that Edmund disapprovingly identifies as "heroism, noise, and fashion," *Mansfield Park* explores the quiet virtues of duty, loyalty, and affection. The ministry, Edmund's chosen profession, calls for such virtues, and Fanny Price is herself the embodiment of them. . . .

Delightful as she is, Elizabeth Bennet needs to be reexamined by both author and reader. In truth, *she* is the one who is too good. Her flaws are minor, and her story, from a certain perspective, unrealistically romantic. In contrast to her, Fanny Price appears dull and everyday, the spiritless product of a chastened Romanticism. Fanny has considerably more than Elizabeth's nominal shortcomings: she is inarticulate and humorless, a young woman of strong moral fiber, but little social grace. She has principles, but lacks presence. What readers dislike most in Fanny is not her morality—Elizabeth Bennet is moral—but her tameness, her want of Romantic stature. They cannot easily accept the superiority of steadfast duty over passionate inclination, or the ascendancy of fraternal love over sexual attraction. But such acceptance is precisely Austen's agenda in *Mansfield Park*. She succeeds in making Fanny interesting by setting her down in an atmosphere charged with sexuality and then showing her surprising attractiveness.

FRATERNAL AND SEXUAL ATTRACTION

Admittedly, Fanny appears the least likely creature to become involved in such a scene. But the fact that she plays a key role in the outcome of the sexual fates of so many characters adds a certain fascination to her story. Although Fanny herself appears immune to sexual attraction, she is not. What she is immune to is superficial sexuality—good

---

EDMUND DISCOVERS HIS LOVE FOR FANNY

In an excerpt from the last chapter in Mansfield Park, *Jane Austen traces Edmund's discovery that he wants to marry Fanny. While Edmund's feelings for Fanny change, her feelings remain as they have long been, too deep and complex to describe.*

Scarcely had he done regretting Mary Crawford, and observing to Fanny how impossible it was that he should ever meet with such another woman, before it began to strike him whether a very different kind of woman might not do just as well—or a great deal better; whether Fanny herself were not growing as dear, as important to him in all her smiles, and all her ways, as Mary Crawford had ever been; and whether it might not be a possible, an hopeful undertaking to persuade her that her warm and sisterly regard for him would be foundation enough for wedded love. . . .

With such a regard for her, indeed, as his had long been, a regard founded on the most endearing claims of innocence and helplessness, and completed by every recommendation of growing worth, what could be more natural than the change? Loving, guiding, protecting her, as he had been doing ever since her being ten years old, her mind in so great a degree formed by his care, and her comfort depend-

looks, easy manners, flirtatious behavior. Her long-standing love for her cousin Edmund stems not from physical attraction but from their common interests and common values. It begins when she arrives at Mansfield Park at age nine and grows steadily instead of suddenly transforming into an adult sexual attachment. But it *is* a sexual attachment—one that causes Fanny pain when Mary Crawford arrives and captivates Edmund and one that later on gives her strength to resist Henry Crawford's insistent attentions.

Without any suggestion of perversion or impropriety, *Mansfield Park* assumes that fraternal love and sexual love may overlap and produce the purest and most enduring form of conjugal love. This love develops somewhat differently in Fanny and Edmund but the result is the same. From the outset, Edmund has treated Fanny with the fondness of a loving older brother. Upon her return from Portsmouth late in the book, after both of Edmund's natural sisters have disgraced themselves by eloping, he greets her as, "My Fanny—my only sister—my only comfort now." She in turn has always

---

ing on his kindness, an object to him of such close and peculiar interest, dearer by all his own importance with her than any one else at Mansfield, what was there now to add, but that he should learn to prefer soft light eyes to sparkling dark ones. . . .

Having once set out, and felt that he had done so, on this road to happiness, there was nothing on the side of prudence to stop him or make his progress slow; no doubts of her deserving, no fears from opposition of taste, no need of drawing new hopes of happiness from dissimilarity of temper. Her mind, disposition, opinions, and habits wanted no half concealment, no self deception on the present, no reliance on future improvement. Even in the midst of his late infatuation, he had acknowledged Fanny's mental superiority. . . .

It remained for a later period to tell him the whole delightful and astonishing truth. His happiness in knowing himself to have been so long the beloved of such a heart, must have been great enough to warrant any strength of language in which he could cloathe it to her or to himself; it must have been a delightful happiness! But there was happiness elsewhere which no description can reach. Let no one presume to give the feelings of a young woman on receiving the assurance of that affection of which she has scarcely allowed herself to entertain a hope.

loved him as intensely as she loves her brother William.

When Edmund finally decides that he loves and wants to marry Fanny, his realization is described as a natural change. But for Fanny, there has been no change: her affection for Edmund has for years been both fraternal and sexual. By not articulating precisely when Fanny's attachment becomes sexual, Austen suggests the extreme closeness of the two kinds of love. Although sexual love can be rooted in superficial infatuation, as is Edmund's early love for Mary Crawford, it can also be a deepening and an extension of the kind of fraternal love that he and Fanny share.

What is suggested about sexuality and fraternal love in Fanny's devotion to Edmund is further articulated in Henry's attachment to Fanny. Once Henry appreciates the depth of Fanny's feeling for her brother William, he stops flirting and actually falls in love with her. He notes "with lively admiration, the glow of Fanny's cheek, the brightness of her eye, the deep interest, the absorbed attention" that she gives her brother as he describes his adventures at sea. The power of her feelings becomes the ultimate sexual attraction for Henry, and he longs to be the object of such fervent emotion: "It would be something to be loved by such a girl, to excite the first ardors of her young, unsophisticated mind!" To his surprise, Fanny interests him a great deal.

Austen mentions more than once that Fanny does not surrender when besieged by Henry's sexual attentions because she is fortified by her love for her cousin. Edmund, however, lacks the shield of a deeper sexual attachment and so he becomes infatuated with Mary Crawford. Unlike Henry, whose broad experience with women allows him to see a sexual appeal in the intensity of Fanny's fraternal devotion, Edmund is still relatively naive. Because of his inexperience, he is temporarily blinded by the more obvious sexual attractions of Mary Crawford's beauty and her flirtatious behavior. He must learn through painful experience the deeper appeal of Fanny's character.

Mary's and Henry's Charm and Limitation

Mary and Henry Crawford figure among Austen's most skillful creations. Representing the "heroism, noise, and fashion" that Edmund so looks down upon, they are nevertheless extremely engaging—even to him. The narrator repeatedly calls them "thoughtless," "careless," and "selfish," but the reader, like Edmund, has difficulty resisting their charm. Part of their appeal lies in a willing admission of their short-comings. Henry owns that he loves to flirt and has no inten-tion of settling down; Mary just as readily admits that she wants to marry money and that she finds religion dull. Both separately refer to their behavior as "noisy." Although they may be considered irresponsible, they cannot be accused of outright deception.

Austen also makes a point of showing in both brother and sister a susceptibility to the unusual appeal of Fanny and Ed-mund. It appears that Henry has actually changed his be-havior once he falls in love with Fanny, especially when he visits her in Portsmouth. Even she cannot help noticing that he is "altogether improved since she had seen him . . . much more gentle, obliging and attentive to other people's feelings than he had ever been at Mansfield; she had never seen him so agreeable." Mary, too, shows promise of reform—al-though more randomly. At one point she kindly rescues Fanny from the persecutions of the other young people when she refuses to take part in their amateur theatricals. Later, she genuinely misses Edmund after he has gone to London, and regrets her ridicule of his chosen profession: "She was afraid she had used some strong—some contemp-tuous expressions in speaking of the clergy, and that should not have been. It was ill-bred—it was wrong. She wished such words unsaid with all her heart."

But the Crawfords are incapable of radical change, and at the novel's end they remain themselves, regretting what they have lost, but unable to break old habits and behave differ-ently. The possibilities of improvement and change and the limitations of education are among the most important of *Mansfield Park*'s themes. Careful nurture and rigorous edu-cation work best on the naturally receptive and agreeable. The advantages that Fanny gains during her stay at Mans-field Park improve her immensely, but only because she is a naturally fine individual to begin with. Fanny's sister Susan will also profit from her stay at Mansfield Park that begins as the story ends, for she, too, is tractable and receptive. But Mansfield Park has done little for Lady Bertram; she is su-perficially more refined than her slatternly sister Mrs. Price because she is wealthier, but the two share an ingrained las-situde, a want of firmness, and a helplessness that neither advantage nor education could do much to alter. . . .

THE SEDUCTIVENESS OF EASE AND ACTING

The easiness of Henry and Mary's social behavior suggests their insincerity, the fact that they are only role-playing. Both are good actors and very much at home during the weeks of preparation for the ill-timed and ill-fated theatricals at Mansfield Park. Fittingly, Henry is said to be the best actor of the group, and he and Mary each admit that they were never happier than during this period. Fanny, in contrast, is extremely uncomfortable, observing with dismay the bitterness, jealousy, and selfishness that surface in the others as they "act." She will not take part, for she thinks that acting makes light of very real and painful feelings.

Edmund articulates other reservations when he observes that acting both encourages egotism and sets aside decorum, giving license to ordinarily unacceptable behavior. He differentiates between "real acting, good hardened real acting" done by professionals and "the raw efforts of those who have not been bred to the trade,—a set of gentlemen and ladies, who have had all the disadvantages of education and decorum to struggle through." His suggestion that his family and the Crawfords are not "hardened" actors is only partially correct. The Crawfords are indeed hardened, callous individuals who do not take seriously the emotions with which they are toying. . . .

Mary and Henry Crawford epitomize the seductiveness of unregulated nature and art, the dangers of ease. Henry can read Shakespeare in such an appealing way that even Fanny, who has resolved to resist him, must put down her sewing and listen with rapt attention. And Mary can play the harp like the angel she clearly is not, drawing Edmund away from conversation with Fanny. The two are so "naturally" gifted at interpreting art that they are unaware of the rigor and discipline that goes into its creation. Because life is so easy for them, they see no need for the guidance of morality. An appreciation of the balance of hard work and sensitivity that goes into any serious endeavor, whether it be acting, landscaping, or writing, is foreign to them. . . .

MANSFIELD PARK AS A FRAMEWORK OF ORDER

The stabilizing and decidedly non-Romantic role of the Mansfield Park estate in Fanny's education is another of the novel's central motifs. Living back in Portsmouth among the

disorderly and crude members of her family, Fanny rhap-
sodizes on Mansfield's value: "In her uncle's house there
would have been a consideration of times and seasons, a reg-
ulation of subject, a propriety, an attention towards every
body which there was not here." At first this tribute seems
excessive, for Mansfield Park is no paradise; it is the home of
the officious Mrs. Norris, the two selfish Bertram sisters,
their inert mother, and their wastrel older brother, Tom. Edmund is the only member of Mansfield society who actually
treats Fanny kindly. Since she has a similar companion and
friend in her older brother William at her home in Portsmouth, what—other than material comfort—has been gained
that makes her think Mansfield so superior to her home? The
fundamental difference between the two environments lies
not in the people, nor in the amount of hardship endured, but
in the amount of structure in day-to-day life.

In Portsmouth, people behave wildly, according to their
lowest natural instincts, while at Mansfield they are civilized
and regulated. The order of Mansfield Park does not render
the life there ideal, but it allows for possibility, and for the
growth of individuality. Left at Portsmouth, Fanny, Susan,
and William would certainly have become either crude like
their father or disorganized and disoriented like their
mother. At Mansfield they have a chance to be something
else. When Fanny muses on the growth of some shrubbery at
the Mansfield parsonage, she could easily be describing herself there: "Every time I come into this shrubbery, I am more
struck with its growth and beauty. Three years ago, this was
nothing but a rough hedgerow along the upper side of the
field, never thought of as any thing, or capable of becoming
any thing; and now it is converted into a walk, and it would
be difficult to say whether most valuable as a convenience or
an ornament." Like the shrubbery she admires, Fanny has
taken on character at Mansfield Park. She has grown into a
useful and pleasant addition to the society there.... Unlike
Fanny, Mary is utterly immune to anything but the material
worth of Mansfield Park. She never considers that a person
might be poor, yet rich in spiritual blessings.

VALUE IN QUIET

In fact, Mary is quite blind to any kind of activity that goes
on below the surface. A most articulate and engaging talker,
she is at a loss to interpret Fanny's silences. She always has

something to say, while Fanny is often mute, especially when she is moved. For Fanny there are emotions of tenderness that cannot "be clothed in words." Because of her deep devotion to Edmund, she is unable to speak to him as she leaves for Portsmouth; similarly, she feels "speechless admiration" for William in his uniform and is all but inarticulate in her letter to Mary when she attempts to rebuff Henry's very unwelcome proposal of marriage. Fanny's inability to speak and her quietness become another of the novel's central themes. In her comment to Edmund that she likes to hear Mary Crawford talk because "she entertains me," she unconsciously puts speech on a trivial plane. To Fanny, words can be diverting even distracting, but they cannot convey deep feeling.

Even more to the point, words can be agents of deception. Fanny understands right away that Mary's "lively and affectionate," letters to her are calculated to be read aloud to an admiring Edmund, who then will praise the literary skill and warmth of affection that her words eloquently convey. Fanny's censure of speech and her mental disgust at the facile uses of language serve to elevate and legitimize her own emotional silences. Although she does engage in conversation with Edmund, much of their communion is either silent or undramatized by the author. As he dances with Fanny toward the end of the evening at the ball given in William's and her honor, Edmund says, "I am worn out with civility. I have been talking incessantly all night, and with nothing to say. But with *you*, Fanny, there may be peace. You will not want to be talked to. Let us have the luxury of silence." Unlike Mary, who sees speech as a weapon to win selfish conquests, Edmund views it only as a component of civility. Speech is not necessary to the silent understanding that he and Fanny share. Fittingly, at the novel's end, when Edmund asserts his love for Fanny, she feels "a happiness which no description can reach."

Because of their deep seriousness, Fanny and Edmund are poor candidates for any authorial irony in *Mansfield Park*. Their stature in the reader's eye is extremely fragile, and it could not withstand the deflation of mockery. If Austen were to poke fun at the two cousins' unbending goodness, she would be allying herself with Mary Crawford, and joining forces with the enemy. Those readers who say that they miss Austen's wonderfully ironic wit in *Mansfield*

Park have failed to understand what the novel is about. The story means to demonstrate that silence is often deeper than words and that seriousness is finally deeper than humor. A witty narrator would only undermine this theme....

Nobody will ever like Fanny Price better than Elizabeth Bennet; in a sense, this very human, ingrained preference is what *Mansfield Park* is all about. The reader, like most of the residents of Mansfield, sees little to become excited over in Fanny Price. In the beginning, only Edmund and Austen feel kindly toward her and appreciate her quiet virtue. As Edmund's kindness helps to educate and bring Fanny out of her shell, so does Austen's skillful narration make the reader look on her with a more kindly eye by the story's end. It is Austen's good judgment not to insist that the Mary Crawfords of the world ever totally lose their appeal, or that Edmund ever totally forgets Mary. Austen's job is not to superimpose Fanny's image over Mary's, but to hold her up as an alternative whose appeal grows stronger as time passes.

Persuasion: Austen's New Kind of Novel

Marvin Mudrick

Marvin Mudrick argues that Austen's unrevised *Persuasion* is a new kind of novel with a different kind of heroine. Written with less emotional distance and more personal feeling, *Persuasion* has a new caustic edge to its criticism of those preoccupied with power, money, and property. Moreover, Austen presents the heroine, Anne, with greater sensitivity. According to Mudrick, Anne Elliot is self-taught. Alone in her new awareness, Anne, learning from her own observations and thought, is transformed in the process. Marvin Mudrick taught at Temple University in Philadelphia, the University of California at Santa Barbara, and at Queens College of the City University of New York. He is the editor of *Conrad: A Collection of Critical Essays* and the author of *On Culture and Literature* and *The Man and the Machine.*

In *Persuasion,* Jane Austen's tone has acquired a sharp personal edge. This edge, which she does not vindicate by any claim of aesthetic or social propriety, emerges in the novel as a compulsive exasperation, turned, at unpredictable moments, against any character who fails—for whatever reason—to advance the interests of her heroine. Her chief target is Sir Walter Elliot; but not until Sir Walter has been solidly created. He sustains himself so well, in fact, that his vitality obscures the directness of her assault, and diverts one's attention from the minor figures whom she attacks with far more damage to their integrity: Elizabeth, Mrs. Clay, above all Mrs. Musgrove and the deceased Dick Musgrove. Of these, not only does she tell us what to think; she seems to resent even the creative effort by which she must embody before she can impale them. . . .

One thing we do know which distinguishes *Persuasion* from the other novels: it was never thoroughly revised. In March 1817, Jane Austen wrote to her niece Fanny Knight: "...I have a something ready for Publication which may perhaps appear about a twelvemonth hence" (13 Mar. 1817). But she was already very ill, and four months later she died. We know that it was her practice to write carefully and to revise intensively: *Sense and Sensibility* and *Pride and Prejudice* were rewritten several times; *Mansfield Park* required two and a half years; even *Emma*, written at the peak of her self-confidence and (however limited) recognition and in her most characteristic style, took well over a year. *Persuasion*, on the other hand, occupied her less than a year.... The first draft was, in fact, the shortest of her full-length novels, until—dissatisfied with the penultimate chapter—she altered and expanded it into two, in the same summer (of 1816) in which she had finished the first draft....

PERSONAL FEELING: A NEW ELEMENT

Never before, at any stage of composition, has Jane Austen been close enough to her material for exasperation. Persistent through all her work has been a sense of distance between author and subject: successfully (as in *Emma*), filled with the cool light of irony; unsuccessfully, when irony fails (as in *Mansfield Park*), obstructed by the flattening mirror of social judgment; always, a distance as much personal as aesthetic. Only in *Persuasion* does the irony coarsen to sarcasm, and the judgment become ardently personal. Reginald Farrer has observed that, as Jane Austen regards the world, "she has no animosity for it; but she has no affection." These words apply profoundly to all her previous work, but they fail to apply to *Persuasion*; and though, in the practice of her art, she might finally have expunged the animosity, which is here the waste energy in the creation of a new image, she could not have expunged the affection without canceling the new image whose very frame it is.

The new element in *Persuasion* is personal feeling. It pervades the characters and settings, it complicates the moral climate. Further revision would—we may surmise—have altered the book for the better, but only by refining and proportioning its novelty. Jane Austen's old need for detachment is gone; and if she is sensitive to the point of vexation and haste in her treatment of villains, she is also, for the first time in her work, sensitive to the point of detailed and sympathetic analysis in her treatment of heroes and heroines. She dismisses Sir Walter only to let Anne come back intensely to herself.

Anne is the heroine, the center of action, and the point of view of *Persuasion*. She must be disposed of in marriage; she

WENTWORTH'S LOVE FOR ANNE

In chapter 23 of Persuasion, *Anne and Wentworth find themselves in the same room at a party after eight years of separation. While Wentworth composes a letter for Captain Harville, Harville engages Anne in conversation near the desk where Wentworth is sitting. Anne and the Captain drift into a discussion about whether a man or a woman suffers longer from the breakup of a relationship. Eavesdropping, Wentworth composes a second letter to Anne, in which he refers to the conversation. His letter illustrates the sensitivity and feeling that Mudrick says characterize this novel.*

'I can listen no longer in silence. I must speak to you by such means as are within my reach. You pierce my soul. I am half agony, half hope. Tell me not that I am too late, that such precious feelings are gone for ever. I offer myself to you again with a heart even more your own, than when you almost broke it eight years and a half ago. Dare not say that man forgets sooner than woman, that his love has an earlier death. I have loved none but you. Unjust I may have been, weak and resentful I have been, but never inconstant. You alone have brought me to Bath. For you alone I think and plan.—Have you not seen this? Can you fail to have understood my wishes?—I had not waited even these ten days, could I have read your feelings, as I think you must have penetrated mine. I can hardly write. I am every instant hearing something which overpowers me. You sink your voice, but I can distinguish the tones of that voice, when they would be lost on others.—Too good, too excellent creature! You do us justice indeed. You do believe that there is true attachment and constancy among men. Believe it to be most fervent, most undeviating in

'F.W.

'I must go, uncertain of my fate; but I shall return hither, or follow your party, as soon as possible. A word, a look will be enough to decide whether I enter your father's house this evening or never.'

must illustrate and resolve, wherever resolvable, whatever conflict surrounds her and cuts her off from a fulfillment; and, finally, she must open her mind to observe and transmit as much as we need to know of the story.

Jane Austen has laid such a responsibility on no other of her heroines. . . . Always Jane Austen supervises: with irony toward Catherine, Elizabeth, and Emma; with a predetermined partiality toward Elinor and Fanny which merely exposes their poverty of substance. But Anne needs no supervision. She sees clearly, without caprice; and even the author's obvious partiality toward her serves only to provide space and light for a mind richly responsive to both.

How can this notion of Anne's personality be reconciled with the distorted images of Sir Walter, Elizabeth, Mrs. Clay, and the Musgroves which she, as the point of view, must have given us? The answer is that no reconciliation is possible: we never do believe that Anne sees them so. These figures, at least in the pattern of the whole novel, represent a failure of technique and a misdirection of feeling. They are never assimilated to Anne's story: the abuse that holds them off is so patently the author's, and generally so amusing, that we neither cavil[1] at it for the moment nor ever trace it back to Anne, who seems incapable of it anyway; but it leaves them all, even Sir Walter, external and wasted. The story of *Persuasion* is, ultimately, Anne's story; as it would have been, perhaps, altogether and from the beginning, if we had had the promised revision. . . .

ANNE: A NEW KIND OF HEROINE

In all her work previous to *Persuasion*, nothing has tempered her protagonists finely and vitally *except* irony; among her "serious" heroines, Elinor is shadowy and blurred, Fanny a model of inappropriate priggish insipidity which cries out for the ironist. Only Anne survives without the dimension of irony. The third dimension of Jane Austen's heroines (except for the embarrassingly live, and finally snuffed out, Marianne) has been the author's irony or nothing at all; but Anne's depth—and her unique quality in the Austen gallery—is the sustained depth of projected and implicit personal emotion.

This emotion is not simply Anne aware of herself: she is

1. to find fault unnecessarily

discriminatingly aware of feeling, and capable of analyzing it with delicate accuracy; but it is as often the feeling of others (not just their principles or prospects, which the other heroines find far more engrossing) and the emotional atmosphere of groups and of places.

Unlike Emma or Elizabeth Bennet, she never imposes her tone upon others; nor in her shyness does she resemble Fanny, crouched fearfully in a corner and ready always with small, sharp teeth against a breach of propriety; for Anne seems to have withdrawn mainly by choice, and without prejudice to her awareness. Identity of interest is no longer prerequisite, as at Mansfield Park, to godliness: Anne has learned, between Kellynch and Uppercross, to accept the emotional disparateness of groups:

> Anne had not wanted this visit to Uppercross, to learn that a removal from one set of people to another, though at a distance of only three miles, will often include a total change of conversation, opinion, and idea. She had never been staying there before, without being struck by it, or without wishing that other Elliots could have her advantage in seeing how unknown, or unconsidered there, were the affairs which at Kellynch-hall were treated as of such general publicity and pervading interest; yet with all this experience, she believed she must now submit to feel that another lesson, in the art of knowing our own nothingness beyond our own circle, was become necessary for her.

Deeply in love herself, she is capable of distinguishing without malice between love and what often passes for love. . . .

Anne is Jane Austen's first heroine to take a detailed and disinterested pleasure in sensory impressions; in the beauty of autumn:

> Her *pleasure* in the walk must arise from the exercise and the day, from the view of the last smiles of the year upon the tawny leaves and withered hedges, and from repeating to herself some few of the thousand poetical descriptions extant of autumn, that season of peculiar and inexhaustible influence on the mind of taste and tenderness, that season which has drawn from every poet, worthy of being read, some attempt at description, or some lines of feeling.

in the "romantic" attraction of Lyme[2] (and it is remarkable that *Persuasion* is the first book in which Jane Austen uses the words "romance" and "romantic" without irony and in their favorable sense):

2. Lyme Regis, a coastal town; Jane Austen's favorite resort

> ... the woody varieties of the cheerful village of Up Lyme,
> and, above all, Pinny, with its green chasms between roman-
> tic rocks, where the scattered forest trees and orchards of lux-
> uriant growth declare that many a generation must have
> passed away since the first partial falling of the cliff prepared
> the ground for such a state.

These descriptions are perhaps the more revealing in their
awkward and breathless, their almost travel-book style; for
Jane Austen is opening compartments of her mind that have
been shut till now, and she has not yet achieved the form
most expressive of her new material. The fact remains that
the world is enlarging—with some loss of hard, sharp con-
tour initially, but with a great potential (and often realized)
gain in variety and power.

Anne's devotion to Wentworth is, of course, the sustained
emotional impulse of the book; and Anne traces it with un-
remitting sensitivity. Her feeling is clear enough in her first
thought of him:

> Anne ... left the room, to seek the comfort of cool air for her
> flushed cheeks; and as she walked along a favourite grove,
> said, with a gentle sigh, "a few months more, and *he*, perhaps,
> may be walking here."

Without bitterness, but with a fixed regret, she recalls her
decision, on Lady Russell's advice, to refuse him. . . .

ANNE'S TRANSFORMATION

Only Anne observes, from its center, the whole history of the
conflict that divides into two camps all the major characters
of the book except herself; and her decision—which she
made before the story begins—is that both sides are wrong.
If it were not for Wentworth's return, however, she would
have lived with her feelings unspoken and unfulfilled.
Throughout the book, she is caught in the center of a struggle whose issues—precedence, power, money, property—
are hateful to her as issues, among people who pursue material goals in a wreckage of personality; and she will
remain caught, forever, because she is a woman and unmarried in a society which maintains unmarried women on
sufferance, because she has nowhere to go and nothing to
say—unless the lover, not suitor but lover, whom she rejected in ignorance of his momentous distinction from the
others, comes back to claim her. The worlds of Anne Elliot
are not nearly so simple and definable as Fanny Price's, for
Fanny could choose Mansfield Park and be sure of heaven.

Anne has either no choice at all, or no need of choice. . . .

It is not that Anne escapes finally, but that she grows through and out of her prison. Understanding is prerequisite to growth and release, and understanding comes only within and through the pull of opposed tensions. . . . Having gone through it in eight years of accumulating observation and judgment, Anne has grown to understand just how rare a lover Wentworth is; but she has learned, even more somberly, how rare love is. . . .

THE THEME OF SENSITIVITY

Persuasion offers a figure caught between pairs of opposites: Anne between Sir Walter and Mr. Elliot, between Mary and Charles, between Lady Russell and Wentworth. The course of the story shows how she was caught and how she is finally able to transcend the conflict. The interest of the story is to illustrate the plight of a sensitive woman in a society which has a measure for everything except sensitivity. And the climax of the story occurs when Anne—Jane Austen's only heroine so aware of, and so irrevocably cut off from, her society—is ready to articulate and define her lonely personal triumph.

So Wentworth is enlightened, and Anne is freed, as the novel rounds to its authentic climax at the White Hart Inn, where Anne can speak at last what she is now so sure of, after eight years. The perfection and emotional resonance of this scene are unique in Jane Austen's work: nowhere else do we grasp so much of personality grown and summed up. Unlike Elizabeth Bennet and Emma, who did not grow except in our aggregating perception of them, bit by bit, through the perspective of the author's irony; unlike Fanny Price and Elinor, who had not even this ironically simulated growth—Anne has grown altogether and truly, out of the constrictions of her group, out of her timidity, out of the defiant need for wit and self-assertion, out of the author's tight, ironic feminine world. *Persuasion* has a new impulse, feeling; and a new climax, self-fulfillment.

What Jane Austen might have achieved if she had been able to revise the whole book as she revised this scene, is no more than interesting speculation. Here is the book, and as it is we must judge it. Certainly, it marks the most abrupt turn in Jane Austen's work: it shows the author closely attentive to personal feeling and to economic tensions for the first time; and—perhaps most notable—it shows that Jane Austen has at last discarded the shield of irony, as in her sharp and brilliant comedies, and the shield of casuistry,[3] as in her heavy failures. Irony has become a controlled and un-compulsive instrument, casuistry must submit to being examined in the light of personality; and the universe is enlarging to include many things undreamed of—or *just* dreamed of—in her youth.

Persuasion has its defects of execution, its languors, its relapses into old bad habits: Jane Austen was, after all, on strange ground, after a lifetime of alternation between amusing and edifying her family, that singular family which must have demanded from its most talented member laughter and moral lessons, but never tenderness, or must at least never have felt the lack of it. If *Persuasion*, however, is a partial failure as a work of art, it is an astonishingly new and sure direction in a great novelist, toward a door that Jane Austen lived only long enough to set ajar. She was even apologetic about this new direction to the end. Writing about *Persuasion* to her niece, she remarked: "You will not like it, so you need not be impatient. You may *perhaps* like the Heroine, as she is almost too good for me" (23 Mar. 1817). She could not be confident about Anne or the new direction: it was still too early.

3. judging conduct on the basis of general ethical principles

Persuasion and the Cinderella Story

D.W. Harding

D.W. Harding contends that Austen's novel *Persuasion* is a more complex version of the Cinderella story. Whereas Cinderella waits passively for the prince to arrive with the glass slipper, according to Harding Austen gives Anne an active role in restoring her relationship with Wentworth. Harding concludes that the Cinderella story clarifies the theme of *Persuasion*—when a woman makes an individual romantic choice in a conformist society, she could be left alone or she could find happiness. D.W. Harding has taught psychology at Bedford College and the University of London. He has edited and written books on psychology and is the author of *Words in Rhythm: English Speech Rhythm in Verse and Poetry*.

The situation of being a poor relation was one that Jane Austen could share with her sister and their widowed mother. The situation of being the most brilliant, the most sensitive and penetrating member of her family, while she filled the roles of affectionate spinster aunt and of dutiful daughter to a hypochondriac mother, was a situation she could share with no one. It is not surprising, therefore, that variants of the Cinderella story, as well as the psychologically allied story of the foundling princess, should be prominent among the basic themes of her novels.

Anne Elliot, the heroine of *Persuasion,* her last novel, is the most mature and profound of Cinderellas. Earlier, in *Mansfield Park,* she had tried an out-and-out foundling princess and Cinderella in Fanny Price—all moral perfection, thoroughly oppressed, rather ailing, priggish, but finally vindicated and rewarded with the hero—and few people can stomach her. The theme is inevitably difficult to handle. . . .

CREATING AN OPPRESSED SITUATION

The novelist's difficulty with this theme is to secure a lively enough interest in the heroine during the early stages, when the reality of her dejection has to be enforced, and to retain interest and sympathy during the necessarily long period before the *bouleversement.*[1] Fairy tale and pantomime can resort to caricaturing the heroine's oppressors. The serious novelist whose heroine must be unappreciated and neglected by a credible social world faces a harder problem.

It is solved in *Persuasion* partly by the dexterity of a practiced writer, and partly through more mature understanding of the basic situation and the forms it may take. The vanity and shallow self-importance of Sir Walter Elliot and his eldest daughter, their heartless worldliness, accompanied by ill-judgement even in worldly things, are handled scathingly but with only a little caricature. The situation used to exemplify the clash between their values and Anne's—the problem of extravagance, debt and retrenchment—is more convincing to modern minds than the episode of the private theatricals in *Mansfield Park.* And the scales that were weighted too heavily against Fanny are here kept nearer level by the presence of Lady Russell, the influential friend, who not only sees Anne's worth (as Edmund did Fanny's) but is in many ways allied with her against the family and serves by her comments to indicate that people of good sense think as Anne does. Ill-health too is dealt with differently. Fanny's debility was presented almost as morally superior to the rude health of her companions. In *Persuasion,* which Jane Austen wrote when she was dying of a malady that gradually sapped her strength (resting on an arrangement of three chairs while her mother monopolized the sofa in the living room), it is the heroine's patience that has to be mustered to cope with the complaining hypochondria of her younger sister. . . .

A MORE MATURE CINDERELLA

Of even greater importance than these changes of treatment is a more mature interpretation of the theme, one no longer presenting the heroine as a passive sufferer of entirely unmerited wrongs. Anne has brought her chief misfortune on herself through a mistaken decision—to break her engage-

1. upset

No Need for a Glass Slipper

In the final pages of Austen's Persuasion, *no glass slipper is necessary to identify the princess. Walking together, oblivious to their surroundings, Anne and Wentworth have the power of their own conversation to convey to each other their feelings, promises, and mutual respect.*

Soon words enough had passed between them to decide their direction towards the comparatively quiet and retired gravel-walk, where the power of conversation would make the present hour a blessing indeed; and prepare it for all the immortality which the happiest recollections of their own future lives could bestow. There they exchanged again those feelings and those promises which had once before seemed to secure every thing, but which had been followed by so many, many years of division and estrangement. There they returned again into the past, more exquisitely happy, perhaps, in their re-union, than when it had been first projected; more tender, more tried, more fixed in a knowledge of each other's character, truth, and attachment; more equal to act, more justified in acting. And there, as they slowly paced the gradual ascent, heedless of every group around them, seeing neither sauntering politicians, bustling housekeepers, flirting girls, nor nurserymaids and children, they could indulge in those retrospections and acknowledgments, and especially in those explanations of what had directly preceded the present moment, which were so poignant and so ceaseless in interest. All the little variations of the last week were gone through; and of yesterday and today there could scarcely be an end.

ment with Wentworth—to which she was persuaded by Lady Russell. Her lapse from her own standard, in letting worldly prudence outweigh love and true esteem for personal qualities, is the error which has also to be excused in her mother, who in marrying Sir Walter was too much influenced by 'his good looks and his rank'. We start then with a much more mature Cinderella, more seriously tragic herself in having thrown away her own happiness, more complex in her relation to the loved mother, who not only made the same sort of mistake herself but now, brought back to life in Lady Russell, shares the heroine's responsibility for her disaster. . . .

In fairy tales the baffling intermingling of the hateful and lovable attributes of all mothers is simplified into a dichotomy between the ideal mother—entirely lovable, dead and beyond the test of mature observation—and the step-mother, living, entirely detestable and doing her worst for the child. In the maturity of *Persuasion* Jane Austen puts her heroine into relation with a lovable but not perfect mother who, in doing her mistaken best for the girl, has caused what seems an irremediable misfortune.

It is Wentworth's hurt feelings and his belief that Anne was over-yielding in giving him up that create the barrier between them when he comes back prosperous, seeking a wife and attracted by the amiable, commonplace Musgrove girls.

THE "PRINCE" ARRIVES

The emotional barriers Wentworth had erected against Anne have been broken down in a graded sequence of incidents, mingling observation and action on his part, which Jane Austen manages with supremely delicate skill: at first, his comment on Anne's altered looks, 'his cold politeness, his ceremonious grace'; then his inquiry of the others whether she never danced (while she is playing for them to dance); later, his quite unceremoniously kind and understanding act in relieving her of the troublesome child, 'his degree of feeling and curiosity about her' when he is told of her having refused a more recent proposal of marriage, his realizing her tiredness and insisting on her going home in Admiral Croft's chaise ('a remainder of former sentiment', Anne thinks, 'an impulse of pure, though unacknowledged friendship'); finally, his noticing the glance of admiration she receives from Mr Walter Elliot at Lyme,[2] followed quickly by the climax of the accident on the Cobb and the instant partnership between him and Anne as the competent and responsible people keeping their heads in a horrifying situation.

From this point onward the tables are turned; Captain Wentworth, in the full return of his early love, has to face the anxieties of his apparent commitment to Louisa and his jealousy at Mr Walter Elliot's wooing of Anne. Although suspense and strong emotion are maintained to the last pages, the visit to Lyme is the turning point at which the earlier sadness—wasted opportunity, regret, misunderstanding—has finally been modulated with infinite skill into comedy.

It remains serious comedy. Captain Wentworth's release

2. Lyme Regis is a resort town on the southern coast of England.

from Louisa, it is true, has the arbitrariness of lighter comedy.... The serious problem lay in managing the psychological terms on which the lovers came together again....

ANNE AS AN ACTIVE CINDERELLA

Anne, who actively caused the breach with Wentworth, must take more than a passive part in its healing if she is to remain consistently more responsible than the simpler Cinderella.... The problem for Jane Austen was how to give her an active part in promoting the reconciliation without the impossible breach of decorum involved in telling him of her love, in effect proposing to him....

The solution lies in Anne's making an almost public avowal, easily overheard in the crowded room, of her ideals of unchanging love and her belief that women have the unenviable privilege 'of loving longest, when existence or when hope is gone'. She could not have spoken like this if she had accepted Mr Elliot, and it tells Captain Wentworth enough.... The chapter goes on to emphasize still more the active responsibility she feels she must take: Wentworth having smuggled his ardent letter to her and gone, she has to make absolutely certain of giving him the word of encouragement he asks for. Her struggles to ensure this, in face of her friends' kind misunderstandings and ill-timed helpfulness, provide genial comedy....

There has been complete silence for several years between Anne and Lady Russell on the subject of the broken engagement: 'They knew not each other's opinion, either its constancy or its change, on the one leading point of Anne's conduct, for the subject was never alluded to'. The result is that Anne Elliot is presented as self-contained, controlled and with hidden power, in spite of her regrets and her real tenderness. She has the quiet maturity of a sensitive individual who is loyal to her own values without colliding needlessly and unprofitably with the social group she belongs to, or with people, like Lady Russell, to whom, in spite of seeing their limitations, she is deeply attached.

ROMANTIC LOVE IN A CONFORMIST SOCIETY

In so compact a civilized society, romantic love between individuals who freely choose each other for qualities not readily identified and categorized by those around them is a disruption.... Lovers assuage their loneliness without pay-ing the price of full conformity. Whether the ideals of romantic love are expressed in an attachment, like Anne's for Wentworth, or in a refusal to marry for anything other than attachment, like her resistance to the match with Mr Elliot, they simultaneously express and support the individual's partial nonconformity, his selection from the values ruling around him. This aspect of romantic love relates it closely to Jane Austen's concern with the survival of the sensitive and penetrating individual in a society of conforming mediocrity.

Although the nucleus of the fable—Cinderella, the foundling princess—has its universal significance, there would be no novel unless it were embodied in a particular time and place, something realized more substantially than the sketchy never-never land of fairy tale and once-upon-a-time. In Jane Austen's society—as indeed in fairy tale—the girl who made an individual romantic choice might well have to defy the standards of class and social position. And in *Persuasion* the story is embedded in a study of snobbery, snobbery displayed amidst the sharply realized detail, social and physical, of life in country houses and Bath at the end of the Napoleonic wars.

ORGANIZATIONS TO CONTACT

The Jane Austen societies have information or publications available to interested readers. The descriptions are derived from materials provided by the societies themselves. This list was compiled upon the date of publication. Names and phone numbers are subject to change.

The Jane Austen Society
Mr. Tom Carpenter, TD
Jane Austen Memorial Trust
Jane Austen's House
Chawton
Alton GU34 1SD
UK
phone and fax: 11420 83262

Founded in 1940, the society raised funds to preserve Jane Austen's cottage in Chawton and turn it into a museum. Besides helping to maintain the museum, the society promotes interest in Jane Austen's life and works. It publishes a report of its annual general meeting, which includes the address given by an invited speaker, historical notes and articles, and a bibliography of articles and book reviews published the previous year. Lists of available publications and souvenirs can be obtained from the Chawton address. Copies of the collected annual reports of the society, videos, cassettes, and all books in print relating to Jane Austen may be obtained from P. & G. Wells Ltd., 11 College Street, Winchester, Hampshire SO23 9LX, UK.

Jane Austen Society of North America (JASNA)
207 Pinecroft Dr.
Raleigh, NC 27609-5232

Founded in 1979, JASNA brings scholars and enthusiasts together to study and celebrate the genius of Jane Austen. It sponsors an annual conference held in various parts of the United States and supports forty-seven regional groups. JASNA publishes a literary journal, *Persuasion,* each December 16, Austen's birthday. It contains reports and papers from the annual conference, articles written by members on Austen, her family, her art, or her times. In addition, JASNA publishes *Persuasions: Occasional Papers* at irregular intervals and the *JASNA News,* a semiannual newsletter. Membership information is available by contacting Barbara Larkin, 2907 Northland Dr., Columbia, MO 65202, phone: 314-474-9682.

CHRONOLOGY

1770
Romantic poet William Wordsworth born

1772
Romantic poet Samuel Taylor Coleridge born

1773
Boston Tea Party in America, a revolt against British taxation without representation

1775
American War of Independence begins; George Washington commands colonial army; Jane Austen born at Steventon, December 16

1776
Thomas Jefferson writes the Declaration of Independence, July 4; Thomas Paine, American political philosopher publishes *Common Sense*

1778
Novelist Fanny Burney publishes *Evelina*

1780
Samuel Johnson, author admired by Austen, publishes *Lives of Poets*

1781
British surrender to Americans in War of Independence

1783
Austen and sister, Cassandra, sent to Mrs. Cawley's school; George Crabbe, Austen's favorite poet, publishes *The Village*; Washington Irving, American writer, born; Treaty of Paris ends American War of Independence

1785
Austen and Cassandra sent to Abbey School at Reading

1786

Scottish poet Robert Burns publishes *Poems*

1787

Constitutional Convention meets in Philadelphia

1788

Romantic poet Lord Byron born

1789

French Revolution begins with storming of the Bastille; William Blake publishes *Songs of Innocence*; George Washington becomes first American president; James Fenimore Cooper, American novelist, born

1791

Austen writes family theatrical *The History of England*; Cassandra illustrates; Washington, D.C., established as U.S. capital; Bill of Rights adopted

1792

Thomas Paine publishes *The Rights of Man*; Romantic poet Percy Bysshe Shelley born

1793

England goes to war with France; Eli Whitney invents the cotton gin

1794

The Comte de Fuillide, husband of Austen's cousin, guillotined in France

1795

Austen writes first draft of *Elinor and Marianne*; Cassandra engaged to Thomas Fowle; Austen's flirtation with Tom Lefroy; Romantic poet John Keats born

1796

Austen begins writing *First Impressions* (later retitled *Pride and Prejudice*); Austen's surviving correspondence begins; John Adams elected second American president

1797

Cassandra's fiancé dies in the West Indies; Austen finishes *First Impressions* and is rejected by Cadell; *Sense and Sensibility* begun; *Susan* written

1798

Wordsworth and Coleridge publish *Lyrical Ballads* with Preface, beginning Romantic period

1800

Napoleon defeats Austrians; Thomas Jefferson elected third American president; Library of Congress founded

1801

Austen's father retires and moves family to Bath; Austen meets man she is expected to marry; he dies

1802

Harris Bigg-Wither proposes to Austen: she accepts and then breaks engagement; Peace of Amiens with France; American essayist and poet Ralph Waldo Emerson born

1803

Susan sold to Crosby, who does not publish it; war with France resumes; United States buys Louisiana Territory from France for $15 million

1804

Austen begins *The Watsons*; Napoleon becomes emperor of France; American novelist and short story writer Nathaniel Hawthorne born

1804–1816

Lewis and Clark expedition explores American west

1805

Austen's father dies; Austen recasts *Lady Susan*, an epistolary novel written before 1793; Battle of Trafalgar establishes England as supreme naval power

1806

Austen moves to Southampton with mother, Cassandra, and Martha Lloyd; lives with brother Frank and his wife Mary; Noah Webster publishes *Dictionary of the English Language*

1807

Abolition of slave trade in Britain; Wordsworth publishes *Poems*

1808

Napoleon captures Madrid; American Congress stops importation of slaves

1809

Austen moves to Chawton with mother, Cassandra, and Martha Lloyd; American short story writer Edgar Allan Poe born; Abraham Lincoln born; Washington Irving publishes *Knickerbocker's History of New York*

1810

Scottish Romantic novelist Sir Walter Scott publishes *Lady of the Lake*

1811

Austen begins *Mansfield Park*; *Sense and Sensibility* published

1812

War of 1812 begins between United States and England; Charles Dickens born; Napoleon's Russian campaign ends with retreat from Moscow; American Academy of Natural Science founded; James Madison elected fourth American president

1813

Pride and Prejudice published; *Mansfield Park* finished

1814

Austen begins *Emma*; *Mansfield Park* published; Scott publishes *Waverly*, begins trend of historical novels; British troops burn Washington, D.C.; Francis Scott Key writes "The Star Spangled Banner"

1815

Austen begins *Persuasion*; prince regent "invites" Austen to dedicate *Emma* to him; *Emma* finished and published; *Susan* bought back from Crosby; Napoleon defeated in Battle of Waterloo; Peace of Vienna; peace with America following War of 1812

1816

Austen's health begins to fail; Scott reviews Austen in *Quarterly Review*; *Persuasion* finished; "Plan of a Novel" finished; James Monroe elected fifth American president

1817

Austen writes *Sandition*; moves to Winchester for better medical care, but dies of Addison's disease on July 18; American essayist Henry David Thoreau born

1818

Persuasion and *Northanger Abbey* published; Scott publishes *Heart of Midlothian*; Mary Shelley publishes *Frankenstein*

1819

Queen Victoria born; American novelist Herman Melville born

FOR FURTHER RESEARCH

ABOUT JANE AUSTEN AND HER WORKS

Walter Allen, *The English Novel: A Short Critical History.* New York: E.P. Dutton, 1954.

J.D. Austen-Leigh, *A Memoir of Jane Austen,* 1870. In *Persuasion* by Jane Austen, ed. with an Introduction by E. W. Harding. London: Penguin Books, 1965.

Albert C. Baugh, *A Literary History of England.* New York: Appleton-Century-Crofts, 1948.

Julia Prewitt Brown, *Jane Austen's Novels: Social Change and Literary Form.* Cambridge, MA: Harvard University Press, 1979.

Douglas Bush, *Jane Austen.* Masters of World Literature Series, ed. Louis Kronenberger. New York: Macmillan, 1975.

David Cecil, *A Portrait of Jane Austen.* New York: Hill and Wang, 1978.

R.W. Chapman, *Jane Austen: Fact and Problems: The Clark Lectures.* Oxford: Clarendon Press, 1948.

Robert Alan Donovan, *The Shaping Vision: Imagination in the English Novel from Defoe to Dickens.* Ithaca, NY: Cornell University Press, 1966.

Christopher Gillie, *A Preface to Jane Austen.* London: Longman Group, 1974.

John Halperin, *The Life of Jane Austen.* Baltimore, MD: Johns Hopkins University Press, 1984.

Michael Hardwick, *A Guide to Jane Austen.* New York: Charles Scribner's Sons, 1973.

Park Honan, *Jane Austen: Her Life.* New York: St. Martin's Press, 1987.

Elizabeth Jenkins, *Jane Austen.* New York: Grosset & Dunlap, 1949.

R. Brimley Johnson, *Jane Austen.* London: Sheed & Ward, 1927.

Margaret Kennedy, *Jane Austen.* London: Arthur Barker, 1950.

Marghanita Laski, *Jane Austen and Her World.* London: Thames and Hudson, 1969.

Juliet McMaster, *Jane Austen's Achievements: Papers Delivered at the Jane Austen Bicentennial Conference at the University of Alberta.* New York: Barnes and Noble, 1976.

Judith O'Neill, *Critics on Jane Austen: Readings in Literary Criticism.* Coral Gables, FL: University of Miami Press, 1970.

Joan Rees, *Jane Austen: Woman and Writer.* New York: St. Martin's Press, 1976.

Annette T. Rubinstein, *The Great Tradition in English Literature from Shakespeare to Shaw.* New York: Citadel Press, 1953.

LeRoy W. Smith, *Jane Austen and the Drama of Women.* New York: St. Martin's Press, 1983.

Stuart M. Tave, *Some Words of Jane Austen.* Chicago: University of Chicago Press, 1973.

Dorothy Van Ghent, *The English Novel: Form and Function.* New York: Rinehart & Company, 1953.

Ian Watt, ed., *Jane Austen: A Collection of Critical Essays.* Englewood Cliffs, NJ: Prentice-Hall, 1963.

ABOUT THE TIMES

Asa Briggs, *The Age of Improvement: 1783–1867.* New York: David McKay, 1959.

Will Durant and Ariel Durant, "Johnson's England: 1756–89," in *Rousseau and Revolution,* vol. 10 of *The Story of Civilization.* New York: Simon and Schuster, 1967.

Howard Mumbord Jones, *Revolution and Romanticism.* Cambridge, MA: The Belknap Press of Harvard University Press, 1974.

Dorothy Marshall, *English People in the Eighteenth Century.* London: Longmans, Green, 1956.

J.A. Mazzeo, ed., *Reason and the Imagination: Studies in the History of Ideas 1600–1800.* New York: Columbia University Press, 1962.

J.H. Plumb, *Studies in Social History: A Tribute to G.M. Trevelyan.* London: Longmans, Green, 1955.

Marjorie Quennell and C.H.B. Quennell, *A History of Everyday Things in England,* vol. 2 1500–1799, and vol. 3 1733–1851. London: B.T. Balsford, 1919.

Alfred Leslie Rowse, *The West in English History.* London: Hadder and Stoughton, 1949.

George Macaulay Trevelyan, *British History in the Nineteenth Century (1782–1901).* New York: Longmans, Green, 1924.

———, *English Social History: A Survey of Six Centuries: Chaucer to Queen Victoria.* London: Longmans, Green, 1943.

———, *History of England.* London: Longmans, Green, 1929.

Earl R. Wasserman, ed., *Aspects of the Eighteenth Century.* Baltimore, MD: Johns Hopkins University Press, 1965.

Basil Willey, *The Eighteenth Century Background: Studies on the Idea of Nature in the Thought of the Period.* New York: Columbia University Press, 1940.

WORKS BY JANE AUSTEN

Sense and Sensibility First written in 1795 as a series of letters entitled *Elinor and Marianne*; recast as a narrative in 1797 and retitled *Sense and Sensibility* (1811)

Pride and Prejudice First written in 1796, entitled *First Impressions* (1813)

Mansfield Park (1814)

Emma (1815)

Northanger Abbey First written in 1797 and sold but not published as *Susan*; revised in 1816

Persuasion (1818)

Lady Susan First written in 1793 or 1794; revised in 1804 (1870)

The Watsons A fragment written in Bath, probably 1805 (1870)

Sandition A fragment written in 1817 (1925)

Letters The standard collection, ed. R. W. Chapman (1932)

The Works of Jane Austen, ed. R.W. Chapman, vol. VI, *Minor Works*, including "Plan of a Novel" (1954)

INDEX

Adams, Oscar Fay, 21
Altick, Richard D., 52
American Revolution, 13
Austen, Cassandra (sister), 15,
  16, 19, 20, 25
  and death of Jane, 31
  at Godmersham Park, 26-27
  and illustrations, 17, 18
  letters from Jane to, 21-22, 23,
    26, 96
Austen, Cassandra Leigh
  (mother), 14, 16, 24, 26, 27
Austen, Edward (brother), 15, 26,
  27, 58
Austen, Frank (brother), 15, 26,
  27, 44
Austen, George (father), 14, 15,
  16, 24, 27
  death of, 25
  letter to publisher from, 21
Austen, Henry (brother), 28, 29-
  30, 31
Austen, James (brother), 14, 19
Austen, Jane, 19-20, 26
  as artist, 78-79, 83, 126, 192
  ahead of her time, 35, 68
  early writing of, 17, 20-22, 28
  influenced by drama, 70
  and satirist, 23-24
  and storyteller, 128
  see also style; themes
  at Chawton, 27-28, 125
  education of, 16
  family of, 14-19, 126
  as gallery visitor, 142-43
  illness and death of, 30-32
  and love of nature, 77
  personality of, 22-24
  romantic connections of, 20, 25
  social background of, 13, 15,
    125-26
  described in *Emma*, 102
  see also England
Austen, Martha Lloyd (sister-in-

law), 44
Austen-Leigh, Anna (niece), 28,
  29
Austen-Leigh, Emma (niece), 18-
  19
Austen-Leigh, James E.
  (nephew), 15, 24, 29, 55, 56
  on appearance of Jane, 19
  on personality of Jane, 22-23

Babb, Howard S., 117
Bath, England, 14, 17, 19, 24, 25
  in *Northanger Abbey*, 106, 107
Bentham, Jeremy, 52
Blackwood's Magazine, 127
Bradley, A.C., 70
Brontë, Charlotte, 56, 57, 58
Brydges, Egerton, 55
Burke, Edmund, 46, 54

Carlton House, 30
Cecil, David, 15, 24, 28
Chapman, R.W., 22, 92
characters, 46, 71, 75, 82, 83
  in *Pride and Prejudice*, 129-30,
    140-41
  in *Sense and Sensibility*, 115
  reflect theme, 118-23
  see also manners
Church, Richard, 156
Clarke, James Stanier, 30
Coleridge, Samuel Taylor, 54, 56
comedy, in Austen's works, 70-
  77, 129, 133-34
  balanced by detached irony, 79-
    83
  balanced by love-story, 75-76
  in *Emma*, 157, 165
  and illusion, 72-73
Constable (publisher), 54
Crosby (publisher), 28, 30, 104

Duckworth, Alistair M., 93
Dwyer, June, 108, 168

Egerton, Thomas (publisher), 28, 29

Elinor and Marianne, 20

Emma, 46, 75, 125, 126
  comedy in, 157, 165
  dedication of, to prince regent, 29, 30
  games in, 94, 99-102
  portraits of characters in, 157-61
    Emma, 65, 67, 68, 110
      as heroine with faults, 72-73, 162-67
        and desire to dominate, 164
        and snobbishness, 127, 158, 159-61
      is redeemed by Knightley's devotion, 160, 161
    Frank Churchill, 61, 63, 71, 156, 161
      as described by Mr. Wood-house, 72
      and flirtation, 68, 167
      as game player, 101, 102
    Harriet Smith, 65, 72, 73, 110, 166
      through Emma's eyes, 158, 160
      and rejection of Robert Mar-tin, 162-63
    Jane Fairfax, 73, 101, 156, 157
      as foil to Emma, 161
      secret engagement of, 61, 68
    minor characters, 72, 100-101, 159, 163
    Miss Bates, 157, 159
    Mr./Mrs. Elton, 159, 160, 163
    Mr. Knightley, 68, 100, 102, 160, 161
      compared to Churchill, 101
      and recognition by Emma, 73, 164, 166
      sense of social responsibil-ity, 99
      vitality of, 67
    Mr. Woodhouse, 72, 159
  sexuality in, 67-68
  style in, 156-57
  written like thriller, 156

Emma: Point Counter Point (Wiesenfarth), 164

England, 13, 14, 35-41, 51-52, 78
  poverty/sickness in, 36-37, 40-41
  snobbery in, 79-81

Fergus, Jan, 60, 64

French Revolution, 13, 19, 41, 161

games, 93-102
  and Austen family, 18, 93-94, 100
  cards, 95-97
  negative significance of, 94-99

Goldsmith, Oliver, 94

Halperin, John, 16, 17, 23, 51

Harding, D.W., 186

Hughes-Hallett, Penelope, 44, 100

James, Henry, 58

Jane Austen (Dwyer), 108

Jane Austen (Lucas), 17

Jane Austen and Steventon (Austen-Leigh), 19

Jane Austen's Letters to Her Sister Cassandra and Others (Chap-man), 22

Jane Austen's Novels: A Study of Structure (Wright), 115

Jefferson, Douglas, 162

Johnson, Dr. Samuel, 130

Juvenalia, the, 17, 23

Kent, England, 15, 16, 18, 19, 26

Knight, Fanny, 179

Knight, Thomas, 14, 15, 16

Lady Susan, 26, 34, 35

Lascelles, Mary, 85-86, 90

Lefroy, Anne, 18, 25

Lefroy, Tom, 20

Lewes, G.H., 54, 57, 127

Life of Jane Austen, The (Halperin), 16

Lloyd, Martha, 24, 25, 26, 27, 44

London, 19, 28, 29, 37

manners, 43, 46-49, 50
  contribute to moral stability, 45-46
  reveal morality of characters in *Pride and Prejudice*, 147-54
  through improprieties of minor characters, 151-54

by standards of Elizabeth
  Bennet, 148-50
Mansfield Park, 18, 29, 74, 75, 125
  characters
    Edmund, 98, 127, 169, 173, 174
    love for Fanny, 99, 170-72,
      176, 177
    Fanny, 45, 89, 110, 111
    attraction to Edmund, 99,
      170-71
    growth of, at Mansfield Park,
      173, 175
    and Henry Crawford, 98,
      172, 174
    as opposite of Emma, 162
    priggishness of, 127, 181, 186
    values quiet, 169-70, 176-77
    Henry Crawford, 89, 97, 98,
      169, 172
    as actor, 174
    as incapable of reform, 173
    Mary Crawford, 170, 171, 172,
      173, 177
    self-absorption of, 168, 169
    shallowness of, 175-76
    social ease of, 174
  as greatest work?, 126
  house
    as framework of order, 174-75
    as symbol, 47
  as rethinking of *Pride and
    Prejudice*, 168-69
  see also themes
Maugham, W. Somerset, 125
Memoir of Jane Austen, A
  (Austen-Leigh), 15, 19, 22-23,
  26, 56
Monaghan, David, 42
Mooneyham, Laura G., 131
Mudrick, Marvin, 23, 178
My Dear Cassandra (Hughes-
  Hallett), 44, 100

Napoleon, 78
Napoleonic Wars, 13, 191
Nardin, Jane, 147
nineteenth-century criticism, 51-
  58, 126, 127
  and campaign against fiction,
    52-54
  by Charlotte Brontë, 56-58
Northanger Abbey, 75, 113, 125
  characters
    Catherine, 71-72, 89, 91, 94

as antiheroine, 105-109
    education of, 109-11
    inner journey of, 108
    General/Mrs. Tilney, 71, 89,
      106, 109
    and suspicion of foul play,
      107, 108
    Henry, 72, 106, 107, 108, 110
    Isabella, 91, 106, 109, 110
    John, 89, 106, 107, 109, 110
  originally titled *Susan*, 21, 25,
    28, 30, 104
  satire and realism in, 104-11
    mocks Gothic fiction, 106, 107,
      108, 111
  structure of, 105-108

Odmark, John, 112
Oxford University, 14, 19

Persuasion, 24, 30, 77, 125, 126-27
  characters
    Admiral/Mrs. Croft, 45, 49, 50
    Anne Elliot, 66-67, 75, 76, 180,
      183-84
    as perfect heroine, 95, 181-
      83, 186
    and Wentworth, 188, 190,
      191
    Captain Benwick, 66, 67, 76
    Captain Wentworth, 76, 183,
      184, 188, 190
    jealousy of, 189
    at Lyme, 66, 180
    and sexuality, 67
    Sir Walter Elliot, 47, 178, 180,
      181, 184
    and Anne, 189
    vanity of, 75, 87
  has rare charm, 128
  judgment in, 148
  and Kellynch Hall as symbol, 47
  as new kind of novel, 178-85
    showing personal feeling, 179-
      80, 184
  written quickly, 179
  written when Austen's health
    failing, 75
  see also under style, irony;
    themes
Political Register, 54
Portrait of Jane Austen, A (Cecil),
  15
Pride and Prejudice, 23, 28, 29,

53, 125
characters
  Charlotte, 35, 43-44, 151, 152
  Darcy, 44, 64, 82, 140, 141
    and Elizabeth, 65, 135
    and enforced meditation,
      133
  Elizabeth, 35, 38, 65, 87, 128
    compared to Charlotte, 152
    compared to Fanny of *Mans-*
      field Park, 74-75, 168-70,
      177
    and Darcy, 48, 65, 137-38,
      139, 142
      initial attraction, 134-35,
        136
      relationship sets pace of
        novel, 132-33
    as favorite of Austen, 129
    independent energy of, 110,
      143
    as model heroine, 64, 162
    at Pemberley, 144-45, 146
    resembles Austen, 82, 83,
      136
    and social propriety, 148
    as standard of excellence, 44
    and walk to Netherfield, 150,
      151
  Jane, 43, 47, 87, 128, 130
    and attraction to Bingley, 63
    and illness at Netherfield,
      150
    as like Cassandra, 129
    as uncorrupted by Mrs. Ben-
      net, 46
  Kitty/Lydia/Mary, 46, 47, 71,
    87, 91
    impropriety of, 153
  Lady Catherine de Bourgh, 97,
    151, 152, 153
    exaggerated character of,
      129, 130
  Miss Bingley, 142, 149, 150,
    153
    and overuse of flattery, 65,
      87
  Mr./Mrs. Bennet, 80, 81, 150,
    153, 154
  Mr. Collins, 71, 97, 149, 151,
    152
    as comic figure, 82, 129
    ridicule of, 86, 87-88, 89, 130
    and use of cliché, 91

Wickham, 63, 64, 82, 140, 141
compared to *Mansfield Park*,
  74-75
earlier called *First Impressions*,
  20, 78
as most humorous novel, 71
nineteenth-century review of,
  53
popularity of, 126, 127
  as most popular novel, 74
significance of pictures in, 141-
  46
  and Darcy's portrait, 144, 145-
    46
and social world, 79-81
structure of, 128, 129, 132-33
see also under characters;
  games; *under* style; *under*
  themes
Priestley, J.B., 78
prince regent (future George IV),
  29, 30

Reynolds, Sir Joshua, 143

Sandition, 31
Scott, Sir Walter, 54, 125-26, 127,
  130
Sense and Sensibility, 21, 23, 29,
  34
  characters, 73-74
    Colonel Brandon, 90, 91, 115,
      116, 118
    Edward, 115, 118, 119, 120,
      121
    Elinor, 90, 95, 96, 119, 122
      contrasted with Marianne,
        113-14, 118
      as ironic symbol, 115
      on the Palmers, 120
      as principle, 116
      special obligation of, 121
    John Dashwood, 73, 74, 90-91,
      122-23
    Lucy Steele, 95, 115, 118, 119
      as manipulator, 120-22
    Marianne, 86, 88, 91, 95, 96
      and attraction to Willoughby,
        63, 65, 87, 90
      behavior governed by feel-
        ings, 113-14, 118
      and decision to marry Bran-
        don, 116
      Willoughby's rejection of, 73,

74, 119
Mrs. Dashwood, 47, 122
Mrs. Ferrars, 90
Mr./Mrs. Palmer, 45, 118-19, 120
  senseless talk of, 118-19
concept of duty in, 154
games in, 95
publication of, 28, 125
rigidity of, 117-18
see also under characters; style; themes
Shakespeare, William, 54, 72, 82, 141
Sherry, Norman, 104
society. *See* England
Southampton, England, 26, 27
Stein, Gertrude, 60
Steventon, Hampshire, 15, 16, 19, 24
  as birthplace of Jane Austen, 13, 14
Story of Jane Austen's Life, The (Adams), 21
style, Austen's, 24, 72, 85-86, 92, 128
  compared with Shakespeare's, 72, 82
  in *Emma,* 156-57
  and irony, 21, 47, 62-63, 71, 86-91
    created by contradiction, 90
    created by elaborate language, 87-88
    created by understatement/ negatives, 88-89
    and distancing of characters, 111
    in *Persuasion,* 179, 185
      absent in portrayal of Anne Elliot, 181
    in *Sense and Sensibility,* 115, 122, 123
      lack of, 113-14, 116
    types of, 112
  and metaphors/clichés, 91
  in *Pride and Prejudice,* 130, 133-34
  reveals good-humored criticism, 80, 86-87
  and significance of pictures, 141-46
  and use of letters, 110-11
  and wit, 69
  see also comedy; manners

Susan. See Northanger Abbey

Tanner, Tony, 140
Thackeray, William Makepeace, 81
themes
  in *Mansfield Park,* 169-77
    fraternal attraction, 170-72
    goodness, 169, 176
    limitations of charm, 172-74
  marriage, 44, 45
  in *Persuasion,* 184-85
    Cinderella story, 186-91
  in *Pride and Prejudice,* 131-39
    conflict/compromise, 132, 134
    reading/writing, 135-36
    self-love, 133
  sexuality and social life, 60-69, 137-39
    and attraction of opposites, 65, 134-35, 136-37
    and conduct books, 61-62
    and flirtation, 63-64
    and love at first sight, 61, 63
  snobbery, 79-81, 121, 158, 159-61, 191
  see also comedy; manners
Trilling, Lionel, 163, 165
Trollope, Anthony, 54, 55
tuberculosis (TB), 37, 41
Twain, Mark, 56, 58

Watsons, The, 26
Weldon, Fay, 34
Wiesenfarth, Joseph, 164
Wilson, Edmund, 54
Winchester, England, 31, 32
Wollstonecraft, Mary, 43, 45, 50
women, 13-14, 24, 41, 126
  in Austen's work, 42-50
    changing roles of, 49-50
    and social stability, 46-49
    value of education for, 44
  and childbirth, 39-40
  and employment, 36-37, 43
  expected to hide intelligence, 42
  lack of rights, 38-39
  and marriage, 37-38
Woolf, Virginia, 23
Wordsworth, William, 56
Wright, Andrew H., 85, 115

DATE DUE

Feb 18			

GAYLORD 234   PRINTED IN U. S. A.